WOLF MARSHALL'S JAZZ GUITAR COURSE

MASTERING THE JAZZ LANGUAGE

PLAYBACK+
Speed • Pitch • Balance • Loop

To access audio, visit:
www.halleonard.com/mylibrary

Enter Code
4244-0762-0923-6550

Photos courtesy of Rick Gould

ISBN 978-1-5400-5412-8

Visit Hal Leonard Online at **www.halleonard.com**

Explore the entire family of Hal Leonard products and resources

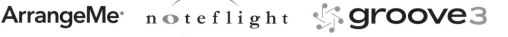

World headquarters, contact:
Hal Leonard
7777 West Bluemound Road
Milwaukee, WI 53213
Email: info@halleonard.com

In Europe, contact:
Hal Leonard Europe Limited
1 Red Place
London, W1K 6PL
Email: info@halleonardeurope.com

In Australia, contact:
Hal Leonard Australia Pty. Ltd.
4 Lentara Court
Cheltenham, Victoria, 3192 Australia
Email: info@halleonard.com.au

CONTENTS

PROLOGUE

I didn't choose jazz; jazz chose me. I wasn't born or raised in a jazz-centric household; my mother was a classical pianist who favored Beethoven, Chopin, and Debussy while my father preferred pop songs like "Que Sera, Sera." My ear training began as a child listening to mom's practicing. I taught myself guitar at 14; there were no methods for learning the music of Link Wray, Dick Dale, the Beatles, Stones, Jeff Beck, Eric Clapton, B.B. King, Jimi Hendrix, or Buddy Guy. I had to rely on my ear and do so to the present. That's a bedrock principle of this course.

Savvy bandmates introduced me to Joe Pass, Howard Roberts, and Jobim, and by 16, jazz began to attract me at the periphery. The road appeared before me when Mick Abrahams (Jethro Tull's original guitarist), whose playing I adored, extolled his jazz influences and advised me (in his best Cockney) to "get a Kenny Burrell album." Good advice. I listened to *Blues: The Common Ground* religiously while adding Johnny Smith, Barney Kessel, and Wes Montgomery to the playlist. Several life-changing events followed: studying with Johnny Smith in Colorado, attending Howard Roberts' seminar at Donte's, taking private lessons with George Van Eps and Joe Pass, and finally meeting and becoming close friends with Pat Martino, who taught me about the art of jazz and how it works on guitar. And he encouraged me to transcribe the music.

Why do I relate all this? Everyone treads a different path yet they all lead to the shared language—if you want to speak jazz. Learning means surrendering to the language with the intention of communicating. The means of gaining mastery are myriad from Wes Montgomery's emulation of Charlie Christian to John Coltrane's lifelong quest to expand and repurpose the language of his forebears. Operating continuously behind the scenes, the ear never stops growing. Listening to and transcribing John Coltrane, Charlie Parker, Hampton Hawes, Freddie Hubbard, McCoy Tyner, and Vincent Herring—and realizing their music on guitar afforded important insights into the language beyond the confines of guitar—further guided this effort as a conduit for enumerable expressions of the jazz language. My seemingly circuitous path shaped the work you are viewing; it wasn't created in a vacuum or to secure academic rewards. The practices and wisdom of my aforementioned mentors are in this book. We're waiting for you to join the queue.

I gratefully acknowledge those who accompanied me on the journey to bring this book about: my colleagues Henry Johnson—who persuaded me to venture out after years in the studio and play jazz live, and Mark Stefani—fellow educator and language disciple who shares my love of documenting the work of our mentors. I must mention gifted graphic artist David Gill, Jeff Schroedl—who suggested we combine five of my books to produce this course, and Derek Volkmann and Kurt Plahna—who shepherded the laborious editorial process. Finally, I am honored to cite my heroes: Herb Ellis, Howard Roberts, George Van Eps, Johnny Smith, Joe Pass, Pat Martino, Hank Garland, and Kenny Burrell. They all inspired me and contributed to this course inadvertently or directly. Hopefully their spirits will touch you in the same way.

FOREWORD

Kenny Burrell

I was impressed with Wolf's music before we met and played together at my 75th birthday concert at Royce Hall in 2006. Next year, when I became too busy to work with my guitar students at UCLA, he was on my short list of guitarists I hoped to have teach with me in the jazz program. I approached Wolf because I was impressed with his playing, and I thought he'd do a good job educating and demonstrating the music. Well, he did a great job and is still doing it. And in the years since, I have come to appreciate his teaching and educational abilities even more.

I am also very impressed with what is offered in this course. It was wise of Wolf to teach guitar from the language of jazz and cite what key players have contributed to the genre. That concept in the presentation of material in this book makes it one of the best music educational methods I have ever seen. His vast experience as a writer, educator, and a fine guitarist brings forth an unprecedented and unique look at how jazz improvisation and harmony are formed. I feel that this book will help guitarists in all stages of development and is yet another example of Wolf's excellent teaching approach. It has my highest recommendation.

ABOUT THE AUTHOR

Wolf (left) with Kenny Burrell (right)

Wolf Marshall is one of the most published and best-known educators in the jazz guitar world. He has authored acclaimed books on the most important artists of the genre such as George Benson, Pat Martino, Kenny Burrell, Barney Kessel, Charlie Christian, Grant Green and others, as well as guitar compilations in many genres and styles, and *Giant Steps for Guitar*, decoding the music of saxophone player John Coltrane, all published by Hal Leonard. He has written articles for major music magazines since 1984, presided over his own magazine *Wolf Marshall's GuitarOne* in the 1990s, and been a monthly columnist for *Vintage Guitar* for over 20 years. As a celebrity, performer, and authority, he has been interviewed by *Just Jazz Guitar*, *Guitar Player*, *Guitar World*, *Vintage Guitar*, *New York Times*, *Wall Street Journal*, and *San Diego Union Tribune*. In his writings, he has shared his expertise on a variety of styles including jazz, blues, rock, folk, classical, metal, country, pop, fusion, and world music, making him a true practitioner and expert in the area of global jazz. He has been a highly visible instructor in new media, lauding a career that began in the 1980s with all-star videos to the present with some of the world's leading platforms for online lessons and content.

Wolf Marshall is also a performing artist, having appeared in live venues from small jazz clubs to large auditoriums. He has worked with Burt Bacharach, Kenny Burrell, Dee Dee Bridgewater, B.B. King, John Pisano, and Eric Marienthal, led his own bands for the last 20 years, and has played as a solo guitarist in numerous clubs, resorts, and restaurants in Southern California, as well as internationally.

Recruited by the founder of the UCLA jazz department, Kenny Burrell, Marshall has been teaching jazz guitar at UCLA since 2007.

INTRODUCTION

Any course in music balances art and craft. This course is designed to strike that balance and unveil the beauty and technical demands of jazz for guitarists. It is divided into three sections: harmony, melody, and improvisation. Harmony (chord types, functions, and usage) and melody (single-note expressions) comprise prerequisites and are well suited to study and practice in step time. The craft is learned in both step and real time.

The art of jazz performance is reflected in improvisation. It is the creative impulse, reflecting the action of harmony and melody in real time. In this course, every music example feeds the ear, intellect, and fingers. They were extracted from the lexicon of the music itself, obtained by transcribing a mountain of recordings from the repertoire or through personal interactions with the masters. Regular references to artists who have pioneered, developed, and advanced the jazz form are cited. In presenting their contributions and formalizing some of their preferences, logical conclusions are drawn about how to *speak* jazz. In that sense, it is the first course of this type. This volume is intended to develop artistry and fluency with the music through a system of immersion. It is not for advanced players only, nor for neophytes. It is a manual for achieving conversant mastery of the essentials and basics of the art with the goal of employing the principles creatively. I call it *jazz language for the guitar*. You can jump in at any point of development of a dialog.

This course can be played in linear or random fashion. The linear approach means following the chapters from beginning to end, in order. This provides a natural, systematic methodology and organic progression from learning your first handful of jazz chords to intelligent and intuitive improvising. In the random approach, a student can plug directly into any chapter at any point in the course and explore the sonic terrain of that sector.

What about rhythm? Rhythm is the heartbeat and soul of jazz. However, no specific exercises are presented in the area of rhythm and its corollary, time. Instead, every demonstration example contains and exploits rhythms and phraseology that are idiomatic and intended to be *felt* and internalized at the outset. In this manner, rhythm becomes second nature and seamlessly joins the aspects of melody, harmony, and improvisation.

About the Audio 🔊

As this book focuses heavily on the language of the jazz masters, it is crucial to understand not only *what* the vocabulary is but *how* it is played. In order to fully grasp the intricacies of phrasing, I've recorded each example to help you understand the nuances of time feel, accents, note lengths, and much more when working through the material. Just head over to *www.halleonard.com/mylibrary* and enter the code found on page 1 of this book to access the audio examples.

PART I:
HARMONY

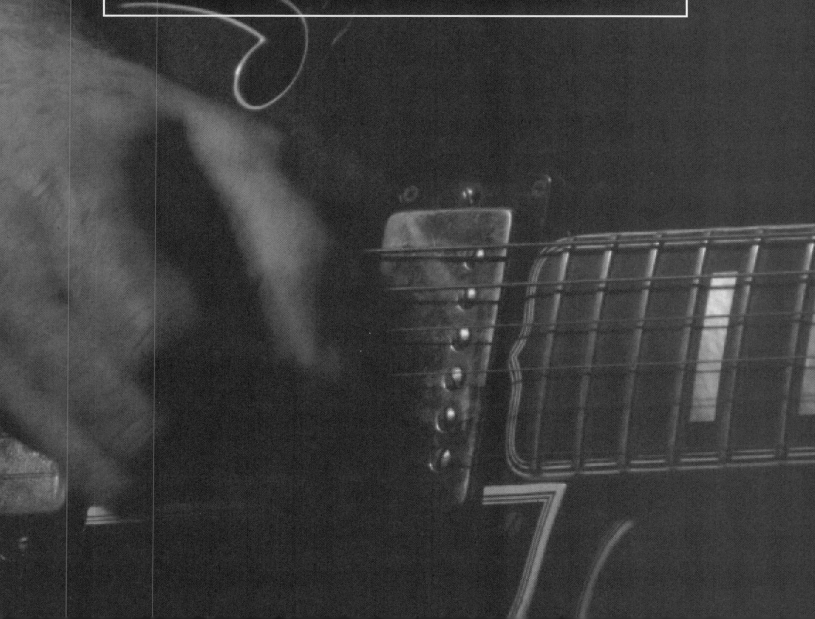

CHAPTER 1

ESSENTIAL JAZZ CHORDS

Essential Elements of Harmony

Jazz guitar is *harmonic* music. It is based on harmony—that is to say, *chords*. Chords are used in rhythm playing and *comping* (accompaniment). They are ideally suited to gaining an understanding of how harmony affects melody and, ultimately, your statement in improvisation. Essential jazz chords, while seemingly an oversimplification, provide a serviceable starting point for learning to use and, more importantly, *hear* the music *harmonically*.

Essential Basic Jazz Chords

While the notion of proposing "essential basic jazz chords" is a risky venture, the knowledge of and fluency with the genre's most-used chords offers an ideal entry into harmony. These are the most common; used frequently in rhythm playing, comping and chord-melody settings. For many, these chords will be familiar. However, in the interest of thoroughness, if you think you know them, challenge yourself by playing the forms and noting their *shapes*.

Each form is a 7th or 6th chord and has a four-note structure that generally contains root, 3rd, 5th, and 7th tones or root, 3rd, 5th, and 6th tones. However, the *voicing*—the arrangement and distribution of *voices*, or tones—is not identical. Compare the *divided voicing* of the first chord (played on strings 6, 4, 3, and 2) with the second shape (played on consecutive strings 5, 4, 3, and 2). Also note that the second and fourth forms of the maj6 series have no 5th in the voicing. This is usually the first tone to be omitted from a 6th or 7th chord, particularly in extended and altered chords played on guitar.

Be aware of Xs in the chord grids above each shape. These indicate tones that are *muted* when strumming and avoided when playing fingerstyle. Also noteworthy is the *barring* in several chords, such as the third and fourth major 7th forms. By the end of the Harmony section, you'll experience and master barring with every finger, including the thumb.

Major 7th Voicings

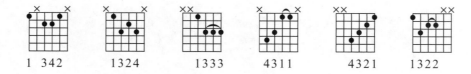

    1 342   1324   1333   4311   4321   1322

Major 6th Voicings

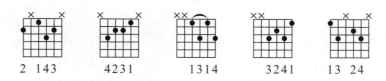

    2 143   4231   1314   3241   13 24

Minor 7th Voicings

Minor 6th Voicings

Dominant 7th Voicings

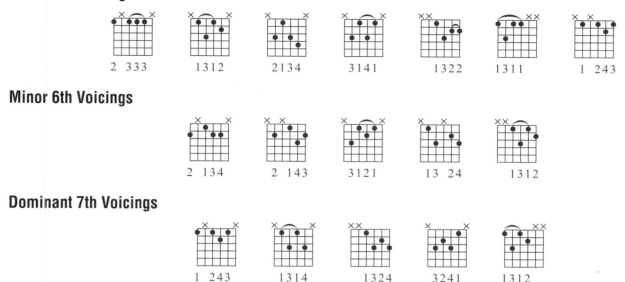

These chords are categorized by quality, or *color*—major, minor, and dominant 7th types. It is useful to initially define chord colors and group them into fingering forms for practice. These forms are in *root position* (the root is the lowest note). Begin by playing each form separately, listening to its color and noting the differences and similarities in each shape. For example, check out the identical shapes of a maj6 form (first chord) and a m6 form (second chord) when fretted on different string sets. Observations like this prove valuable as you begin to amass and manipulate chords in your repertoire and create a visual picture of guitar harmony on the fingerboard.

Next, move each form up and down chromatically one fret at a time from the lowest position to the tenth fret and back, concentrating on maintaining accurate fingering and a clean, buzz-free sound. This inherently mechanical process isolates the acquisition, memorization, and assimilation of physical forms, generating a simple exercise that develops mobility and fretting technique. No chord names are necessary at this stage. In fact, in the spirit of Joe Pass, assimilate these forms first as shapes and sounds.

As you play the chords, be aware that various fingerings are possible and indeed, many will be revealed as we progress through chord changes. George Van Eps taught me that fingering is situational and will vary, depending on the harmonic motion of voices in a progression—that is, what's required to move efficiently from one chord to another.

Basic Progressions

Let's move on to the real world. The jazz language becomes a priority once the forms are learned and comfortable to finger. Chord names are used here, and we'll work with simple chord progressions using a single shape of each color. The following three examples are common patterns using each chord in a functional situation.

This chromatic phrase, based on a familiar rhythm pattern in "Watch What Happens," is used to apply *major 7th* chords to a simple progression. It involves movement around the I chord, here Gmaj7, to the same shape a half step above and below the tonic chord. Chromatic motion of a single maj7 chord is heard prominently in Wes Montgomery's opening phrase of "Days of Wine and Roses," the standard "You Stepped Out of a Dream," and Thelonious Monk's "Well, You Needn't."

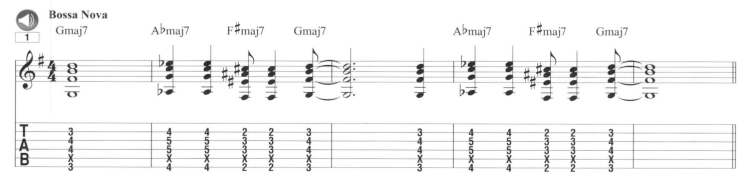

This phrase subjects *minor 7th chords* to ascending and descending chromatic motion within a minor third (three steps distance). Miles Davis used this sound to begin "There Is No Greater Love." Horace Silver applied the motion to his arrangement of "Silver's Serenade" in measures 10–11 (Am7–Cm7). This type of movement was common in the hard bop era, and subsequently modern jazz, but has its origins in big band swing figures.

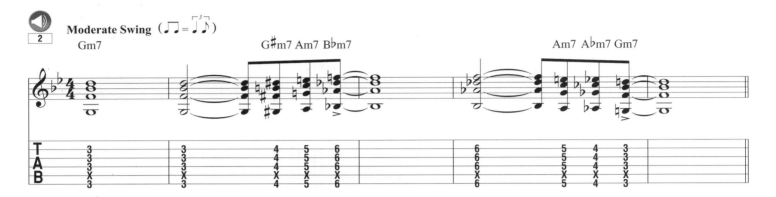

The *dominant 7th chord* is synonymous with the blues, in jazz, and elsewhere. This phrase alludes to Benny Golson's "Killer Joe," a popular soul-jazz piece. Here, a C7 chord is moved down a whole step to Bb7, emphasizing the dominant quality not only in the shape itself but with the toggling of the same form played on the tonic and lowered seventh tone, Bb—a familiar component of the blues. The added B7 acts as a typical chromatic passing chord in the progression.

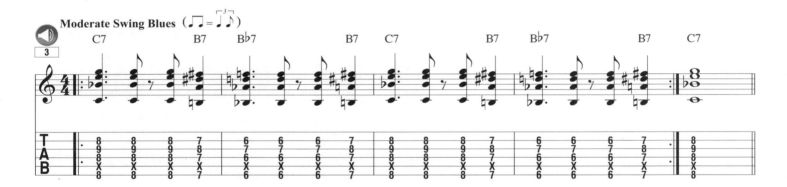

Now, apply the above progressions to every basic form in the Essential Jazz Chords diagrams. For example, use every maj7 and m7 shape with the rhythm patterns of Tracks 1 and 2 and every dominant 7th with Track 3, and listen for the difference an alternate voicing makes.

Essential Extended Jazz Chords

Jazz is renowned for its sophisticated harmony. Even rock groups like the Beatles, the Police, and Steely Dan have harnessed its power. An understanding of and facility with more advanced sounds begin once we venture past the basic forms and start to explore other colors. Like the last group of shapes, these essential chords are common forms but are enriched and *extended* with added tones beyond the simple one-octave confines of the previous section.

Extended Major Chords

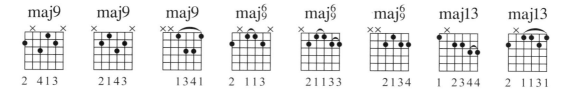

Extended Minor Chords

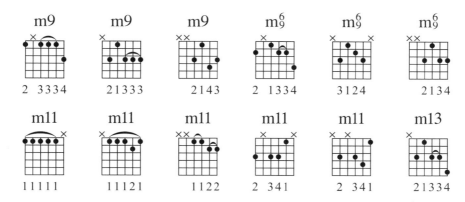

Extended Dominant Chords

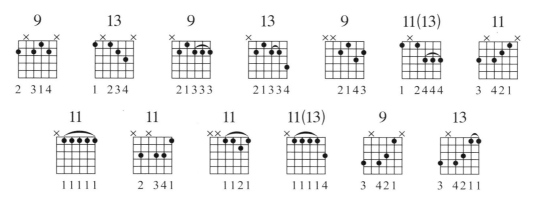

Though these chords are extended, they are still *diatonic*, using only existing notes from the seven-note major scale and its modes. They are not altered and have no chromatic tones but produce a richer sound and pleasing mild dissonance due to the free use of the diatonic scale. Try toggling back and forth from these extended forms to the basic forms and listen for a "pandiatonic" effect. This is jazz-harmony ear training at its most fundamental.

Several forms necessarily have an abbreviated structure; after all, we don't have 13 strings on the guitar! Notice the extended versions of *maj6/9* and *maj13* forms in the major series, which are enriched by the presence of a 7th and 9th in the voicings. Also noteworthy is the use of consecutive 4th intervals in several 6/9, 11th, and 13th chords. This is an aspect of jazz, and chordal music in general, called *quartal harmony*, to be discussed in an upcoming chapter.

It is worth mentioning the distinction between the upper and lower parts of the chord. Chords containing 6th and 7th tones are within the first octave (eight notes). Chords with 9th, 11th, and 13th tones extend into the second octave. Various enriching combinations of 6th, 7th, 9th, 11th, and 13th chord tones are indigenous to modern jazz and affect single-note improvisation significantly. Alto saxophonist Charlie Parker, the father of bebop and modern jazz, was reported saying his style was informed by playing the "higher intervals of chords as a melody line," thereby extending the harmonic content in his solos (*Downbeat*, 1949).

These essential extended chords should also be played using the progressions and rhythms of Tracks 1, 2, and 3. Hear the sound of the chord in the context of its color. Then, simply think major but respond by playing an enriched maj13, because now you hear it.

Essential Altered Jazz Chords

Altered chords are exactly what is specified by the term: chords that contain altered notes, typically the 5th and 9th tones. These chord tones are either lowered (♭5, ♭9) or raised (#5, #9). Alterations produce strong dissonance and can be applied to major, minor and dominant chords with differing coloristic results. They are essential to jazz. Altered chords serve as an important introduction to the first stage of playing *outside* of a diatonic scale or tonality. This diagram shows the most common altered chords with one altered tone, such as a maj7♭5, m7♭5, and dominant 7♭9.

Altered Major Chords

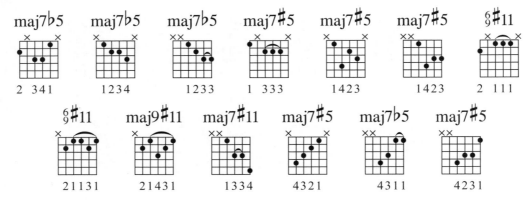

Altered Minor Chords

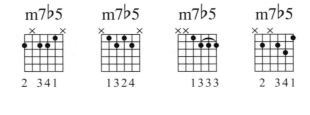

Altered Dominant Chords

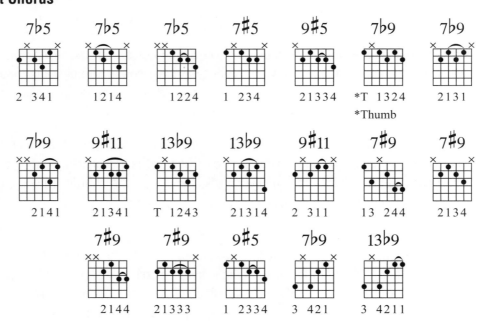

This set of shapes depicts common altered dominant 7th forms with two altered tones. They are more dissonant and sound more active.

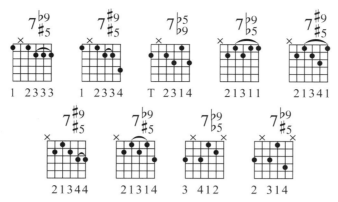

The tension of these forms demands a stronger resolution. Most altered dominants function as enriched V7 chords resolving to I: a major, minor, or unaltered dominant chord, as in the case of the blues. The Roman numeral *V* indicates a dominant 7th chord built on the fifth step of a scale. It is valuable to subject these forms to a *V–I cadence* and listen to the gravitational pull of the harmony.

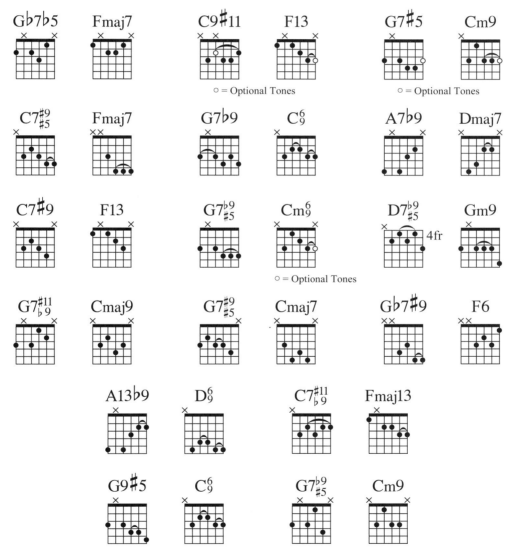

Select your favorites from this list and add them to your repertoire in standards and blues tunes. Then, experiment with your own combinations in the assimilation phase of your learning.

Altered Chords in Context

Each altered chord has its own mood and often works to facilitate voice leading in a chord progression. Listen to this phrase with descending chromatic motion in the top voice: E–E♭ (D#)–D. The G7#5 supplies a connecting sonority that unites the extended Dm9 and Cmaj9 chords.

This is not a random grouping of unrelated chords, rather it is a key phrase from the jazz language. It is also your first example of a *ii–V–I* progression (the most important in jazz) in a major key.

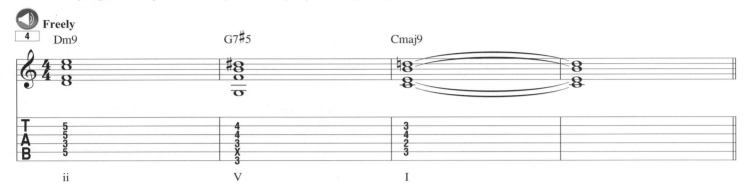

In a 12-bar blues, an altered chord commonly defines the all-important I7–IV7 cadence in measures 4–5. This demonstration phrase applies only dominant 7th chord colors. It exploits chromatic motion with neighboring D♭9 and F#13 forms and a ii–V–I move to C9.

The D♭9 and F#13 are *substitution chords*, used as *tritone (♭5) substitutes* for G7 and C7, respectively. The formula: think G7 but play D♭7.

The ii–V–I to C9 is an example of *harmonic superimposition*—essentially placing a two-chord progression over a single chord. G7 is expanded into Dm7–G7, often referred to a *ii–V of IV*. This emphasizes and strengthens the resolution to C9 (IV chord). Listen to its expansive effect in the blues.

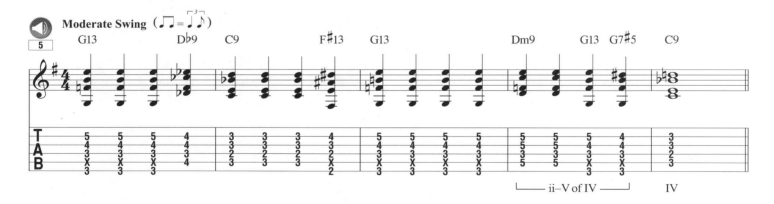

The *m7♭5 chord* (also called a *half-diminished chord*) is typically found in minor keys, where it exists diatonically as a ii chord and is not a true altered chord. There, it generally leads to an altered dominant 7th chord and a resolution to the tonic minor. In symbols, it is also written as a half-diminished, as in this sequence: ii7ø–V7alt–i.

In this case, G7#5 produces the *enharmonic tone*, E♭ (D# = E♭, same sounding pitch) that reflects the C minor tonality. The m7♭5 is often borrowed and placed into the parallel major mode where it becomes an altered chord with a ♭5 tone, as in "What Is This Thing Called Love?" and "Hot House." This is an example of that ii–V–i, first in its natural minor key and then in its parallel major key. Listen and compare.

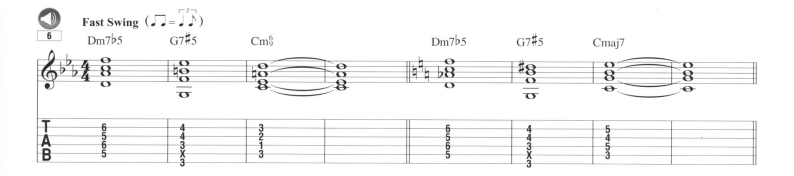

The #11 label is commonly used when a 9th tone is in the chord voicing, as in 9#11 forms. This sound is prevalent in jazz and frequently enriches the dominant II7 chord in standard tunes, such as "Take the A Train" and "Desafinado." It is often approached from the I chord. That's what you hear in this characteristic phrase.

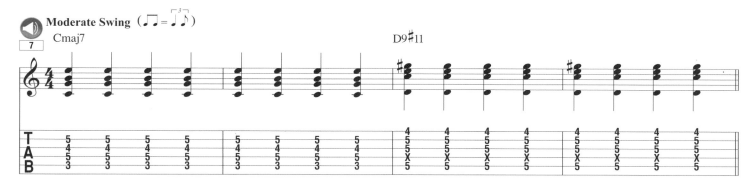

The raised 11th (#11) is enharmonic with the lowered 5th, but when the spelling contains an unaltered 5th in the lower part of the chord, it is heard and functions as a colorful extension rather than an altered tone (see maj7#11). This type of chord is a common modal jazz sound, as in Bill Evans' first chord of "Blue in Green," where it's played with a G bass note to create a Gm13 sonority.

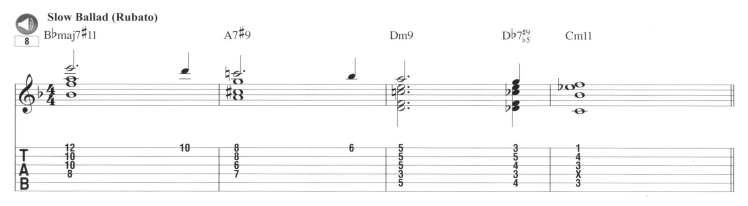

The altered maj7 chord, *maj7b5*, or *maj7#11*, is frequently found in post-bop jazz. Consider the chromatically tinged modern compositions of Joe Henderson, Wayne Shorter, Freddie Hubbard, and Pat Metheny, like "Inner Urge," "E.S.P," "Povo," and "Bright Size Life." This phrase is based on the unusual treatment of parallel maj7b5 chords in "Inner Urge." They are moved in descending whole steps: Fmaj7b5–Ebmaj7b5–Dbmaj7b5, which defies any conventional tonality, and are embellished with various *chromatic passing chords*. In the lexicon of post-bop, they function as independent dissonant sonorities establishing a unique constellation of sounds where every chord has equal weight. (You can see this in action on the next page.)

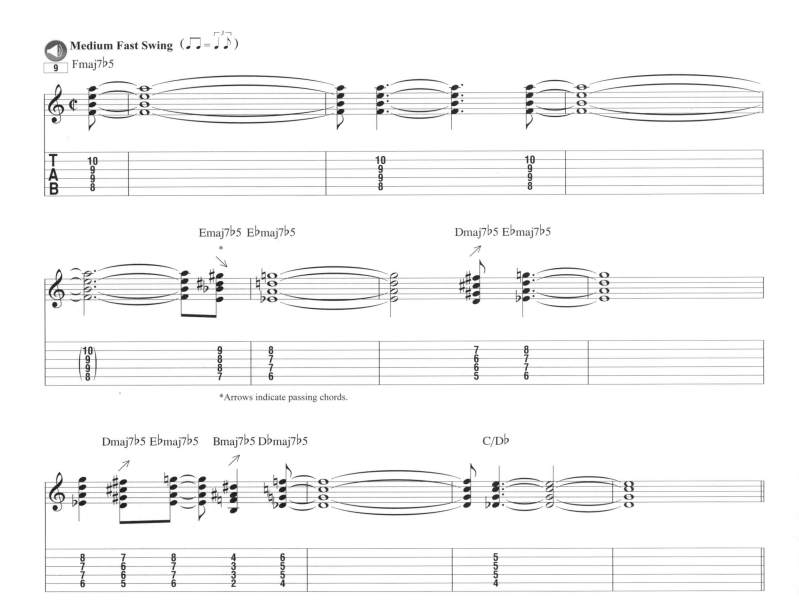

*Arrows indicate passing chords.

Minor-Major 7 Chords

The *minor-major 7th chord*, written *m(maj7)*, is a special case in music. For decades, it has provided a strong, exotic color to tunes like "It Don't Mean a Thing, "'Round Midnight," "Blue Skies," "Hot House," "In a Sentimental Mood," "Yesterdays," "How Deep Is the Ocean?," and "Maybe September," and while we're at it, don't forget the Beatles' "Michelle." Though the m(maj7) sounds dissonant and altered in effect, it is actually a diatonic 7th chord. It's usually played as the tonic chord naturally occurring in minor keys that use the harmonic minor and melodic minor scales as the tonal center. Some of its dissonance is the result of the *augmented triad*, a simple altered chord (root–3rd–#5th), contained in the upper part of the basic form. These are the most common forms of the chord and its extended versions.

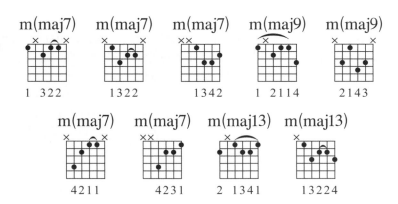

Play the first three shapes in this series and notice the top three strings are augmented chords. In other voicings, like the fourth, sixth, and ninth shapes, an augmented triad is found on the middle strings.

An indispensable minor-mode progression in jazz involves applying the m(maj7) form as part of a *voice-leading pattern* over a static minor chord. This creates motion, color, and harmonic interest without changing the chord itself: Gm–Gm(maj7)–Gm7–Gm6. Grant Green's "Idle Moments" is an example of this sequence in the jazz repertoire.

This pattern uses forms with a sixth-string root. Listen for the chromatic descent of the voice on the fourth string.

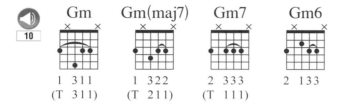

In this pattern, you'll notice alternate fingerings for Cm(maj7), Cm7, and Cm6. Referring back to the wisdom of George Van Eps, these changes make playing the phrase more efficient and feel more connected. Notice the fourth finger is used as a *guide finger* to hold the common tone, G, in the progression.

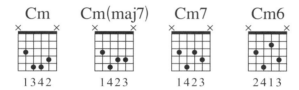

The third finger provides a guide finger for this version of the pattern played from a fourth-string root.

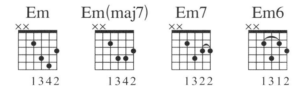

Minor-major 7 voice-leading patterns above inform single-note improvisation in the jazz language. This melody illustrates the chord motion in melodic form. Play the phrase, listen, and connect the single-note sounds with their related chord forms.

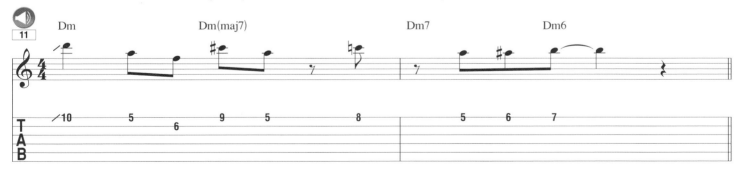

This variation depicts another common application of the pattern in the jazz language, this time over a ii–V progression: Dm7–G7. Note that the voice-leading melody over a G7, essentially superimposing an implied Dm–Dm(maj7)–Dm7–Dm6 progression on the dominant 7th chord. This sound became a staple in the bebop era and subsequent modern jazz.

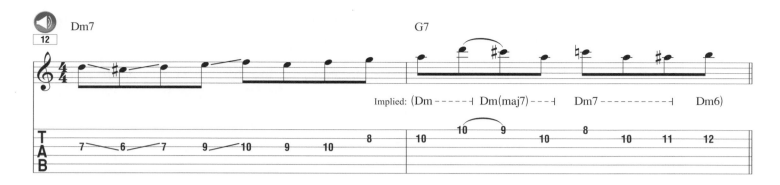

John Coltrane frequently applied the voice-leading pattern to single-note improvisations in the late 1950s. This characteristic phrase from a 12-bar blues in E♭ finds him sequencing the idea to navigate Gm7–F♯m7–Fm7–B♭7 chord changes. Note his clever melodic and rhythmic variations of the pattern.

Suspended Chords

The *suspended chord* has an almost opposite color compared to the m(maj7). Both are diatonic—however, where the m(maj7) has a restless, dissonant sound the suspended is perceived as unresolved but neutral and milder. In a *7sus4 chord*, a 4th replaces the 3rd; it is suspended above the replaced tone. That's why the same form can be used over minor and dominant 7th chords freely when a suspended sound is desired. While 7sus4 chords are related in quality to 11th extended chords, it's not quite the same, as true suspended chords don't contain a 3rd. Play the basic forms and listen to their unique color.

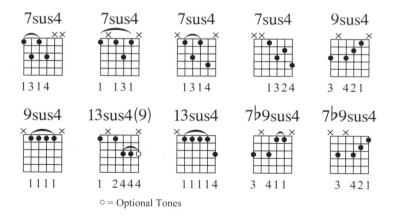

○ = Optional Tones

Like altered dominant 7th chords, suspended forms should be placed into harmonic context in V–I cadences. These four examples present a starting point. All four contain motion to a dominant 7th before the resolution to the tonic. The first is diatonic and maintains a common tone (E) in the top voice: G13sus4–G13–Cmaj7. The second is a blues application. Here, an altered dominant following the suspended chord resolves to a dominant 9th form. Note the harmonizing of a chromatic melody (A–A♭–G) in the top voice and the resulting parallel triads on strings 1–3: G13(9)sus4–G7♯5♭9–C9. The third contains an essential 11th-chord resolution. Here, the C♯ is maintained as a common tone into Dmaj7 in the top voice. The fourth is an example of the sus4 chord in a minor mode. The A7♭9sus4 is a suspended altered chord that places a Gm triad over an A bass note. It is resolved to A7♭9 and a Dm(maj9).

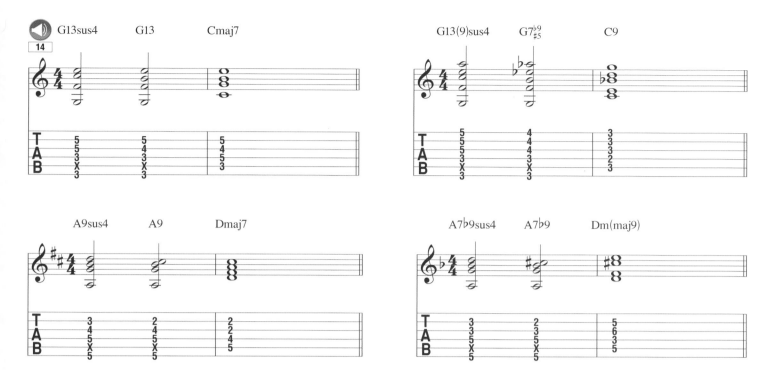

Once you have mastered these patterns freely create your own combinations and variations—and listen.

Diminished Chords

The *diminished 7th chord* (°7) is a unique sonority. Among its unique attributes is its structure, called *symmetrical* because it consists of four equidistant tones, each a minor 3rd apart. Thus, the same diminished form can be moved symmetrically every three frets and still be the same chord with a different voicing. The equal distance simply allows the same notes to be rearranged on different strings as the chord's position is changed. The diminished 7th chord divides the octave into four equal parts. These three shapes are the most common forms of the diminished chord.

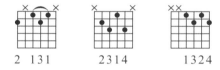

Added tones are frequently used to further color diminished chords. These can be considered suspensions in or extensions of the forms and will sound like close relatives of altered dominant 7th chords, specifically 13♭9 forms.

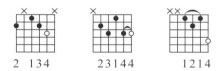

Consider the diminished shape on the top four strings. It can be E°7, G°7, B♭°7, or D♭°7. Play the forms at the second, fifth, eighth, and 11th positions. Notice the obvious symmetry and listen to the recurring tones. This is one of the most common ways a diminished chord is played in jazz. This maneuver is called *inversion* (more on this in Chapter 4).

With a diminished chord and its symmetrical structure, the inverted forms maintain an identical fingering. Many players, Wes Montgomery chief among them, have used this device to great musical effect.

Diminished Chord

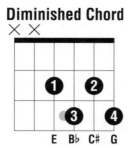

E B♭ C# G

Diminished Forms

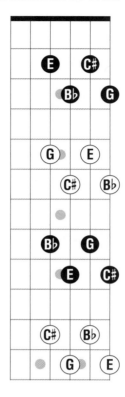

The diminished chord is, as Pat Martino has put it neatly, one of the *parental forms* on the guitar. Lowering any of its tones a half step generates an unaltered dominant 7th chord. Raising any of its tones produces a m6 chord.

This set of forms reveals the connection between E° and its related dominant 7th chords: E♭7, A7, C7, and F#7, as well as its related m6 chords: B♭m6, Em6, Gm6, and D♭m6.

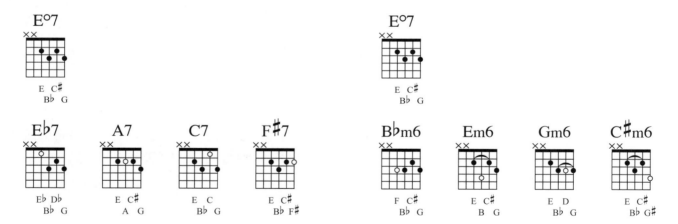

E°7
E C#
B♭ G

E°7
E C#
B♭ G

E♭7
E♭ D♭
B♭ G

A7
E C#
A G

C7
E C
B♭ G

F#7
E C#
B♭ F#

B♭m6
F C#
B♭ G

Em6
E C#
B G

Gm6
E D
B♭ G

C#m6
E C#
B♭ G#

In jazz harmony, the diminished chord is closely related to a 7♭9 altered dominant chord, and indeed, the diminished is often used as a substitute for a 7♭9 altered chord. That's because each tone can be the ♭9 of a dominant 7th chord. Furthermore, a single diminished chord has the potential of going to four different keys a minor 3rd apart. What does all this mean to a player? It means the diminished is a valuable and flexible device for substitution and modulation. An E° can be E♭7♭9 going to A♭ major, minor, or dominant 7th. Or, it can be an A7, C7, or F#7 going to D, F, or B, respectively. John Coltrane used a similar *3rds-related* procedure and the outline of a diminished chord to produce the chord progressions in "Central Park West," a standout composition from his "Giant Steps" canon.

The diminished chord, with its tremendous flexibility, has seen a variety of functions in jazz progressions. The most common is the *diminished substitution* for a dominant 7th chord. In this application, the diminished chord becomes a *rootless* voicing of the dominant—for example, D° becomes G7♭9 without a G root. This example is a ii–V–I progression in C using this substitution concept.

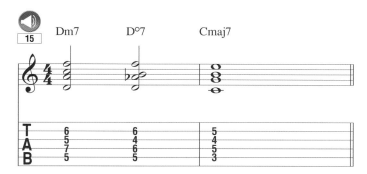

In countless standards, the diminished chord is used as an approach chord to a ii–V–I progression. There, it functions as a *flatted iii diminished* (♭iii°). Many jazz musicians, pianist Mark Levine among them, perceive this chord as a rootless substitution for a "disguised" A♭7♭9 or D7♭9 on its way to resolving to G7. Some of the greatest composers in the Great American Songbook, like Jerome Kern, George Gershwin, and Cole Porter, have woven the ♭iii° sound into tunes, such as "All the Things You Are," "Embraceable You," and "Night and Day."

Two versions of this progression should be learned. Offered are two instructive examples back-to-back. Note the use of Em7 to replace the Cmaj7. This is a familiar substitution and here, has the additional benefits of generating a descending chromatic bass line (E–E♭–D) and descending melody in the top voice.

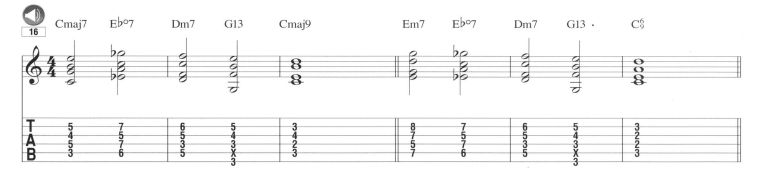

The diminished chord can also function as a *vii diminished* (vii°). In this case, the diminished leads to a tonic (I) major, minor, or dominant chord a half step higher. This phrase, based on a classic big band figure, uses the G#°7 and C#°7 forms to approach and target Am7 and Dm7 chords in a minor blues progression. Note the common tone, E, maintained through the first three forms.

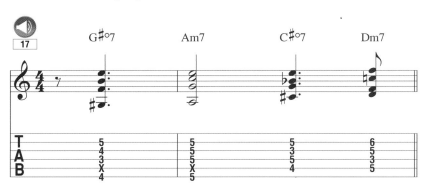

The *vii°* is sometimes used in reverse to lead away from a minor chord and modulate elsewhere. The voice leading created by this type of harmonic movement has been used by Antônio Carlos Jobim, Luis Bonfá, and other Brazilian jazz composers. This phrase, similar to the progression in "Corcovado," depicts motion from Am to F major. The G#°7 chord acts as a *pivot chord*—as both a vii° in relation to Am6 and ♭iii° in relation to F, underscoring the utility of the diminished chord in context.

Johnny Smith once mentioned he thought of the fully diminished chord as the logical resolution of a half-diminished (m7♭5) chord. Half-diminished resolving to fully diminished makes for a tidy and efficient formula. This phrase exemplifies the idea in a sequential cycling progression à la Dizzy Gillespie's "Woody'n You (Algo Bueno)" and "Stella by Starlight." Notice the tight voice leading—only the note on the 3rd string changes for each two-chord pattern.

Augmented Chords

We've already seen and played some of the commonly used augmented chords as altered 7th forms: the maj7#5 and the dominant 7#5 and 9#5. To deepen an understanding of augmented chords, it is useful to reduce the 7th chord to its triad form and observe a similar parental relationship as we saw with diminished chords. And indeed, again in Pat Martino's view of the guitar's nature, the augmented chord is the second parental form. This occurs because like the diminished chord, the augmented chord is built on equidistant intervals, but spaced a major 3rd apart. This divides an octave into three equal parts and exemplifies the idea of 3rds-related harmony in jazz. The augmented chord is frequently written with a "+" designating the raised 5th step. This is a G+ triad.

By moving any voice down a half step, a major triad is created. Thus, three different major triads are possible. G+ becomes G, E♭, and B. Or, put another way, the seemingly remote keys of G, E♭, and B are closely related by the augmented chord.

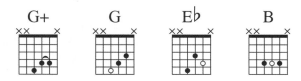

Conversely, moving any voice up a half step produces a minor triad. Thus, three minor triads are possible. G+ yields Em, Cm, and G#m. Interestingly, these chords are the relative minors of the aforementioned major triads.

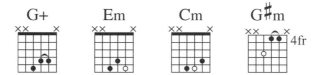

So what? Why does this bit of theoretical minutiae matter? It is one powerful illustration of how chromatic harmony and 3rds-relations work in a jazz context. At least, that's what John Coltrane thought. He used his knowledge of the augmented triad and its symmetry to compose one of his most iconic pieces, "Giant Steps," and other 3rds-related works in the modern jazz canon. Furthermore, awareness of the harmony informed his improvisations and were reflected in his melodies.

Trane based his ii–V–I changes throughout "Giant Steps" (C#m7–F#7–B, Fm7–Bb7–Eb, and Am7–D7–G) on the augmented chord's parental relationships and the resulting key centers of B, Eb, and G. Play these ii–V–Is, note common tones shared by chords, and *listen*.

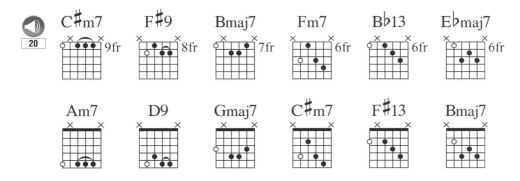

A Tip from Wes, Kenny, Barney, and Tal: Thumb Fretting

Thumb fretting is prevalent in jazz guitar, and has been used regularly by Wes Montgomery, Kenny Burrell, Howard Roberts, Barney Kessel, Tal Farlow, and many others. Why? Some chords require barring across the fingerboard with the index finger to fret all the tones. However, this makes muting with that finger impractical, if not impossible. Moreover, barring across the entire fingerboard does not allow for strumming the chords because unwanted notes aren't muted. Thumb fretting of bass notes alleviates problems of strict barring and in the process simplifies complicated fingerings, making it easier and more efficient to play the forms and make smooth connections in progressions. It often provides a more relaxed grip and enables you to play chords with an "extra" finger when needed. Thumb fretting is a universal guitar technique also found in country (Merle Travis), rock (Jimi Hendrix and Eddie Van Halen), and blues (Stevie Ray Vaughan).

I encourage you to make thumb fretting part of your chord approach to complement conventional fretting. Begin by checking out Barney Kessel's intro in "Tenderly" on *Easy Like*, Howard Roberts' opening phrases in "Mr. Lucky" on *All-Time Great Instrumental Hits*, and Kenny Burrell's final chord (G/Ab) of "In a Sentimental Mood" on *Lucky So and So*. Their thumb-fretted chords are beautifully woven into chord-melody passages that contain a variety of fingered forms.

On the next page are several practice phrases that utilize thumb fretting. Note the advantages the technique provides for muting the 5th string in several forms. As before, play these chords within V–I cadences and ii–V–I progressions to place them in musical context.

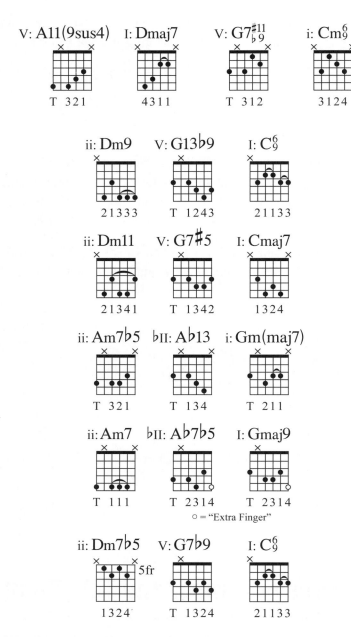

○ = "Extra Finger"

Wes Montgomery, Howard Roberts, and Kenny Burrell sometimes fretted the 6th and 5th strings with their thumbs. Here are three typical forms used in a ii–V–I progression:

CHAPTER 2

PLAYING CHANGES

As previously mentioned, chords break down into basic colors. This affects their function in progressions and the way you hear them. Consider the most common and prevalent progression in jazz: ii–V–I. The color or quality of each chord contributes to the overall movement: ii is a minor 7th chord color and has a subdominant function that sets up the V chord, V is a dominant 7th with an active function demanding strong resolution, and I is the tonic that provides an arrival and has a grounded, home-base quality.

Think of each chord as a group of voices, like a small choir, string quartet, or horn section. This was a premise embraced by Howard Roberts, George Van Eps, and Johnny Smith. Each voice has a determined and often logical melodic destination to another note within a chord change. Listen for voice leading in every chord change and note the color, function, and activity. This can occur in the shortest progressions or longest chord phrases. Listening closely develops your ear for the emotional impact of the chords you choose to play in your personal statement. This in turn will inform and guide your melodic improvisation.

Shell Chords

Shell chords are ubiquitous and are an essential asset in the jazz harmony toolbox. They are simple and standardized—the equivalent of rock's power chords. A shell chord is similar to converting a large barre chord into a smaller, more malleable form on three strings. Shell chords are used by most jazz guitarists to play a variety of chord phrases, and they are particularly effective in rhythm guitar and comping situations. George Van Eps, the undisputed chord genius of jazz guitar and one of the genre's greatest rhythm players, explained the transformation to me in a few simple steps:

First, play a *chord-scale* in triads. The top voice is the tonic of each form.

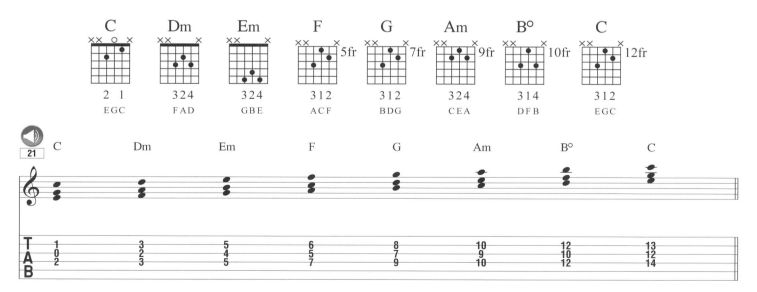

Next, add a lower tone a 5th below each form to produce a full, four-note 7th chord. Notice that the addition of that lower note puts a new root under the chords. C major becomes Am7, Dm becomes Bm7♭5, Em becomes Cmaj7, and so on. This is an important observation: The upper part of the chord (triad) is a diatonic extension. It defines a strong harmonic relationship, as in the case of C and Am7 being relative major and minor key centers. C and Em7 can be considered secondary relative major and minor key centers. We'll apply this harmonic thinking often in chord playing and improvised jazz melodies. Play the forms in a chord scale. This generates a *chord family*.

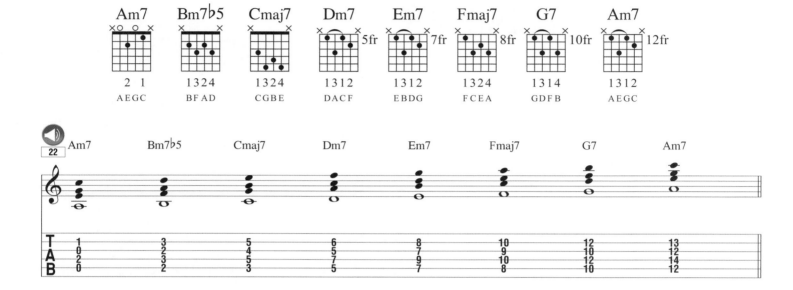

Now, remove the note on the fourth string to convert the form into a three-note shell chord. Van Eps called these "divided voicings" because they are not on consecutive strings. There is a division between fifth and third strings. The voicing now contains only the root, 7th, and 3rd—all the vital information. Note that the chords all have the same fingering: middle, ring, and pinky. Play these forms as a chord scale.

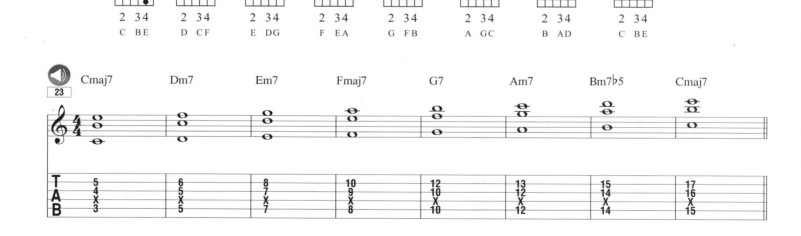

While they are simple, there's nothing simplistic about shell chords. By changing one note in a shape, it's possible to play two chords that are very closely related and share common tones. Move the B tone on the third string down one step in the scale, and Cmaj7 becomes C6 or Am (with C in the bass, an inversion). We can also look at it as a rootless Fmaj7 or F#m7♭5, both with the 5th in the bass. These transformations make shell chords, which by themselves are extremely valuable, exponentially more useful. Play the forms as two-chord patterns and listen to the progressions they create: Cmaj7–C6, Dm7–Dm6, Em7–C/E, Fmaj7–F6, G7–G6, Am7–F/A, and Bm7♭5–G/B.

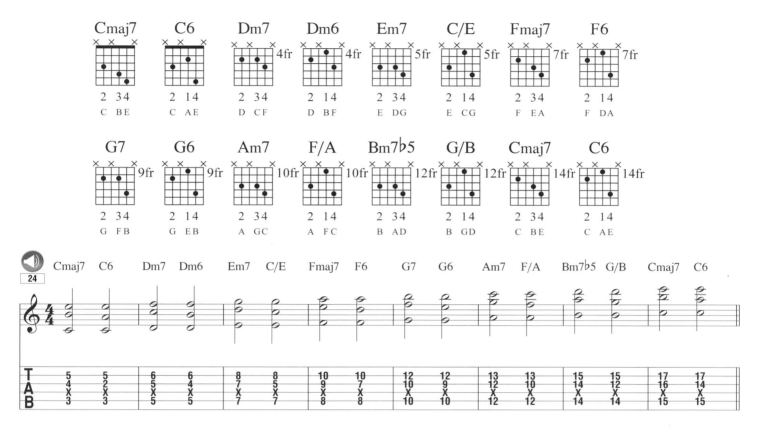

That's only part of the shell chord's utility. Consider the first four forms: That same set of shapes can be heard as Cmaj7–Am7–Dm7–G7, the all-important *I–vi–ii–V* progression used frequently as the simplest diatonic *turnaround*. Note that the Am7 and G7 are incomplete forms; Am7 is missing the 7th and G7 is missing its root. Nevertheless, the sound of the chord progression remains strong and identifiable. Play that group of four chords and listen to their new identities.

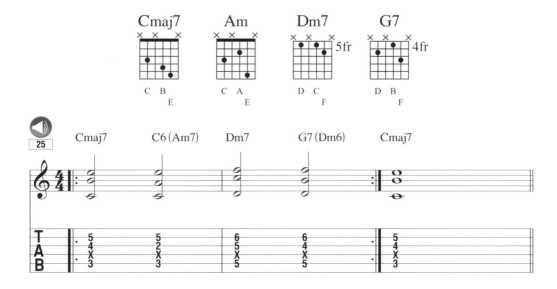

Shell chords can be expanded with simple chromatic alterations to form other progressions. In this phrase, the second shell chord can be seen as a C#°, the vii° of Dm7, or a rootless A7♭9. This is a very useful tactic in jazz harmony and enriches the turnaround progression with a dominant 7th sound resolving to Dm7. Notice two other refinements in the phrase: By lowering the D to D♭ (5th string) in G7, a D♭7 occurs. This is a tritone substitution in shell-chord form: G7 becomes D♭7. By lowering only the D to D♭ and keeping the C in the form, a half-step substitution or upper-neighbor figure is created: Dm7–D♭maj7–Cmaj7.

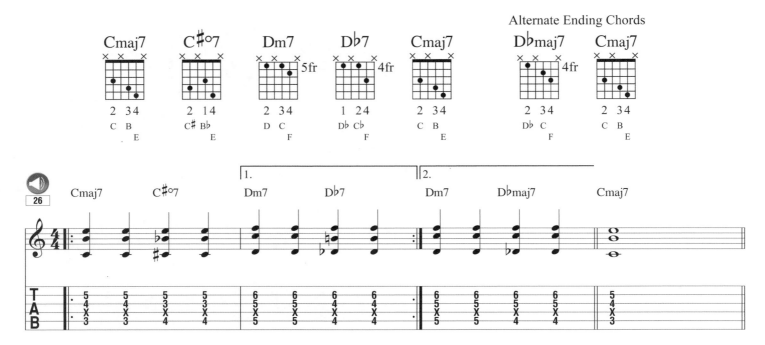

This longer phrase is an indispensable progression in jazz, heard in renditions of "Rhythm Changes" ("I Got Rhythm" verse, first half of the A sections) and many other tunes. Here, both the Cmaj7 and Dm7 shell chords are transformed into diminished chords, C#°7 and D#°7, that progress to Dm7 and Em7, respectively. This alteration generates an attractive ascending chromatic bass line: C–C#–D–D#–E, which gathers momentum as it rises. Listen to this figure and process it as a musical feeling. The Em7–A7–Dm7–G7 that concludes the progression provides a contrasting descending pattern and is another version of the turnaround.

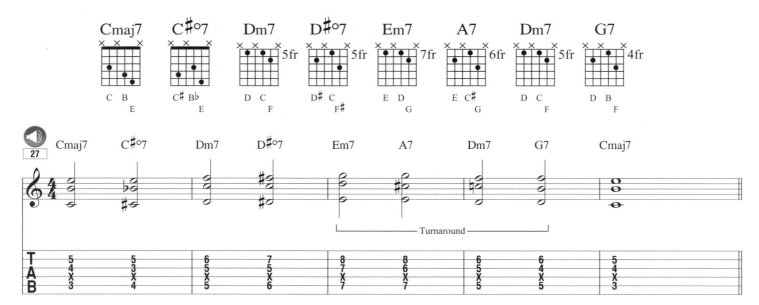

Shell chords merge and combine smoothly when diatonic and altered chords are mixed in a progression. This example uses a diatonic "walk-up" line: Cmaj7–Dm7–Em7–Fmaj7 in the first two measures. The descending section, a turnaround, is begun with an Fm7 passing chord, an alteration made by lowering the A and E to A♭ and E♭, respectively. This leads down and provides a smooth connection to Em7, the first chord of the turnaround. Listen to the voice leading and strive to internalize harmonic sensitivity for the subtle differences in the chord changes.

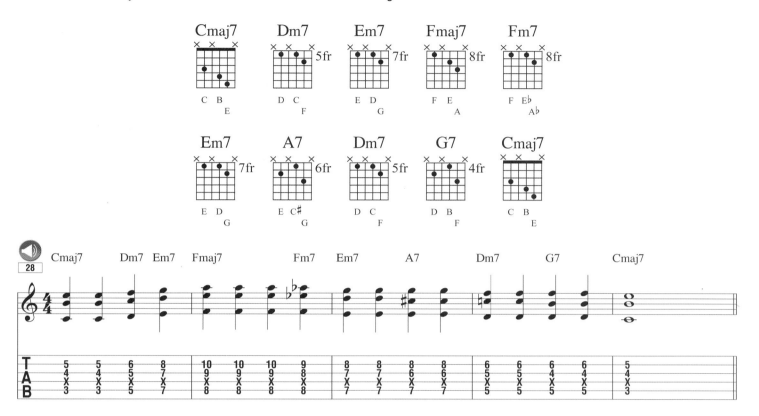

Shell-Chord Progressions

Let's put shell chords to work in a few standard progressions. This pattern is based on the chords of "All the Things You Are," one of the most important set of changes in the jazz repertoire. It is a *cycle-of-4ths* phrase, which moves through the key center of A♭ in 4ths: Fm–B♭m–E♭7–A♭–D♭ and then modulates to a new key, C major. Using shell chords and chromatic alteration, it's easy and efficient to make the D♭maj7 into a G7 form and resolve smoothly to the remote key of C.

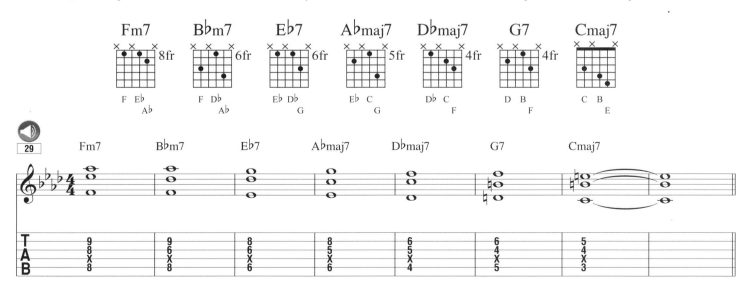

In the jazz vernacular, cycle harmony is often enlarged with additional chromatic passing chords. Here, an added A7 creates a stronger pull to A♭maj7 and the final cadence is expanded with a ii–V–I: Dm7–G7–Cmaj7.

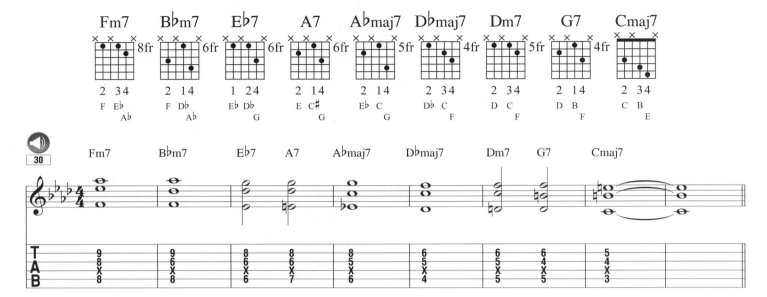

The progression can be further expanded with a chromatic ii–V cadence, Em7–A7, inserted into the changes, here before the A♭maj7. This is a strategy that enriches standard changes and is employed by countless jazz musicians, Wes Montgomery chief among them. In a 1965 European video (*Jazz Icons* series), you can watch Wes counsel his Dutch sidemen to play similar chromatic changes in the verse of "The End of a Love Affair."

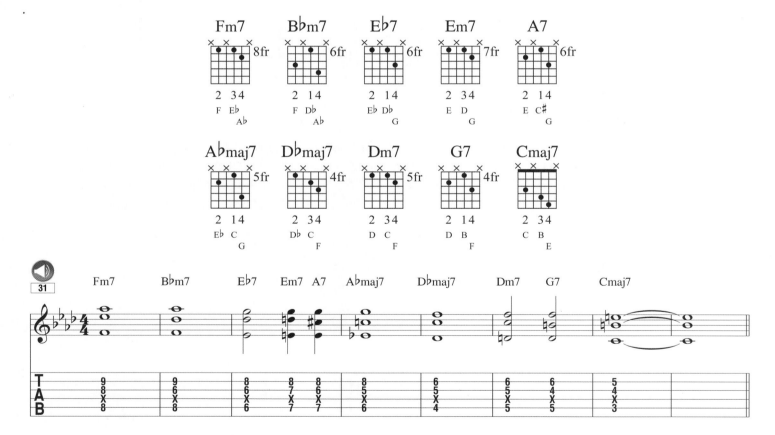

Any progression is possible with shell chords, even the most challenging and intricate. In fact, shell chords often provide a smoother way to play changes in remote keys and modulate. This demonstrative phrase applies shell chords to John Coltrane's "Giant Steps," comprised of 3rds-related changes. Using shell chords simplifies the guitar approach to the modulating progression.

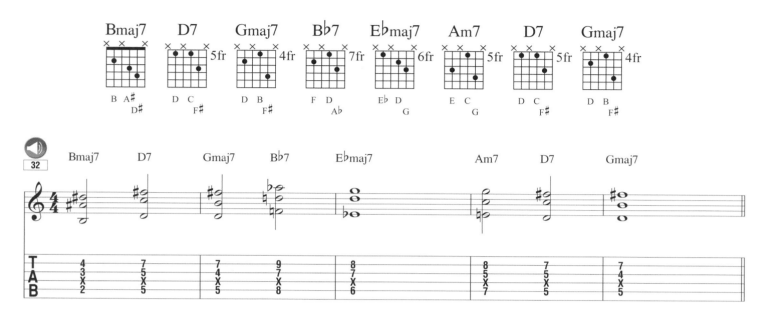

The modulating cycle of ii–Vs in tunes like "Woody'n You" and "Stella by Starlight" is also expedited with shell chords. Note that this entire progression is played with three forms that exemplify smooth voice leading. Another advantage is the missing 5th from the minor 7th chords, which allows the player to use the unspecific form over a minor 7th or minor 7♭5 chord.

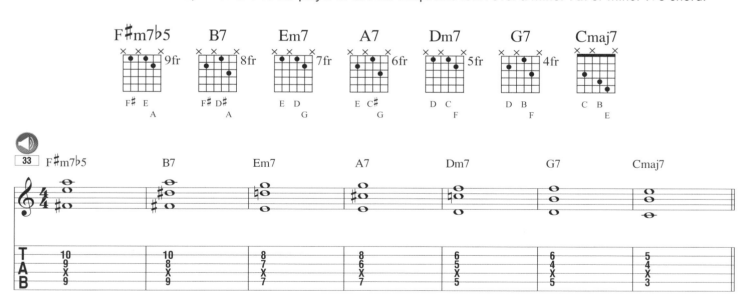

Shell chords should also be learned in the lower register on the sixth, fourth, and third strings. Here are the same forms played as a chord scale in the key of G, a 4th below, with root tones on the sixth string. Note the slight variations in the shapes, all shown on the next page.

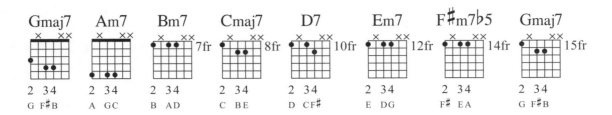

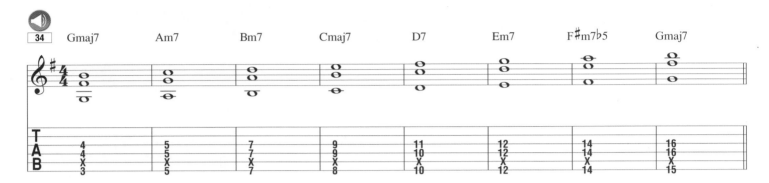

Play these lower shell chords with a moving inner voice on the fourth string, as previously seen in Track 24. After you have mastered these forms and combined them with shell chords having fifth-string roots, virtually every progression will fall comfortably under your fingers.

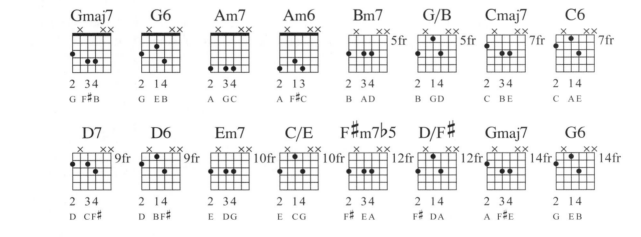

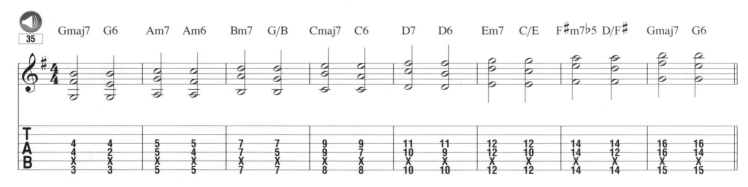

Let's combine the various shell-chord forms studied thus far in some essential progressions from the jazz repertoire. The first example is a phrase from Dizzy Gillespie's "Con Alma." V–I(i) cadences and ii–V–I changes are marked throughout. Note the connections and transitions of string groups.

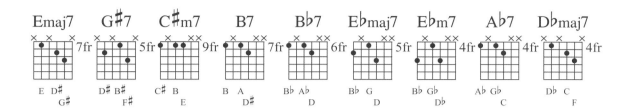

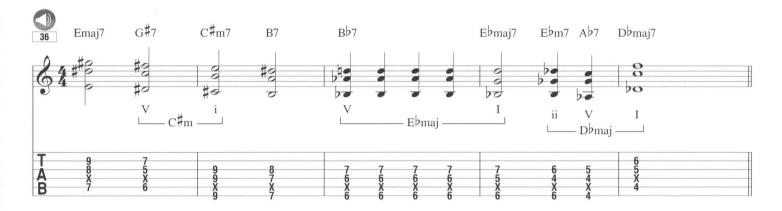

Duke Ellington's "Satin Doll" contains modulating patterns that recur in many tunes of the repertoire. Note the first three ii–Vs that modulate but don't resolve to their tonics: Dm7–G7, Em7–A7, and Am7–D7. These progressions normally resolve to C major, D major, and G major, respectively. The final Abm7–Db7 is a tritone substitution for Dm7–G7 and moves to Cmaj7 by half-step motion, another idiomatic jazz connection. There are two basic possibilities for rendering these progressions as shell chords.

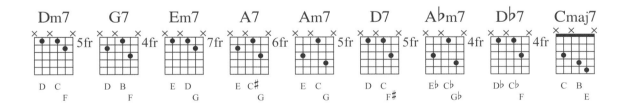

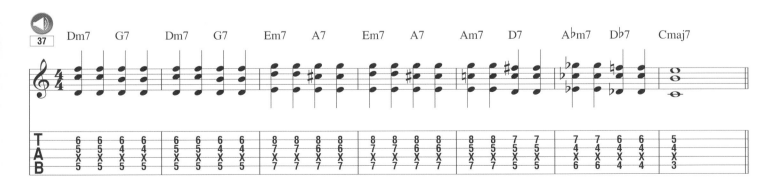

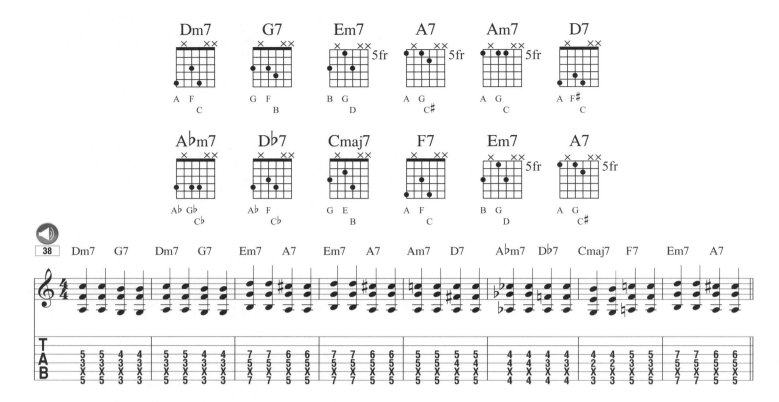

"I Got Rhythm" is the forerunner of practically every jazz tune to follow. Kenny Burrell once mentioned that no aspiring jazz player should sidestep this important piece in their learning and formative years. We made it a priority in the UCLA jazz program. "Rhythm Changes" have been a popular, reliable, and flexible progression with numerous options for harmonic variation. It has been used as a structure for *contrafacts* (a new melody written over a preexisting chord progression) by countless jazz musicians from Lester Young ("Lester Leaps In") and Duke Ellington ("Cottontail") in the swing era through modern jazz artists like Thelonius Monk ("52nd Street Theme"), Charlie Parker ("Anthropology"), Sonny Rollins ("Oleo"), Miles Davis ("The Theme"), Sonny Stitt ("The Eternal Triangle"), Michael Brecker ("Third Rail"), and Pat Metheny ("What Do You Want?"). This example in shell chords is the A section of the AABA form of the tune.

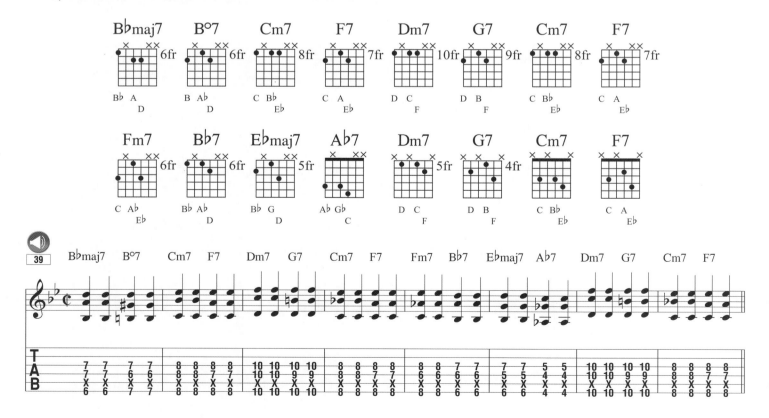

John Coltrane's "Moment's Notice" provides an ideal setting for advanced use of shell chords. This harmonic maze is essentially a series of fluid, modulatory ii–Vs and ii–V–Is that visits numerous tonal centers. Some patterns remain unresolved, like "Satin Doll," and are treated chromatically: Em7–A7 in the first phrase and Dm7–G7 in the second. Others resolve to temporary keys like E♭, D♭, Cm, A♭, and G♭. To assimilate the unusual changes, play the patterns in shell chords slowly and listen carefully.

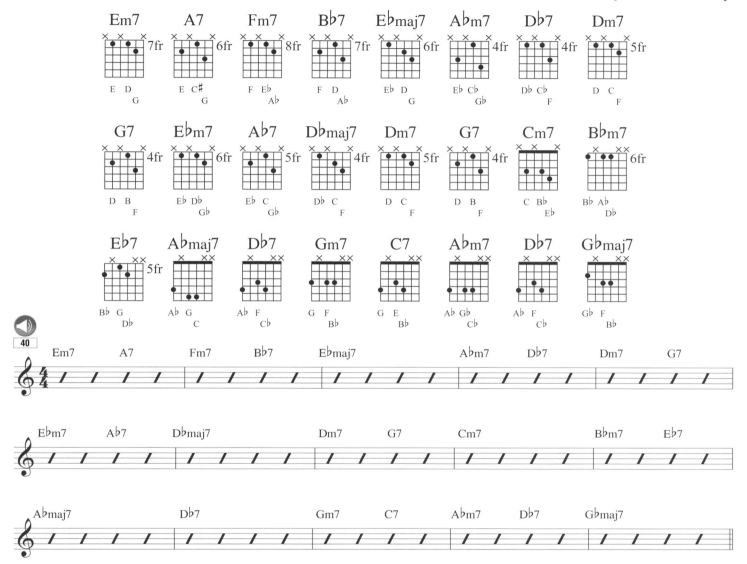

Shell chords on consecutive strings, sometimes called "small chords" or "short chords," provide additional valuable forms for comping, rhythm playing, and alternate voicings and textures in chord-melody work. This series of forms depicts this type of shell chord. It is used to play the "Woody'n You" or "Stella by Starlight" progression. Note the rootless V7 chords in the phrase. B7, A7, and G7 are dominant 7th voicings lacking a root tone; however, the voice leading is smooth due to common tones maintained through the ii–V cadences and the harmonic motion remains identifiable and convincing.

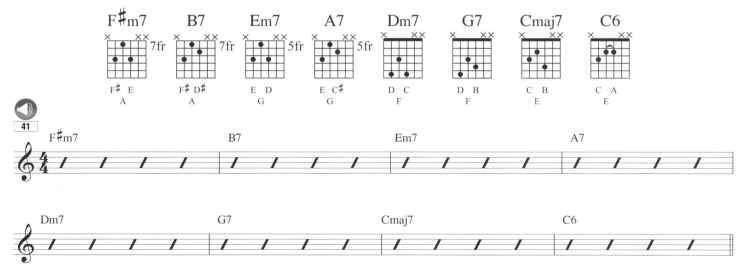

Compare these shapes with previous shell chords in this chapter. You'll see in this example that the two types are closely related and share the same exact tones. In minor 7th forms, such as F#m7, they are simply *re-voiced* to span the shorter outside interval distance of a 7th (F#–E) instead of a 10th (F#–A), or made "smaller." It's akin to a "juggling" effect where the A note on the fourth and second strings exchanges places, or is juggled. This holds true for major 7th chords. Check out Cmaj7: Its span of a 7th (C–B) is the smaller version of the 10th voicing (C–E). The dominant 7th (B7) and major 6th (C6) forms place the 3rd of the chord (D#) and 6th of the chord (A) in the top voice, which generates additional harmonic possibilities for chord-melody. Moreover, in a ii–V progression, it places the strong resolution tones, E–D# in F#m7–B7, in the higher register where it stands out to the listener.

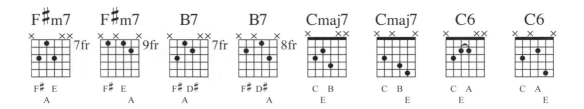

These small forms are well-suited to players first getting acquainted with jazz chording and progressions and are very efficient. They belong in every player's harmonic arsenal. Caveat: In the real world, these more tightly voiced forms sound best on the fifth–third string set. The 3rd of the chord on the middle string can sound muddy on the sixth–fourth string set and can lose its appeal quickly, especially if overused in a combo or large ensemble context where the guitar's low frequencies may result in sonic conflicts with the bass or low piano chords.

As an example of their efficiency and simplicity, here are the small shell-chord forms used to play the bridge of "April in Paris." Note how they expedite chromatic motion as well as ii–V–I progressions.

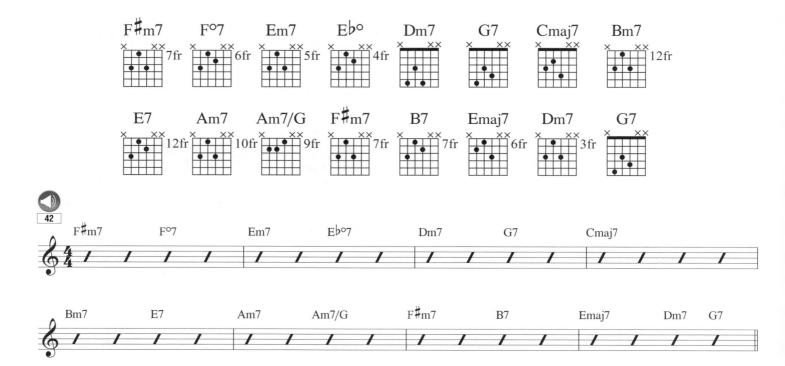

Guide Tones

There are smaller forms that naturally arise from shell chords. These are two-note chords, or *dyads*. Dyads are extremely useful in comping situations where the *density* of chords, i.e. how many notes are in the actual voicing, must be kept to a minimum so as not to interfere with other instruments in an arrangement, but still reflect the harmony. This awareness is mandatory when playing in ensembles of any size. In assessing the guitar's comping role, it often comes down to two notes. But which two notes? This question leads directly to the subject of using *guide tones*.

In jazz harmony, the content of dyads guides the movement of the two voices in relation to an underlying chord progression. Put succinctly, guide tones guide the activity. When playing these two-note chords, the sound should strongly imply the voice leading of a progression with its most active tones. These are most often the 3rd and 7th of a chord, such as E and B of Cmaj7, E and Bb of C7, and Eb and Bb of Cm7. In devising guide-tone forms, dyads are generally voiced as the interval of a 4th, 5th, or tritone (flatted 5th or raised 4th) and played as a chord. Harmonically, the 3rd determines the quality (major or minor) and is stable while the 7th is dissonant and produces melodic motion towards resolution in a chord change.

The distilling of harmonic information down to its "essence" makes for compact and versatile sounds and shapes that can fit a variety of situations. In this chapter we have explored several important shell-chord forms and their use in common chord progressions. A logical starting point for understanding and applying guide-tone chords grows directly from these shapes and patterns.

Guide Tones and Shell Chords

A *guide-tone chord* may be considered a "shell inside a shell." To develop understanding and facility, it's instructive and practical to extract guide-tone dyads from three-note shell chords and apply them to existing progressions. Consider this simple progression seen earlier as Track 25. By removing the bass note (root tone), we automatically generate a guide-tone chord from each shell chord. The changes are Cmaj7–C6–Dm7–G7–C, played with only two-note chords defining the voices in the progression. Notice that all three qualities of the intervals are present: B–E is a 4th interval, implying Cmaj7 with a major 7th and major 3rd. A–E is a 5th that spells C6 with a major 6th and major 3rd. B–F is a tritone that defines G7 with a major 3rd and flatted 7th. Each interval has a mood or color: The 4th is moderately active, the 5th is stable, and the tritone is the most active and unstable. By combining these qualities and their chord inferences, a variety of chords can be generated with two notes.

The dyads in this example have been moved to the third and fourth strings. In rhythm guitar and comping contexts, the most basic guide-tone chords occur on the third–fourth and fourth–fifth string sets, in the mid-range—the guitar's "sweet spot." Play these shapes and listen for the implied chord movement of a progression.

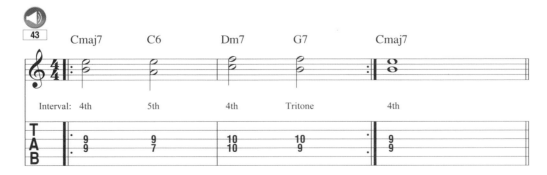

This progression is a guide-tone repurposing of Track 27 and presents a similar fingering transposition. It includes chromaticism, diminished chords, and a turnaround pattern in measures 3–5. The phrase connotes more activity. Why? The dyads are either 4ths or tritones, the less stable intervals.

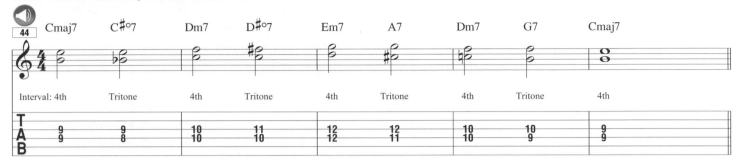

Guide-Tone Chord Progressions

Guide-tone chords are ideal for conveying the harmonic movement of cycle progressions. This sequence defines the cycle-of-4ths changes and modulations of "All the Things You Are." These two cycle phrases are played on different string sets, second–third strings and third–fourth strings. Play the guide-tone chords and listen for the resolution of the tritone to either 5th or 4th interval.

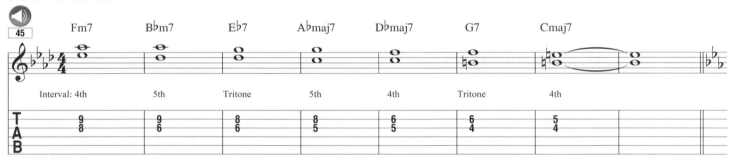

Guide-tone chords are well suited to virtually any standard progression. This example is a variation of Track 37 and presents a guide-tone framework for comping on "Satin Doll" changes.

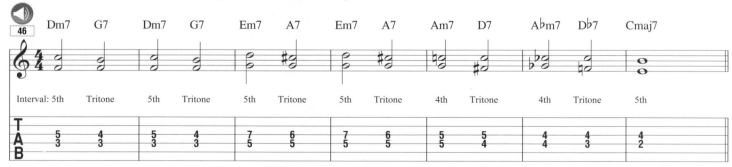

Imagine you're confronted with a chord chart for "Rhythm Changes" à la "Anthropology" or "Oleo" to be played at an up-tempo pace. It's essential you visualize and manage guide-tone chords effortlessly in response to the written symbols.

This progression portrays the first eight bars of "Rhythm Changes." There are several refinements in this example, offered as suggestions to aspiring rhythm guitarists. Check out the characteristic "Charleston" rhythm pattern employed in measures 1–2 and 5–6. This is an idiomatic comping figure favored by countless jazz pianists and guitarists. It is contrasted by straight, half-note rhythms in bars 3–4 and 7–8. After you become comfortable with these options, try mixing and matching or adding your own variations. With practice, you'll soon create a personal rhythm-guitar arrangement spontaneously.

Notice a wider variety of dyad forms and plural applications of shared interval structures in the phrases. This is the musical equivalent of a homonym in language and permeates jazz harmony. A 4th is used for both B♭maj7 and Cm7 in measures 1–2, a tritone for diminished and dominant chords throughout, and 5th–tritone sequence for the Dm7–G–Cm7–F7 turnaround in measures 7–8.

Guide-tone chords provide effective uncluttered accompaniment. The blues is a prime candidate for this treatment. This 12-bar progression in G is suitable for comping in a rhythm section behind a keyboard solo or lightly behind a bass solo. If you are playing without a drummer, play straight, quarter-note rhythms and maintain a steady pulse, thus providing a different type of accompaniment—a more basic form of rhythm guitar. Using guide-tone chords, there's enough harmonic content to convey the intent and feeling of the blues changes without interfering with another player's improvisations. Note the chromatic motion in bars 7–8 and the turnaround sequence in 11–12.

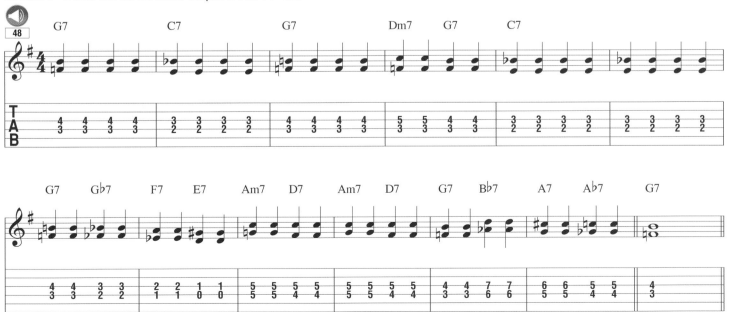

Guide-tone chords facilitate fast moving changes. This example applies dyad shapes to the complex harmony of "Moment's Notice." These forms are reductions of the shell chords used in Track 40. Play the progression and listen for smooth voice leading in the chord connections. Be cognizant of common tones in chords as remote as D♭maj7 and Dm7 in measures 7–8. Guide-tone chords have a leveling effect that boils the most intricate harmony down to two notes, the smallest and simplest essential unit. That is part and parcel of their allure and utility.

CHAPTER 3

PLAYING BLUES CHANGES

Blues is central to the jazz experience. The greatest musicians in the genre have been devoted blues advocates since its inception—Louis Armstrong, Lester Young, Charlie Christian, Nat Cole, Oscar Peterson, Thelonious Monk, Charlie Parker, Dizzy Gillespie, Dexter Gordon, John Coltrane, Cannonball Adderley, Jimmy Smith, Kenny Burrell, Grant Green, Wes Montgomery, and George Benson are just a few exponents on the short list. Blues harmony in jazz begins with the understanding that it is not that far removed from the most basic rural and urban blues heard in the music of Robert Johnson or B.B. King.

The commonalities are myriad. The standardized 12-bar form remains the underlying edifice. The practice of employing three complementary four-bar phrases, statement–reiterated statement–answer to the statement, is also heard prominently. The *call-and-response* phrase structure prevails in many jazz-blues tunes, as does the riff-based melodic procedure. Consider the use of riffs and imitative question-answer phraseology in Charlie Parker's "Cool Blues," Horace Silver's "Doodlin'," Sonny Rollins' "Tenor Madness," John Coltrane's "Blue Train," Cannonball Adderley's "Barefoot Sunday Blues," Wes Montgomery's "West Coast Blues," and Kenny Burrell's "Chitlins Con Carne."

In jazz-blues pieces, most of the harmonic movement from tonic (I) to subdominant (IV) and dominant (V), is very similar in its broad strokes. What is striking is its variety and sophistication. Blues can be cast in the simplest 12-bar, riff-based format or make use of alternate meters, like 3/4 and 6/8 (or even odder time signatures), and employ chord substitutions, harmonic enrichments, dissonance, and angularity. But as Kenny Burrell maintained, "Throughout the history of jazz, people play the blues in many forms—fast, medium, slow, funky, sophisticated, in different meters, and avant-garde. *It's still blues.*"

Basic 12-Bar Blues in Jazz

The most common form of blues changes in jazz is the traditional 12-bar progression with three phrases in a major/dominant tonality with characteristic moves to the IV and V chords. In jazz, these 12-bar progressions are enriched and expanded harmonically with the use of *secondary chords*—secondary diatonic 7ths and secondary dominant 7ths. The latter ingredients signify the move away from traditional folk blues and urban blues à la Muddy Waters and Howlin' Wolf and open the door to blues in jazz.

Let's begin our investigations with a standard 12-bar blues enhanced with secondary chords. This basic progression in B♭ provides a typical example with minimal complexity in shell chords. Play the changes and listen to the enriched colors and activity in measures 4 and 8. The Fm7–B♭7 in measure 4 is an expansion of the B♭7 chord through a process known as *back-cycling* (a term I learned from Joe Pass) and acts as a ii–V to establish E♭7. The G7 in measure 8 is the secondary dominant V7 of Cm7 and emphasizes the motion to the ii chord. Also note that the secondary 7th, Cm7, in bar 9 expands the usual V chord into a ii–V–I progression headed back to the tonic B♭7.

The turnaround at the end of the form is the standard I–vi–ii–V or I–VI–ii–V progression. Many of these harmonic enhancements are the direct result of strides made in the bebop era by players like Charlie Parker and Dizzy Gillespie. (This is demonstrated on the next page.)

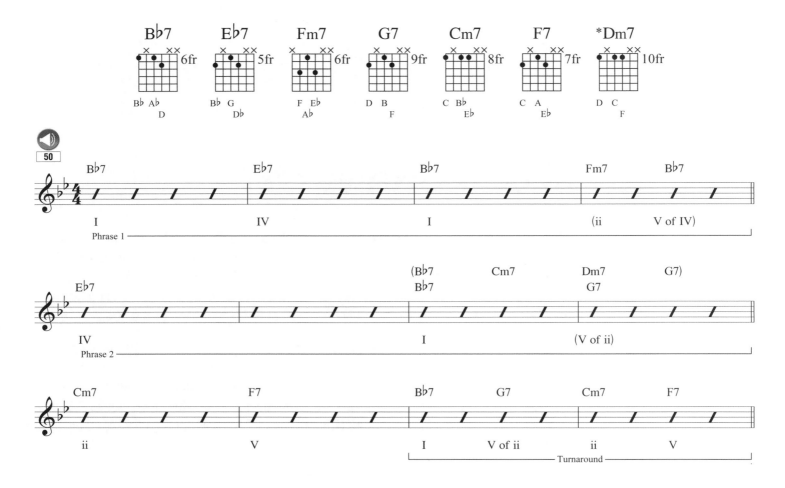

*The G7 in measure 8 is often preceded by Dm7, another secondary 7th chord, to produce a short, one-bar ii–V pattern (Dm7–G7), also via back-cycling.

Once a fundamental understanding of the basic changes is grasped, the creative process–the fun–begins. In this enriched version of the 12-bar blues, again in shell-chord forms, a number of chromatic *push chords*, based on neighboring forms a half step away from their destination, are applied: upper-neighbor E7 to Eb7 in measures 1–2, lower-neighbor A7 to Bb7 in measures 2–3, the chromatic sequence Fm7–E7–Eb7 in measures 4–5, and B7–Bb7 in measures 10–11. Also, check out the use of a superimposed ii–V change, Ebm7–Ab7, to color and expand the return to the I chord in measures 6–7. This common borrowing from the temporary key of Db produces a type of *deceptive cadence*.

Passing-tone chords are found in the chromatic descending figures of measures 7–8, highlighting the G7 chord, and act as a *substitute turnaround* with chromaticism in measures 11–12. Substitute turnarounds are common in the blues but may also be used freely in standards and any jazz composition with turnarounds in their structure. In this case, the time span stays the same (two bars), but the colors and motion are different: Db7 is the tritone substitute of G7, C7 replaces Cm7, and B7 is the tritone substitute of F7.

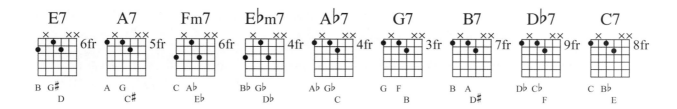

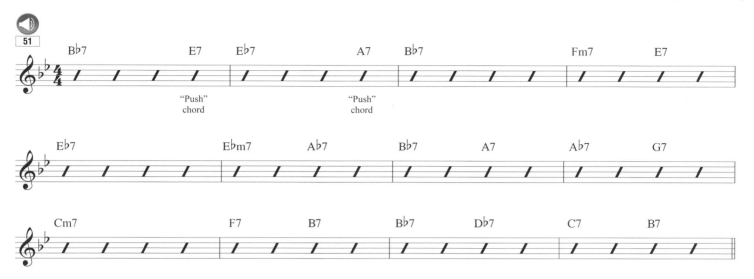

Combining larger chords from Chapter 1 with shell chords, a different and more varied 12-bar blues progression with mixed textures and voicings is made possible. This example applies extended voicings, like 9th and 13th chords, and altered chords: Bb7#5, G7#5, and F13b9. The latter is a member of the diminished chord family, as is the substitute Db°7 in measure 2, which functions as a rootless Eb7b9 (more on this later). Dm7b5 is applied here as a rootless substitute for Bb9 (Bb9/D) in measures 3–4. The superimposed ii–V pattern Ebm7–Ab7 is enlarged to Ebm9–Ab13 in measure 6. A cycle-of-4ths pattern replaces the chromatic descent in measures 7–8. Note the use of chromatic push chords in measures 1, 3–4, 9, and particularly in the turnaround of measures 11–12. Here, the two-bar progression makes use of chromatic neighbor chords in the "stride-piano" style popularized for guitar by Joe Pass. A chord change on every beat produces the familiar walking effect of stride piano. Only simple shell chords are used in the turnaround phrase, which facilitates the quicker harmonic rhythm.

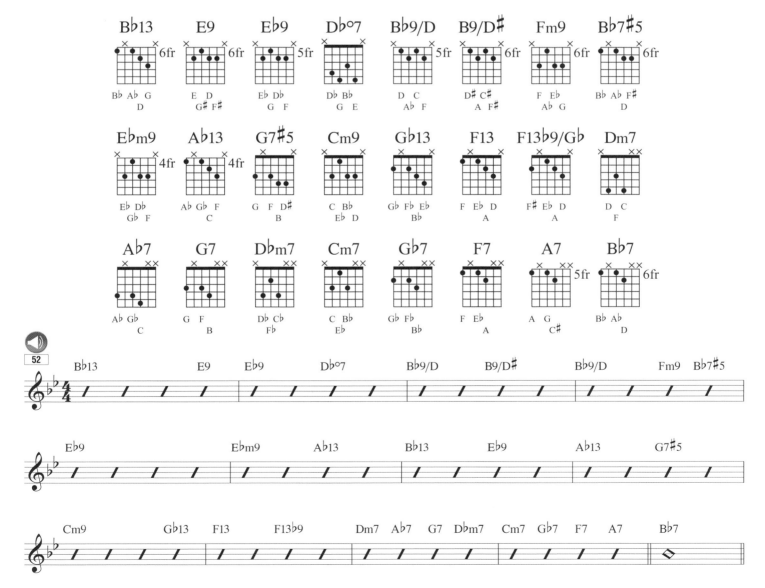

Bird Blues

A common variation of blues harmony in jazz has been called the "Bird Blues" progression, sometimes referred to as "modern blues" or "bebop blues." "Bird Blues" gets its name from Charlie "Bird" Parker, a founding father of bebop who used the altered and enriched changes in "Blues for Alice" and "Laird Baird." Similar changes were used by Sonny Stitt in "Jack Spratt" and Tommy Flanagan in "Freight Train."

"Bird Blues" contains numerous substitutions and alternate chord patterns. This 12-bar progression in F illustrates the expanded harmony and colors of "Bird Blues." The first four bars are, in essence, the "Confirmation" changes grafted onto the blues form, a descending sequence that employs three modulating secondary ii–V patterns in a row: | F | Em7–A7 | Dm7–G7 | Cm7–F7 |. This section represents extensive back-cycling in the blues form. Note that the final Cm7–F7 provides the all-important resolution to the IV chord, B♭. Toots Thieleman's "Bluesette" also employed this pattern. A similar sequence of ii–Vs in descending chromatic motion occurs in measures 5–8: | B♭m7–E♭7 | Am7–D7 | A♭m7–D♭7 |. This pattern was used by Wes Montgomery in "Missile Blues" and "West Coast Blues."

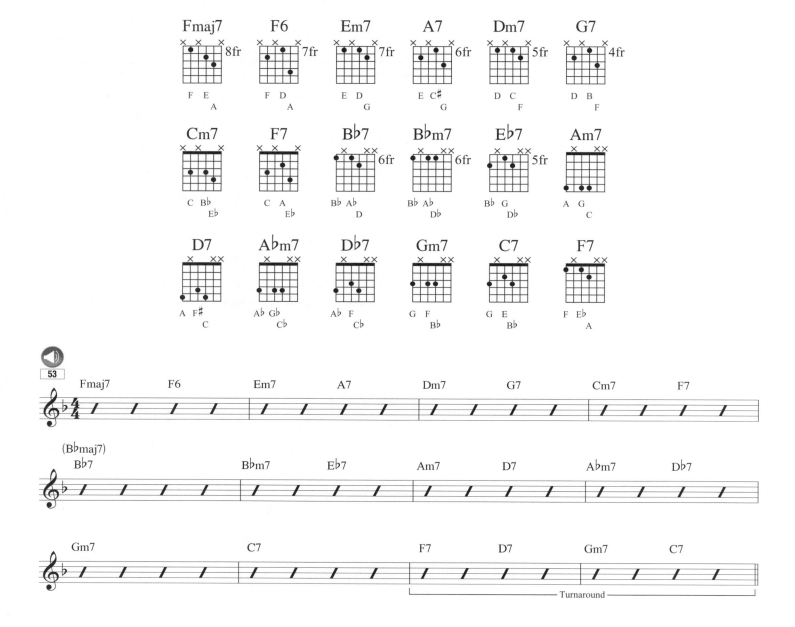

"Bird Blues" is sometimes expanded with a major 7th chord as a substitute IV, replacing the customary dominant 7th—B♭maj7 instead of B♭7. Another common variation is the use of iii–VI–ii–V progression (Am7–D7–Gm7–C7) in the turnaround. Both are heard in Track 54, starting with bars 1–5 of "Bird's Blues."

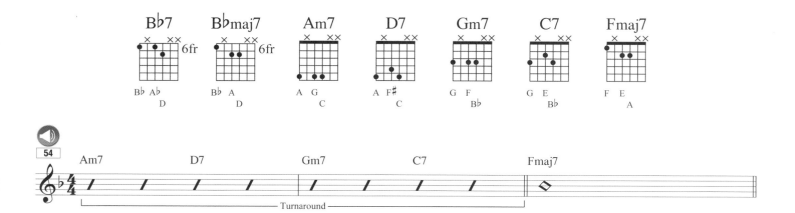

"Bird Blues," with its larger harmonic palette, invites *alternate turnarounds*. Once you've become comfortable with the basic progression, it is valuable to apply different patterns and colors to the final two bars of the form. Here and on the next page are several idiomatic possibilities from the harmonic lexicon of bop and post-bop jazz. Note the mixture of secondary, extended, and altered chords with chromatic motion and substitutions.

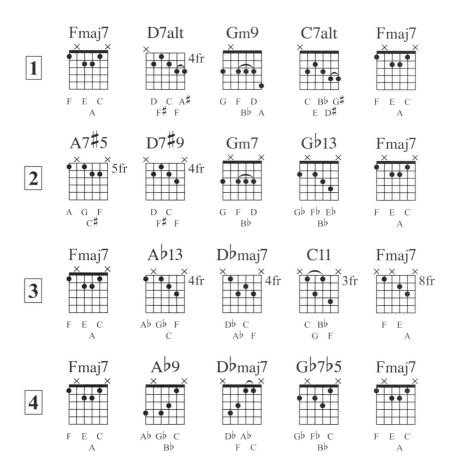

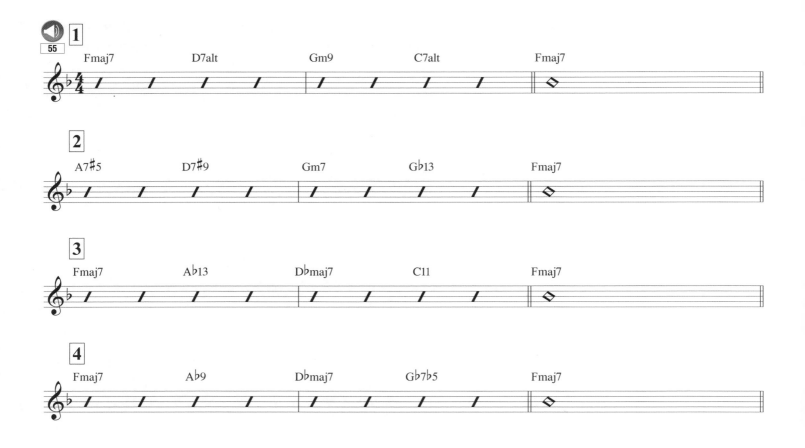

Minor Blues

Minor blues projects an important contrasting mood and color in jazz. Countless artists have explored the parallel minor mode for its distinctive qualities and tendencies to enrich a 12-bar blues progression. Salient examples include Dizzy Gillespie's "Birk's Works," Oliver Nelson's "Stolen Moments," John Coltrane's "Equinox" and "Mr. P.C.," and Kenny Barron's "Minor Blues." Minor blues has inspired jazz composers like Nat Adderley, Stanley Turrentine, and Charles Mingus in tunes as diverse as "Work Song," "Sugar," and "Goodbye Pork Pie Hat," respectively, which are undeniably blues-based, though not in the strict 12-bar structure. Moreover, the feeling and colors of minor blues informed many composers in the Great American Songbook. Consider tunes like "Summertime," "Angel Eyes," "Cry Me a River," "Fever," and "In a Sentimental Mood," as well as more recent popular pieces such as "This Masquerade" and "The Thrill Is Gone."

The 12-bar minor-blues progression retains the standard form, harmonic rhythm, and i–iv–V chords but replaces the major/dominant tonality with minor modality and its indigenous harmony. This example presents the simplest form of minor blues, heard in John Coltrane's "Mr. P.C." and "Equinox." Note the harmonic scheme: i in measures 1–4 (first phrase), iv–i in measures 5–8 (second phrase), and ♭VI–V–i in the final cadence of the third phrase. The most common form of the basic changes uses a ♭VI–V progression in measures 9–10. In this part of the progression, the secondary ♭VI is usually voiced as a dominant 7th chord, generating a convenient neighbor effect a half step above, leading to the V chord, a subdominant to dominant function. Remember, in a major/dominant tonality, this cadence is played as ii–V–I, but functions similarly as a subdominant–dominant–tonic pattern. Put another way, ♭VI–V–i and ii–V–I are functionally equivalent, and in many tunes, are used interchangeably.

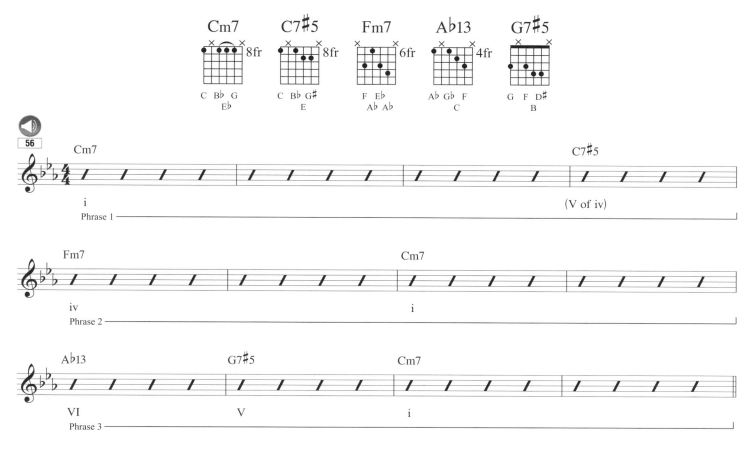

Jazz players frequently use minor 6th and minor 7th forms on the i and iv chords: Cm7–Cm6 and Fm7–Fm6. These generate more harmonic color and motion.

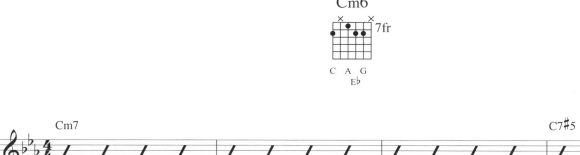

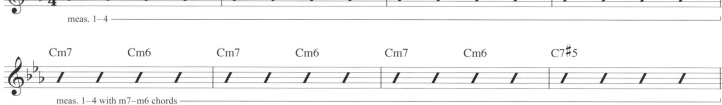

The minor-blues progression is made more interesting with additional secondary chords. This example illustrates refinements used by Dizzy Gillespie in "Birk's Works." It embodies a standard approach to 12-bar minor blues. Note the short ii–Vs in measures 2, 4, 9, and 10. The Dm7♭5–G7 is diatonic to C minor. However, in measure 4, the same progression is a modulating ii–V leading to iv, Fm7: Gm7♭5–C7, the m7♭5 color indigenous to a minor key. In C minor, it can be seen as a ii chord (Dm7♭5, measures 2 and 10) and can also be used as a iv minor 6th chord (Fm6 in measures 5–6). Why? Both have a subdominant function. In measure 9, E♭m9–A♭13 is a superimposed ii–V cadence on A♭13, a characteristic back-cycling pattern in jazz/blues. (This is shown on the next page.)

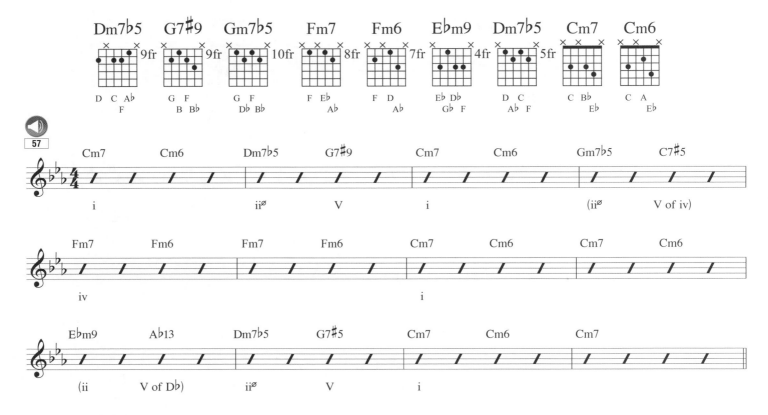

Another option is to use the ii–V–i in the final four bars of the changes and consider the Dm7♭5 to be a type of tritone substitute for A♭7.

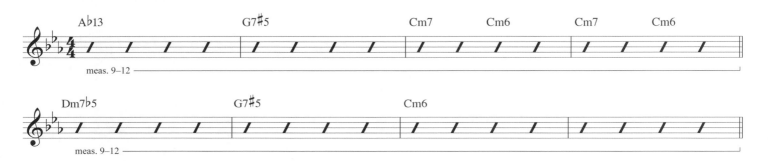

Many other forms of colorizing the minor-blues progression are heard in the repertoire. The following examples are four common alternative approaches to the first four measures of the form.

1. Cm7–Cm6 replaces a static Cm6 chord in measures 1 and 3, increasing the harmonic motion. Also note the mixture of shell-chord forms with larger shapes from Chapter 1.

2. The Am7♭5 provides a different expansion of the progression and superimposes a minor-mode turnaround on measures 1–2. Am7♭5 is essentially an inversion of Cm6: C minor with the major 6th (A) in the bass. Note the use of Gm7 as an alternative for Gm7♭5.

3. A♭13 replaces Dm7♭5 in measure 2. This generates an attractive chromatic bass line in the progression and emphasizes the motion to G7: A–A♭–G. In measure 4, the move to Fm7 is strengthened by two diminished chords, D♭°7 and E°7. These are substitutes for C7♭9.

4. Occasionally, a modal approach is desired in minor blues. In this phrase, Cm7–Dm7–E♭maj7–Dm7 forms in shell chords create a diatonic walking impression.

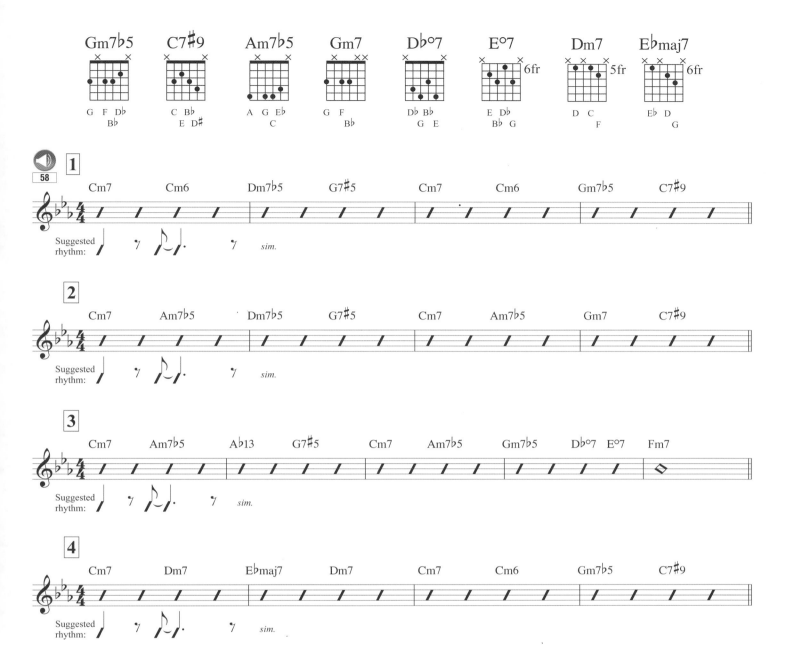

A common enrichment of minor blues changes occurs in measure 8. This example begins on measure 7 of the form. Note the Bbm7–Eb9 in measure 8. It is essentially a short ii–V headed to Ab (measure 13). This maneuver is heard in "Little Shannon," the opening minor blues number on Don Patterson's *Opus De Don* (featuring Pat Martino).

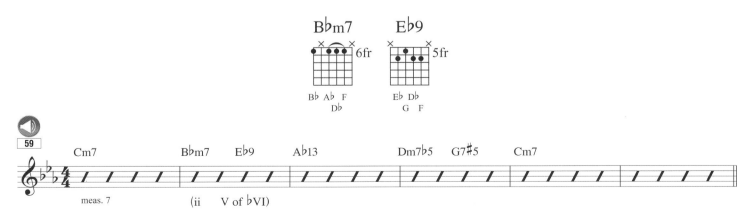

Sometimes, the progression is enlarged further by placing an altered II7–V7 (D7#9–G7#5) cadence in measures 9–10 of the changes. This color is found in Stanley Turrentine's "Sugar."

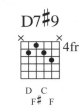

Let's dig deeper into the repertoire and its harmonic language. Here are two exemplary minor-blues progressions exhibiting alternate harmonic pathways.

Trumpeter Clifford Brown experimented with minor-blues changes and the structure of the progression in "Minor Mood." He delayed the return to I (Fm) in measure 7 by substituting a ii–V (Gm7b5–C7) in its place. The resolution to Fm instead occurred a bar later in measure 8. Also note a more extensive use of the ii–V pattern (Gm7b5–C7), in both long and short form, throughout the changes in measures 2, 7, 9–10, and 12.

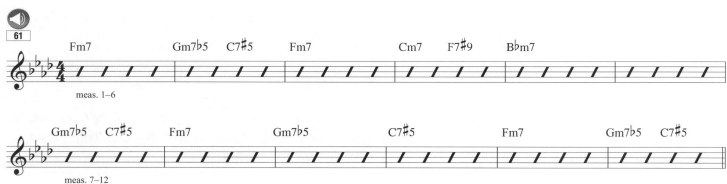

Pianist Bill Evans presented his own interesting minor blues experiments in "Interplay." Note the use of a "quick iv" maneuver from Fm to Bbm in measure 2. This is a more obvious modal application of the subdominant, which provides a nice contrast to the more typical, tonal ii–V pattern used in "Birk's Works," "Minor Mood," and many others, in the same part of the changes. Also note that the Ab13 chord in measure 8 acts as a push chord to the Gm7b5–C7 progression in measures 9–10. The unusual alternate turnaround in measures 11–12 is indicative of Evans' advanced harmonic conception. This turnaround begins traditionally with Fm7–Dm7b5 in measure 11 but departs into tritone substitution chords in measures 12, where Dbmaj7–Gbmaj7 replace the normal Gm7b5–C7 changes.

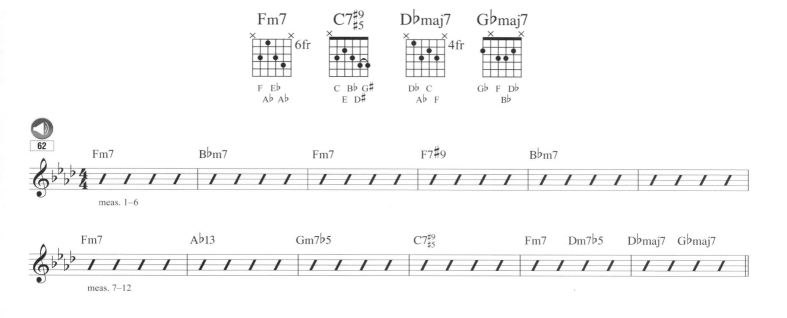

Altered Blues

Blues in jazz welcomes innovation. Many of the greatest composers and performers in the genre have used the blues as a springboard for experimentation, altering existing norms along the way. Reharmonization, harmonic substitutions, alternative meter, and alteration of the 12-bar form itself were common points of departure. The following tunes are exemplary.

In Miles Davis' "All Blues," written as either 6/4 (retaining the 12-bar form) or 3/4 (doubling the number of measures into a 24-bar form), a jazz waltz pulse replaces the usual swing or shuffle feel of medium-tempo blues. The harmony reflects the modal, modern-jazz environment of *Kind of Blue* with simple 7th chords, G7 and C7, over a pedal-point bass riff in measures 1–8 and more dissonant altered chords, D7#9 and Eb7#9, played in chromatic parallel motion in measures 9–10.

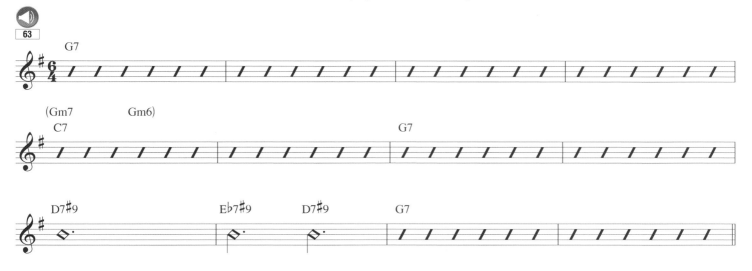

Like Miles Davis, John Coltrane kept the 12-bar form but expanded the harmony in "Some Other Blues." The chords in the first phrase are largely traditional except for a tritone substitution push chord, B7, in measure 4 resolving to Bb7. In measure 5, Trane began on the IV chord, Bb7, but used it to commence a cycle-of-4ths progression: Bb7–Eb7–Ab7–Db7. This replaces the return to I (F7), normally in measure 7, with an Ab7. The Db7 at the end of the second phrase functions as both the final chord of the cycle and a push chord to C7. C7–Bb7–F are reversions to the simplest blues harmony of V–IV–I. (See this in play on the next page.)

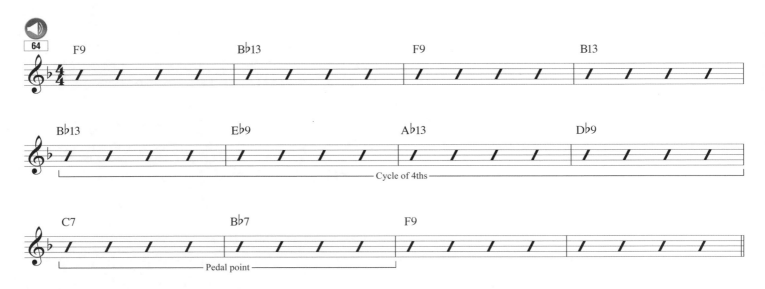

John Coltrane may have gotten the idea from his former employer, Thelonious Monk, who used a similar chord substitution (Ab7 in conjunction with Bb7) in measures 5–6 of "Blues Five Spot."

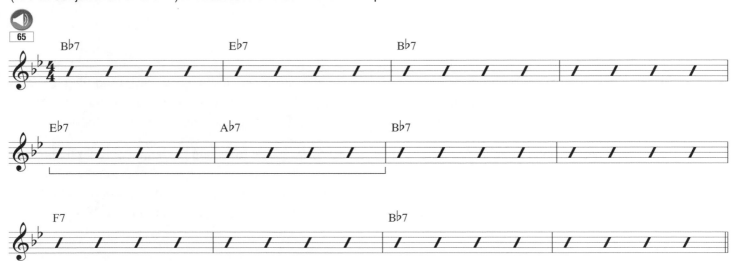

In "Freddie Freeloader," Miles Davis' 12-bar blues was altered by simply substituting an Ab7 for the final Bb7 (and any other changes) in measures 11–12.

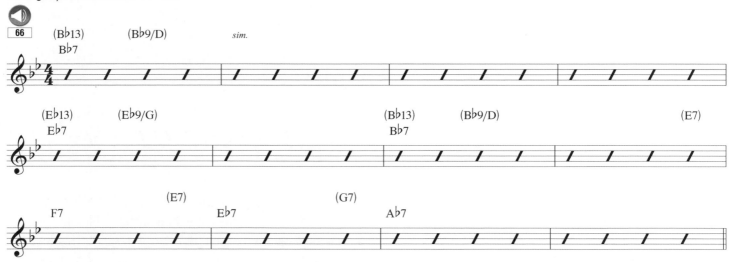

Wes Montgomery employed similar whole-step motion (Bb7–Ab7–Bb7), 6/4 meter and a repurposing of the "Bird Blues" changes (in the second half of the form) in "West Coast Blues." His refinements also included the 3rds-related progression in measures 11–12.

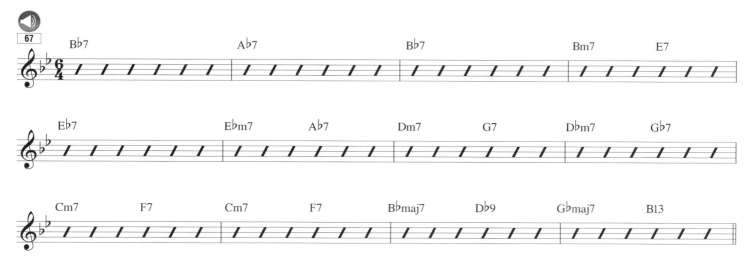

Other jazz musicians have altered the 12-bar blues form itself. These pieces invariably enlarge the number of bars into larger structures. The varied approaches are telling and indispensable in the repertoire.

One of the most straightforward altered blues approaches is found in Herbie Hancock's 16-bar blues composition "Watermelon Man." Played over an even-eighths rock beat, it splits the difference between a blues and a groove tune. Herbie's solution was simple and effective. He built the first half, measures 1–8, on a riff and stuck to only I, IV, and V chords. In the second half, he added four measures to the form in measures 11–12 by repeating the last two chords of the traditional blues progression, C9–Bb9. Count Basie pursued a similar strategy in the 16-bar blues "Blues Five Jive."

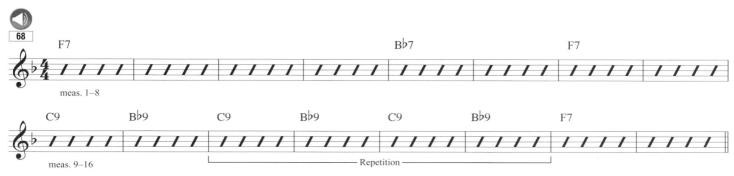

Dave Brubeck thought along similar lines in "Travelin' Blues" (*Nightshift: Live at the Blue Note*). Compared to his earlier medium-tempo, 12-bar rendition on *Time In* (1966), the later slow-blues performance found him repeating a four-bar segment with chromatic changes to produce a 16-bar form. Also note the B°7 chord used in measure 6. This is a typical substitution for the IV chord: The B°7 is essentially a Bb7b9 with the flatted 9th (B) in the bass. It has been in the repertoire since the 1940s and was made famous in Charlie Parker's "Now's the Time."

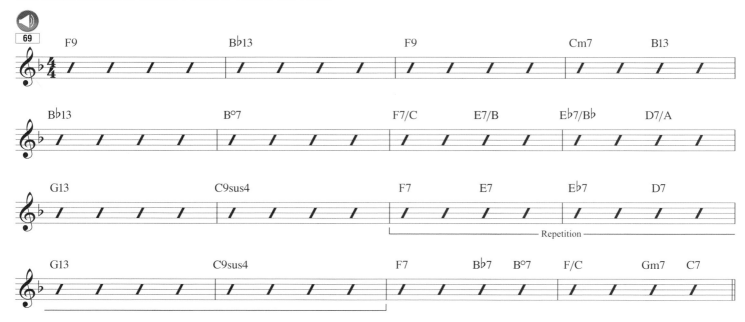

The blues form was expanded further in Lee Morgan's "The Sidewinder." This piece used a 24-bar form created by doubling the time span of each chord. For example, instead of four bars of the I chord (Eb7) in the first phrase, the I chord occupied eight bars and had two riff-based, question-answer phrases. This was followed by four bars of IV (Ab7), another four bars of Eb7 and Gm7b5–C7, four more bars of Fm7 to Bb7, and a final four bars of Eb7 without a turnaround. The entire structure was carried along by the tune's funk rhythm groove.

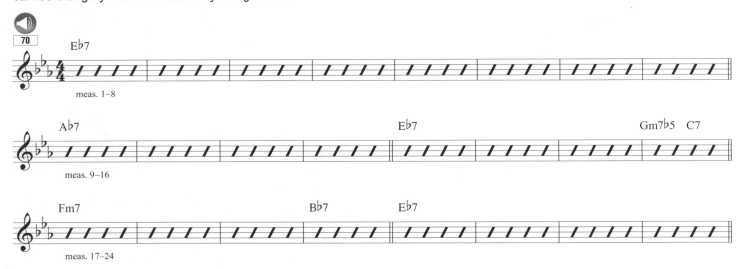

Harmonic expansion and substitution were taken to new heights in the bebop era. Clifford Brown's "Gerkin for Perkin" is a case in point. Though it retains the 12-bar form, it is distinguished by harmonic excursions and colorful modulations in the second half of the progression. Here, a ii–V (Bbm7–Eb7), played typically as an extension of the minor iv sound in measure 6, begins an active modulating cycle of ii–V–I changes: Bbm7–Eb7–Abmaj7, Abm7–Db7–Gbmaj7, and Gm7–C7–F7. The third pattern modulates back to the tonic F7 and a turnaround in measures 11–12.

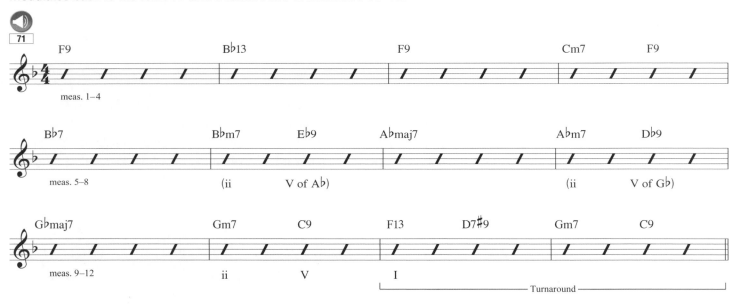

Bud Powell was an important innovator in the bebop age. His "Dance of the Infidels" contains numerous tonal expansions within the 12-bar blues form and reconciles many of Bird's refinements with more chromatic harmony. Notable are his use of the tonic major 7th chord (Fmaj7) in measures 1 and 11 instead of F7, Bbm7–Eb7 instead of the standard Bb7 (IV) chord in measure 2, and the back-cycled tritone substitution F#m7–B7 in measure 4, replacing the normal F7 chord resolving to Bb7. A similar tritone substitution occurs in measure 10: Dbm7–Gb7 resolving to F7. Measures 6–9 are an application of "Bird Blues" chromatic changes.

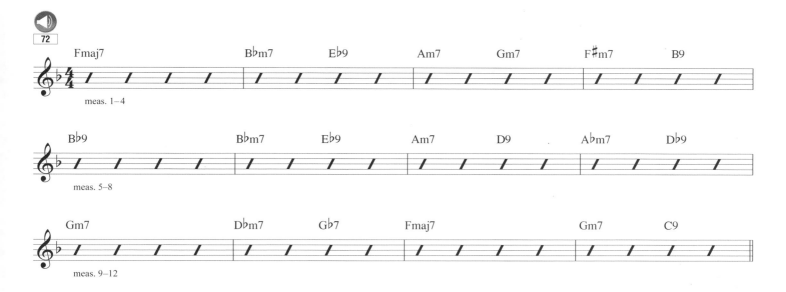

Miles Davis brought modal jazz to the fore. "Eighty One," his collaboration with bassist Ron Carter, is a definitive example of 12-bar blues subjected to modal harmony. In this progression, the I, IV, and V chords are all voiced as 11th forms. In measure 3–4 and 7–8, the F11 receives a rhythmic treatment (indicated in the music as "Rhy. Fig.") similar to Herbie Hancock's "Maiden Voyage," a classic modal tune. This progression has two possible conclusions in the last two bars of the form, written here as a 1st or 2nd ending. It can be played as an F11 or as the more exotic D♭maj7♯11/F, a favorite sonority in the post-bop era. John Coltrane also subjected the 12-bar blues to a modal treatment with suspended chords in "Mr. Day."

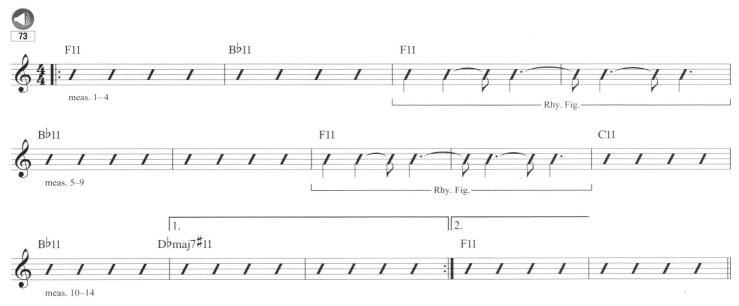

Another strategy for expanding a standard blues is to convert its 12-bar form into an AABA structure, similar to countless pieces in the Great American Songbook. In this case, the 12-bar blues most often becomes the A section and a new B (bridge), often a variant of the "Rhythm Changes" bridge, is added to the form, commonly resulting in a 44-bar arrangement. John Coltrane's "Locomotion" followed and expounded upon this procedure. He used a standard 12-bar blues in B♭ in the A sections and an eight-bar cycling chromatic bridge as the B section: A♭7–G7–G♭7–F7 (two bars each). The bridge is essentially a modern "Rhythm Changes" bridge with tritone substitutions for the first and third chords, normally D7 and C7. Kenny Burrell's "K.B. Blues," Joe Zawinul's "Scotch and Water," and Sam Jones' "Unit 7" are other significant examples of blues-with-a-bridge compositions worth exploring.

Altered Minor Blues

Minor blues has also been subjected to numerous alterations in the jazz world. Similar guidelines are applied: reharmonization, increased dissonance, substitutions, different grooves, odd time signatures, and extended forms. However, in the jazz lexicon, minor blues benefits from the stylistic practice of applying a variety of scales to the tonal center. This results in options from at least five possible sources: Aeolian, Dorian, and Phrygian modes as well as harmonic minor and melodic minor scales.

"Jody Grind," Horace Silver's altered minor blues tune, reflects the artist's fascination with groove music. Played in a rhythm feel reconciling Latin, rock, and even-eighths jazz, it presents several interesting twists on the classic, 12-bar formula. Note the use of Eb9 in measures 5–6, supplanting the usual minor iv (Ebm7) with a dominant chord, typical of ii–V vamps in Latin and R&B tunes. The return to the tonic in measures 9–10 is made with an unorthodox A13–B13 progression, which replaces the traditional VI–V changes (Gb7–F7). A13 and B13 are tritone substitutions for Eb7 and F7.

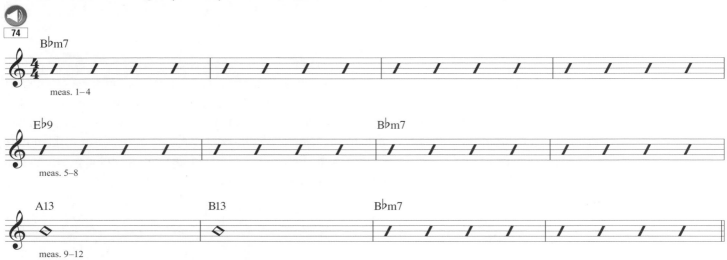

Lee Morgan colorized his swinging minor blues, "Party Time," with greater dissonance and numerous substitutions idiomatic to the hard bop genre. This 12-bar progression illustrates the expanded application of secondary dominant 7th chords in the piece, many of them altered chords or tritone substitutions. Note the use of Bb7–A7 in measure 2 and Bb7–Eb7 in measure 6, both of which resolve strongly to the tonic Abm from different directions. In measure 4, a ii–V change, Ebm7–Ab7#5, emphasizes the resolution to iv, Dbm7. The F7#9 push chord in measure 8 is a substitute for the diatonic Fm7b5 of the key.

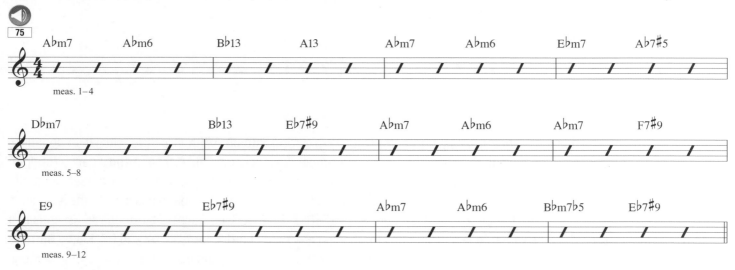

Freddie Hubbard's "Down Under," an important piece in the Jazz Messenger's playlist, presents a simpler, more modal variant of the minor blues progression with a surprise sonority. Note the use of an altered dominant, Ab7b5, a half step above the tonic Gm to replace the customary iv chord, Cm, in measures 5–6.

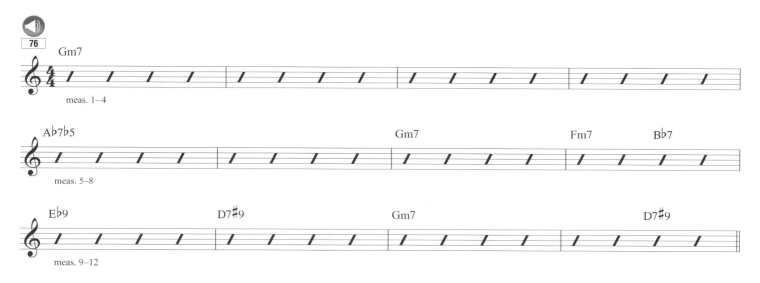

Hank Mobley used this minor blues variation for the head (theme) in "Dig Dis." In this B♭ minor progression, the VI7 (G♭7) is a substitute for the iv chord (E♭m). Herbie Hancock used this change in his well-known groove tune, "Cantaloupe Island."

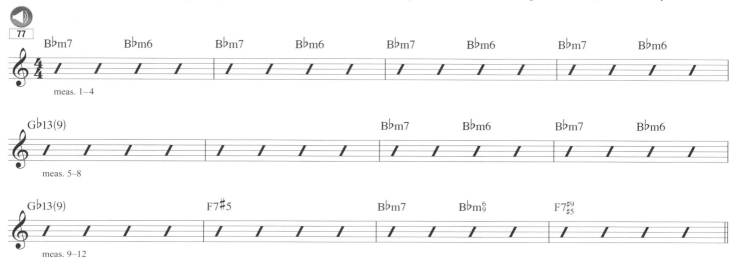

One of the best-known pieces in the jazz repertoire is Wayne Shorter's "Footprints." It retains many aspects of a standard 12-bar minor blues in its proportions, harmonic rhythm, and chord types, but it also adds modal colors, a 6/4 jazz-waltz meter, and a number of interesting substitutions in the final part of the form. Note the extended and altered sonorities in measures 9–10: F#m11, B7#5#9, E7#9♭5, and A7#5#9. These exotic harmonies supplant the usual VI–V changes (A♭13–G7) and add considerable harmonic activity and dissonance to the surrounding modal and suspended sounds in the progression.

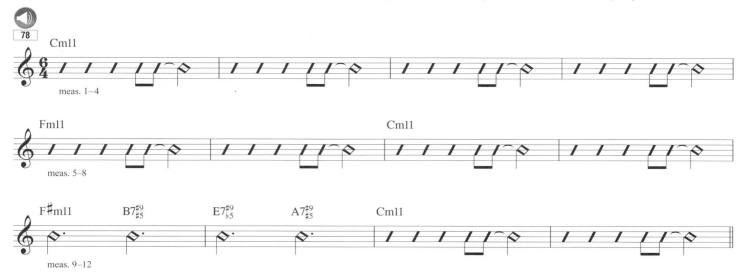

The harmony in measures 9–10 is also sometimes played in these variations.

The minor-blues progression has been altered through numerous experiments with extended form. J.J. Johnson created a simple solution in "Shutterbug," lengthening the time spans of the i and iv chords in measures 1–16 to produce a 20-bar blues. Note that only the standard four chords of minor-blues changes, i, iv, VI, and V, are used in the progression.

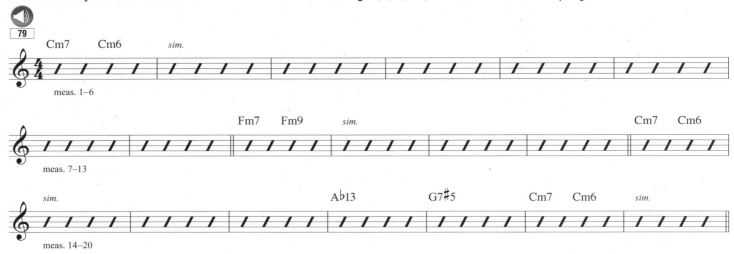

Alterations in the minor blues form by the masters continued on to larger structures. Check out Horace Silver's "Nutville" as a starting point. Silver multiplied the number of bars, creating a 24-bar structure with the same harmonic proportions, and substituted a chromatic progression of VI–V–♭V–IV (all dominant 7th chords) for the normal VI–V–i in the final section. Also notable is Dexter Gordon's "Blues Bikini" (*Dexter Gordon on Dial—The Complete Sessions*). This is a 44-bar, AABA tune in which the 12-bar minor blues progression was used as A sections with an eight-bar bridge.

Listen to the Blues

It is never too soon (or late) to begin active listening. Your vocabulary and feel are greatly improved by assimilating the sound of the repertoire as played by the greatest musicians in the genre through *listening*—in this case, to the blues. This selected list is diverse but by no means exhaustive and is offered to get you started. While in the active listening mode, make note of how the various forms of the blues feel and how they sound different from each other. With repeated exposure familiarity increases—as does your discernment of the blues' modality and chord changes, and your ability to identify the various rhythmic and melodic procedures at work.

Start with the fundamentals; here are some suggestions. Listen for complexity in the harmony of "Blues For Alice" versus simpler changes in "Low Down and Dirty Blues" and "Soulful Brothers." As you listen, imagine the chord of the moment. Are you on the I chord, IV chord?... and so on. And what does that feel like? Does it feel minor, modal, and brooding like "Equinox?" Or does it have a traditional major/dominant tonality like "Back at the Chicken Shack?" To make the experience even more active, find a simple chord chart or lead sheet of a piece. While listening, tap along to keep your place rhythmically and relate the sound of what you're hearing with what is happening in the music at the moment. Your listening skill improves with repetition.

Also ask yourself: Is the melody riff-oriented, like "Cool Blues" and "Tenor Madness," or does it seem more like a through-composed solo with less obvious repetition, as in "Billie's Bounce" and "Freight Train?" Rhythmic aspects involve tempo and feel. Compare the speedy pace of "Mr. P.C." to the slower walking-ballad feel of "Parker's Mood." Check out the funky commercial groove of "The Sidewinder," the R&B dance beat and contrasting swing rhythm of "Sack O' Woe," and the shuffle/boogie-woogie delivery of "Grand Slam." Listen for Latin rhythms in "Barbados," "Nutville," and "Cariba," and jazz-waltz rhythms in "All Blues" and "Footprints." Most importantly, make mental and aesthetic notes of your reactions and how the various blues pieces make you feel.

Charlie Parker
"Au Privave," "Barbados," "Billie's Bounce," "Blues for Alice," "Bloomdido," "Buzzy," "Cheryl," "Cool Blues," "K.C. Blues," "Mohawk," "Now's the Time," "Parker's Mood," "Perhaps," "Relaxin' at Camarillo," "Hootie Blues"

John Coltrane
"Bessie's Blues," "Blues Minor," "Blues to Elvin," "Blues to You," "Blue Train," "Chasin' the Trane," "Cousin Mary," "Equinox," "Locomotion," "Mr. Day," "Mr. P.C.," "Some Other Blues," "Trane's Blues," "Village Blues"

Thelonius Monk
"Blue Monk," "Blues Five Spot," "Blue Sphere," "Misterioso," "Straight, No Chaser," "Blues for Tomorrow"

Miles Davis
"All Blues," "Blues by Five," "Freddie Freeloader," "No Blues," "Vierd Blues," "Two Bass Hit," "Walkin'"

Benny Goodman (with Charlie Christian)
"Benny's Bugle," "Blues in B," "Gone with 'What' Wind," "Grand Slam," "Wholly Cats"

Kenny Burrell
"All Night Long," "Chitlins Con Carne," "K.B. Blues," "Soulful Brothers," "The Common Ground," "Bluescape"

Wes Montgomery
"Cariba," "Fried Pies," "Missile Blues," "Sun Down," "West Coast Blues," "Movin' Along," "Naptown Blues"

Dexter Gordon
"Blues Bikini," "Gotham City," "Long Tall Dexter," "Sticky Wicket," "August Blues," "Soul Sister"

George Benson
"Clockwise," "Hello Birdie," "Low Down and Dirty Blues," "The Cooker," "The Shape of Things That Are and Were"

Horace Silver
"Doodlin'," "Filthy McNasty," "Nutville," "Señor Blues"

Dizzy Gillespie
"Birk's Works," "Blue 'n' Boogie," "The Champ"

Clifford Brown
"Sandu," "The Blues Walk"

Lee Morgan
"The Sidewinder," "Speedball," "Midtown Blues"

Freddie Hubbard
"Birdlike," "Down Under," "Hub-Tones"

Oliver Nelson
"Stolen Moments," "Teenie's Blues"

Dave Brubeck
"Here Comes McBride," "Travelin' Blues"

Duke Ellington
"C Jam Blues," "Things Ain't What They Used to Be"

Count Basie
"Blues in Hoss' Flat"

Lionel Hampton
"Red Top"

Lester Young
"D.B. Blues"

Oscar Pettiford
"Blues in the Closet"

Benny Golson
"Blues March"

Sonny Stitt
"Blues for Prez and Bird"

Benny Carter
"Doozy," "Some Kind of Blues"

Cannonball Adderley
"Sack O' Woe," "Them Dirty Blues"

Joe Zawinul (Cannonball Adderley)
"Scotch and Water"

Sam Jones (Cannonball Adderley)
"Unit 7"

Barney Kessel
"Barney's Blues"

Milt Jackson
"Bags' Groove"

Sonny Rollins
"Tenor Madness," "Blue Seven"

Bobby Troup
"Route 66"

Jimmy Smith
"Back at the Chicken Shack," "Midnight Special"

Tommy Flanagan (with John Coltrane)
"Freight Train"

Grant Green
"Blues in Maude's Flat"

J.J. Johnson
"Shutterbug"

McCoy Tyner (with Joe Henderson)
"Blues on the Corner"

Joe Henderson
"The Kicker," "Isotope"

Wayne Shorter
"Footprints," "Mahjong"

Cedar Walton
"Cedar's Blues"

Pat Martino
"A Blues for Mickey-O," "The Visit"

George Russell
"Stratusphunk"

Woody Shaw
"Blues for Wood"

Chick Corea
"Matrix"

Pat Metheny
"Soul Cowboy"

Stanley Turrentine
"La Place Street," "Soft Pedal Blues"

Oscar Peterson (with Herb Ellis)
"Blues Etude"

CHAPTER 4

INVERSIONS

Understanding and Hearing Inversions

Inversions were introduced when playing diminished chords in Chapter 1. Let's take a deeper dive. Any chord is subject to inversion. Inverting a chord simply involves placing a different chord tone, other than the root, in the bass. This is done to achieve harmonic variety and interest, to produce melodic motion in the lower register, and often to facilitate smooth connections in voice leading.

Using inversions requires a more elaborate system for naming chords. They are most often written with a slash specifying the different bass note. For example, an Fmaj7 has four notes: F, A, C and E (root–3rd–5th–7th). Each tone in a 7th chord can be the bass note. When F is the lowest note, it is in *root position*, because the root is in the bass and is written without a slash. When the Fmaj7 has the 3rd, A, in the bass, it is called *1st inversion* and is written as Fmaj7/A. Fmaj7/C has the 5th in the bass and is in *2nd inversion*. The *3rd inversion*, Fmaj7/E, places the 7th in the bass.

Play these chords and listen. Each begins with a basic, root-position form (a parent chord) on a particular string set that establishes the voicing. It generates a fundamental family of inversions when moved up the fingerboard. The first example is made from the typical divided voicing of Fmaj7 found in Chapter 1 and simply follows the natural ascending motion of chord tones in the form. Note that the root tone, F, indicated by a circled note in the chord grids, is on different strings as the chord is moved through its inversions. It is useful to visualize and aurally distinguish that note in the forms.

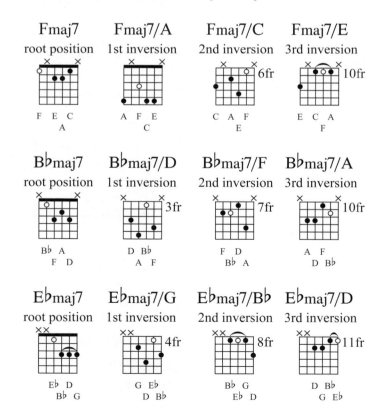

Play the next two sets of inversions, in Bbmaj7 and Ebmaj7, and similarly listen to their qualities. These forms are often used as mid-register and higher-register comping chords and are also useful for chord-melody playing.

Play the inversions freely and listen for the feeling and color of each chord. For example, the root-position Fmaj7 has a stable, grounded feeling, and the 1st-inversion Fmaj7 feels slightly less stable, suggesting it wants resolution. If you're hearing that effect, you're intuitively sensing why the 1st-inversion chord is often used to go to a root-position chord a 4th higher: Fmaj7/A to Bb. The A–Bb bass line has a feeling of movement that is begun with the 1st-inversion form. In jazz, that could be a major 7th, minor 7th, or dominant 7th chord. Fmaj7/C has a more open, and in this case, dissonant quality due to the half-step rub of E and F on adjacent strings in the voicing. Fmaj7/E is a less stable chord that demands resolution because the most active tone, the 7th, is in the bass. It is therefore frequently used as a passing chord.

The guidelines for major 7th chords also apply to minor 7th chords. These are the equivalent forms for minor 7th chords in Fm, Bbm, and Ebm families. Keep track of the root tones in the shapes and listen for the feeling and color of the chords.

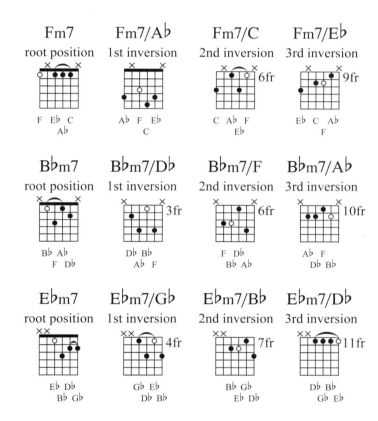

At this point, it is useful to investigate the Fm7/Ab in the first set of minor chords. Note that the form is identical with an Ab6 in Chapter 1. This not only drives home the idea of relative minor and major relations, but it opens the door to viewing the form as a *plural chord* with more than one use.

The dominant 7th chord has a unique quality of dissonance that makes it ideal for the blues, as seen in the last chapter. This series of forms, F7, Bb7, and Eb7, presents the dominant 7th versions of the root-position chords and their inversions. Listen for the bluesy feeling of these chords. You've heard them all in the blues comping and chord-melody phrases of players like Joe Pass, Wes Montgomery, and Kenny Burrell.

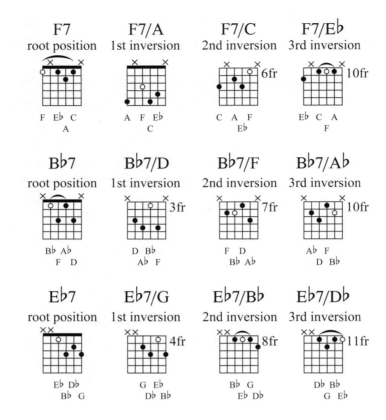

Inversions in Progressions

Inversions are very useful in playing chord changes. Not only do they provide color and interest to the harmony but add close connective motion to the forms. The following four examples illustrate these aspects in common chord progressions.

The 1st-inversion dominant 7th form is particularly effective in a simple I–IV cadence in a 12-bar blues, but it is also viable in a pop song or "Rhythm Changes." This V–I cadence employs the motion of root-position to 1st-inversion chords and its resolution to another root-position chord. It produces that familiar root–3rd bass line movement found in many swing-era jazz tunes like "Tuxedo Junction" and "Straighten Up and Fly Right." Check out the second chord, F9/A. It is identical to an Am7♭5, but here, it functions as a 1st-inversion dominant chord and would be considered a rootless form. It is both a substitution and a plural chord. When using the first three chords, F13–F9/A–B♭maj7, think of a V–I change in B♭. When using the alternate progression, F13–F9/A–B♭7, think of a I–V in an F blues.

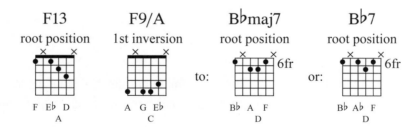

Inversions can be combined in many interesting ways. This progression uses two rootless dominant 7th chords in 1st and 2nd inversion, F9/C and F9/A, to *enclose* the destination chord, B♭ (major 7 or dominant 7).

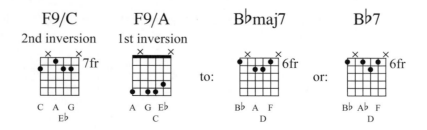

The 3rd-inversion dominant 7th chord has a strong dissonance because the active 7th tone is in the bass. It is often used as a passing chord with a resolution to a chord a 4th above: F7 to B♭. Here, the progression is decorated with a descending stepwise bass line: F–E♭–D. Preceded by a root-position F9, the E♭ tone is harmonized with F13/E♭ and pulls downward a half step to B♭/D, either as a B♭6/9 or B♭9 chord.

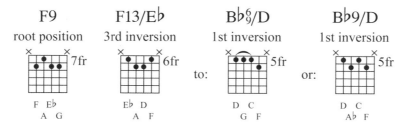

Inversions facilitate rootless chord movement in progressions. This phrase exemplifies the scenario. Every chord in this progression is rootless and can be considered a plural form. Cm9/B♭ is identical with E♭maj7/B♭, F13/A with Am7♭5(add4), B♭maj9/A with Dm7/A, and B♭13/A♭ with A♭maj7#11. But don't let the nomenclature or vagueness confuse you. The lack of rigidity is an asset that opens the door to creativity and multiple applications. Remember—*trust your ear*. Listen to the sound of smooth voice leading within the progression via its common tones and tight chord-tone connections.

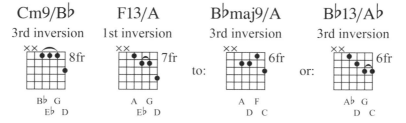

Using Inversions

Inversions are ideal for adding interest to simple accompaniment figures. This progression mixes a number of inversions of major, minor, and dominant chords with root-position forms and is suitable for comping, chord-melody applications, or to simply realize jazz harmony on the fingerboard. It is based on the bridge changes of "Have You Met Miss Jones?," an important standard tune in the jazz lexicon. Note the use of ii–V–I phrases in 3rds-related keys: B♭, G♭, and D major. The final Gm7–C7–F is a ii–V–I returning to the original tonality of F major. Note that these chords are basic and extended diatonic forms, not yet containing alterations. The changes emphasize common tones for smooth voice leading.

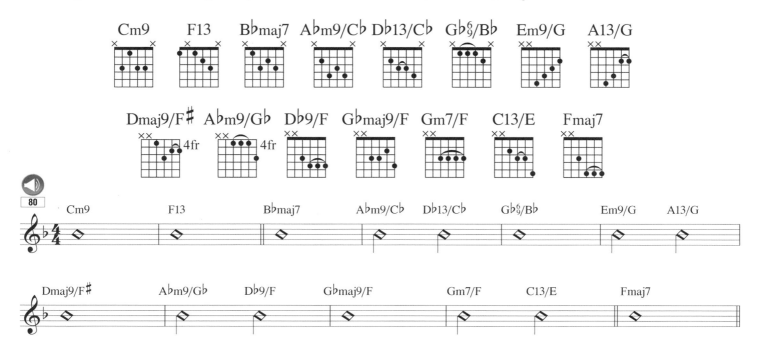

As you play the chords make a note about their shapes and where common tones occur in the changes. For example, check out the use of the same shape for both the root-position Bbmaj7 and a rootless Abm9/Cb. Notice the sustained D melody note on top of Cm9–F13–Bbmaj7 changes. Common tones are also found in Abm9/Cb–Db13/Cb, Em9/G–A13/G, Abm9/Gb–Db9/F to Gbmaj9/F, and Gm7/F–C13 to Fmaj7. And the F# in the bass of Dmaj9/F# is enharmonic with Gb in Abm9/Gb, so it is heard as a common tone, regardless of spelling.

Chord Strategies

It is advantageous to develop a chord strategy as soon as possible. Each tune with its unique changes will suggest a chord strategy. How a player responds to the tune's environment is what differentiates a Joe Pass from a Johnny Smith, or a Tal Farlow from a Kenny Burrell. A chord strategy puts the various shapes and sounds you're accumulating into context and, ideally, *into practice*. With experience and regular application, the strategy becomes an internalized intuitive response and will allow you to create variations "on the fly."

Here are some basic guidelines:

- Isolate a set of chord changes, like the "Have You Met Miss Jones?" bridge.
- Make a chord chart with basic changes. This needn't be fancy or elaborate, just a simple reference sketch that you'll memorize.
- Produce a preliminary set of fingered forms, as in Track 80, with basic and extended diatonic voicings.
- Use devices like inversion and common tones, striving for smooth voice leading and tight connections.
- Work on your "arrangement" until you collect the combinations you want to hear. Think like an arranger writing for a choir or horn section.

Next, create variations of your basic strategy. Where to start? In this example, all the ii and I chords of the ii–V–I progressions are identical to Track 80. However, variation in the form of *reharmonization* is applied to the dominant (V) chords. Each dominant 7th uses alterations (7b9 chords), and in one case, 13b9, based on *diminished substitution*.

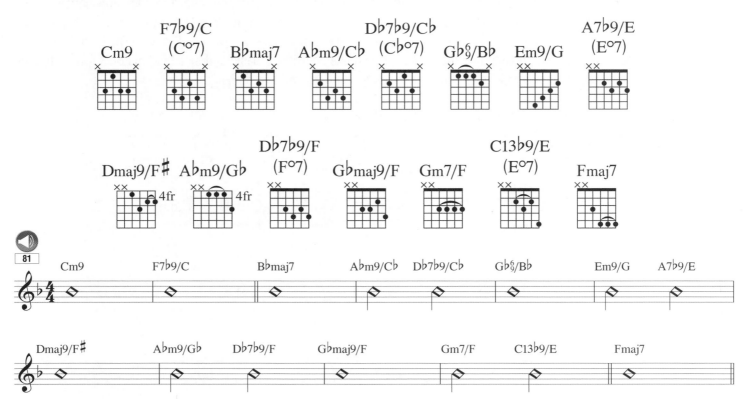

Make a note of the sound and connections, as well as the emotional feeling of each substituted dissonance as you play. Diminished chords, with their natural symmetry, fit neatly into the world of inversions. Remember, every diminished chord can be four different altered dominants (7♭9) in different inversions, sharing the same fingering, and therein lies the payoff. These chords came into regular use with bebop players like Charlie Parker, Dizzy Gillespie, and Bud Powell and are essential elements in the jazz language. When creating melodies over changes this harmonic information will be of great help in decorating and expanding your lines. That's another reason to build a chord strategy—it's a pathway to more colorful melodic improvisation.

A second variation to consider is *tritone substitution*. This will also affect only the V chords in the progression. Here, play the same changes as found in Track 81, but replace each 7♭9 chord with its equivalent tritone substitution. For example, play the B7♯9 instead of F13 in the progression: Cm9–B7♯9–B♭maj7. You'll hear the common tone, D, maintained on top—called *oblique motion*—but you'll now have a chromatic bass line: C–B–B♭. Similarly, a G6/9/B replaces the D♭13/C♭ in measure 4 and produces *parallelism* (G6/9 to G♭6/9) and chromatic movement in the top voice: E♭–D–D♭. A simple E♭ major triad (in 1st inversion) is used for A7 in measure 6. When heard as an A7 sound it is a highly altered chord, A7♭9♭5. The G13 and F♯13, both in 3rd inversion, depict descending and ascending motion using the same form. G13/F goes down to G♭maj9/F (common tone in the bass) while F♯13/E goes up Fmaj7. Note that in the latter, the fingered form is very closely related. F♯13/E and Fmaj7 share a similar fingering a half step apart.

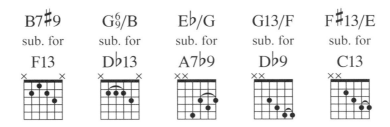

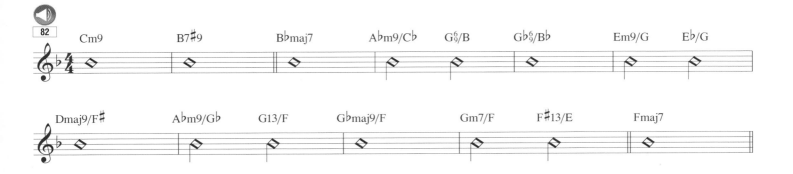

Inversions and Block Chords

Wes Montgomery was a master of block chording on the guitar, drawing his approach from piano players like George Shearing, Red Garland, and Oscar Peterson as well as sax sections in big bands. And why not? Those are the origins of the sound in jazz. On the guitar, they are distinctive and immediately recognizable. The following variation on the "Have You Met Miss Jones?" bridge employs *block chords* exclusively. Note the consistent texture and timbre established by voicing the forms on the top four strings, as well as the use of plural chord forms. The same shape is used to play B♭maj7/F and A♭m9/G♭. That allows you to use it like a chromatic push chord—you can target the higher chord from a half step below. Common shapes also apply to G♭maj7 and Em9/G as well as A♭m7 and G♭maj9/B♭—where a root-position G♭maj9 becomes a 1st-inversion Em9 and root-position A♭m7 becomes a 1st-inversion G♭maj9. By now you're seeing, hearing, and appreciating the utility of these basic shapes and their possibilities. Check out the more dissonant altered chords, D♭7♭9♯5/F and C7♯5♯9/B♭, in the progression. When viewed as tritone subs, they become simpler extended chords, G9/F and G♭13/B♭—two handy inversions. (See this in action on the next page.)

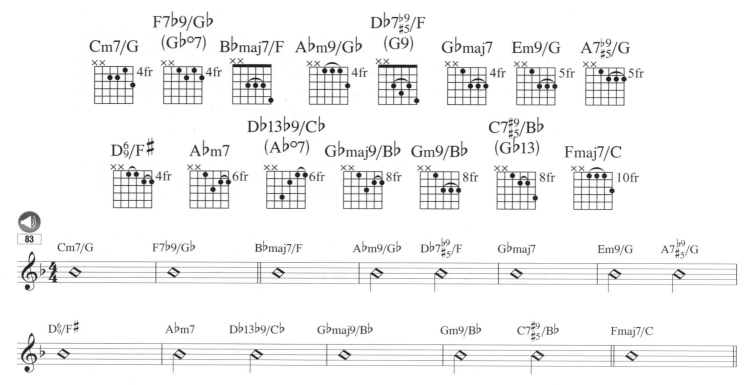

This variation demonstrates a more active approach to the progression with greater motion. Two common moves begin the section: Cm9–Cm6 (seen earlier in the minor blues) and B♭maj9–B♭6. Note the similar shapes and voice leading even though the chords are of different qualities, minor versus major. Over F7, two diminished chords act as inversions of F7♭9 and move in parallel motion. Note the ascending stepwise motion in measures 4–5: G♭–A♭–B♭ and the skipping contour in measures 6–7. The latter is the harmonization of a common jazz melody. Oblique motion is heard in the last two patterns: A♭m11–D♭9/C♭–G♭6/9/B♭ and Gm11/B♭–C7♯5/B♭–Fmaj9/A. In this case, the top note is stationary while the other voices in the chords change—a common harmonic situation.

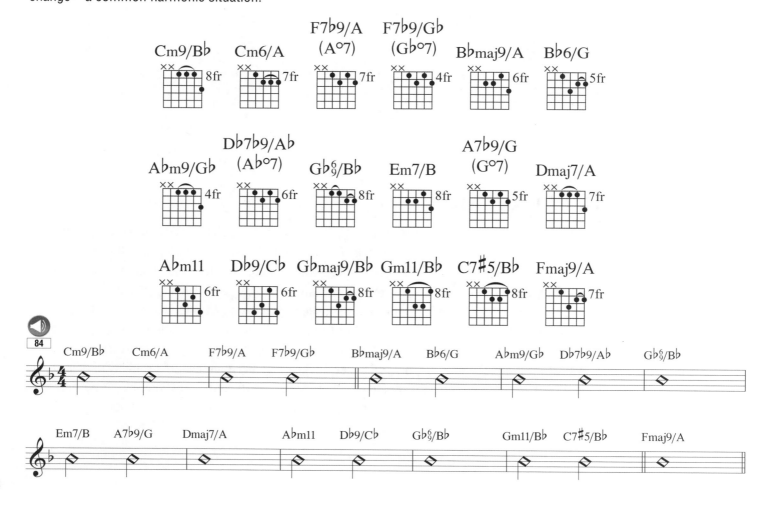

Using Inversions in Cycle Progressions

Inversions are very effective in cycle progressions, where they supply more harmonic and melodic interest than basic, root-position forms. This example subjects inversions of dominant 7th chords to a cycle-of-4ths sequence. This can also be seen as a chromatic cycle in which each chord moves down in half steps. The lowest note in each of these shapes can be the 3rd or 7th tone of a chord—a clear illustration of plural forms. Spelling aside, in jazz harmony, they are often interchangeable, as in Duke Ellington's "Prelude to a Kiss," Sonny Rollins' "Doxy," or the standard "There Is No Greater Love"—three versions of a similar cycle progression. Here, only the last chord in each phrase is in root position. All the rest are inversions. You'll hear chromatic harmony, tritone substitution, and parallelism at work in the two phrases.

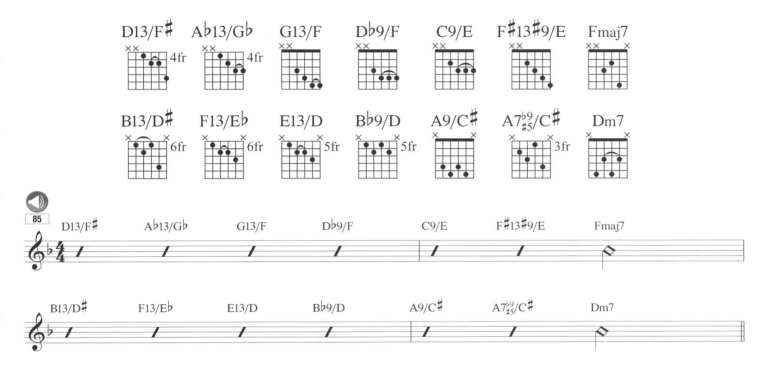

Inversions and Rootless Chords

Play these four chords and listen. This is a progression used often in blues turnarounds and cycle phrases and contains only inversions of rootless chords. Note their physical shapes and names.

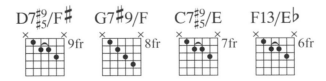

How is it possible that the tension chord (V), C7#9#5, has the same shape as the resolution chord (I), F13(9)? Part of the answer lies in the chromatic parallel motion on the fingerboard. With chromatic parallel motion, complex chords (extended and altered types) having the same or similar structure can be strung together in a progression. It is natural enrichment created by adding extended and altered colors to the simplest type of shell chords: dyads (two-note chords). Notice that the two lowest notes comprise a tritone interval and, when moved down, create a chain of dissonant chords and resolutions. As they are moved, the notes in the forms are juggled and produce a directional, harmonically active voice-leading result unique to the guitar.

Now play those chords again and listen more carefully. Notice that the apparent dissonance of each chord is mitigated by the continuous chromatic voice leading and the resolving effect of the tritones on the lowest two strings. This is comparable to a harmonic kaleidoscope in which the same internal parts assume different shapes with different meanings, depending on how the user manipulates the apparatus. In this case, it's how a guitarist manipulates shapes on the fingerboard. Or, perhaps it's more like a musical Rorshach test? The same forms can be heard as two different sounds, depending on context and the listener's experience. Another part of the answer lies in the phenomenon of rootless chords, which, having no roots, are by definition inversions.

Let's explore the rootless-chord world in more depth. To begin an understanding, it is helpful to compare a root-position chord with its rootless counterparts. These four shapes are all F9 chords. The first is the familiar root-position form while the other three are typical inversions on the same string set. The most commonly used are the 1st and 3rd inversion, F9/A and F9/Eb, favored largely for their voice-leading effects: the 3rd of the chord ascending a half step and the 7th of the chord descending a half step.

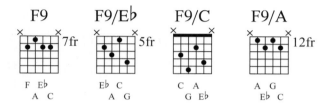

The motion of F7/Eb resolving to either a Bb chord in 1st inversion (Bbmaj7 or Bb7 with D in the bass) or a parallel chromatic chord, such as E7/D (same chord a half step lower), is particularly strong and found throughout the repertoire and the vocabulary of the greatest chord players. Often, the F7 or F9 in 3rd inversion is expanded with a 13th, F13(9)/Eb. Resolve each to Bb⁶₉.

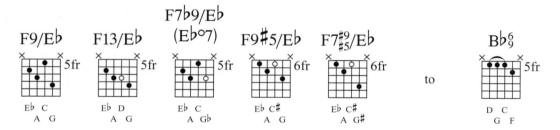

It is also common to see an F7/Eb with alterations, such as a flatted 9th (F7b9/Eb), alterations and extensions, an augmented 5th and natural 9th (F9#5/Eb), or even two alterations in the same rootless form (F7#5b9/Eb). The spelling of chords can be a useful mental exercise initially to describe theory in step time and is part of a complete musician's resources. However, it doesn't necessarily lead to satisfying musical applications in real time. That requires playing and *listening*.

The purpose of learning rootless forms is not to master the spelling but to put them to effective functional use in the music, in chord progressions. That's what Joe Pass explained when he demonstrated many of these shapes and their connections horizontally on the fingerboard as pure harmonic motion. His premise was that they are fluid, changing sonorities used to harmonize a melody, not rigid vertical structures. Even his 1971 chord book contained only shapes categorized by sound and eschewed the naming of specific chords. This basic blues turnaround in F depicts that mindset. Check out the use of rootless chords as inversions in descending parallel motion, similar to passages heard in Joe Pass' and Jim Hall's chord playing. It harmonizes a typical Fm pentatonic blues melody in the top voice.

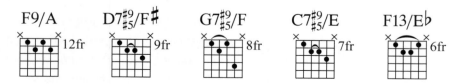

CHAPTER 5

ESSENTIAL CHORD PROGRESSIONS

Harmonic Formulas

The number of chord combinations in music is limitless. However, as in pop, blues, and rock, the number of effective, idiomatic, and widely-used chord combinations in jazz is considerably smaller. Some educators and scholars have boiled down the essential progressions to less than 50. In this category are those must-know nuclear progressions that, in combination with other patterns, yield an unlimited amount of music. We refer to these progressions as *harmonic formulas*. Consider them a list of essential ingredients from which most music using chords is constructed. Or, put another way, they are the harmonic cells from which the body of the music is formed.

Almost every standard song in jazz as well as many original compositions make use of harmonic formulas. It stands to reason that they are prerequisites for developing fluency with chord usage. Among the most prevalent are turnarounds, ii–V and ii–V–I changes, cycles in 4ths/5ths, chromatic cycles, and 3rds-related progressions. The following phrases present some of the most characteristic formulas in jazz harmony.

Basic Progressions

The most fundamental harmonic formulas are largely diatonic with only minimal use of secondary chords. The following progressions are some of the most common in jazz. They are presented in the key of C, but they should also be learned in all keys using the chord types studied in the previous chapters. Be inventive. Apply all the forms you now know: the essential jazz chords, shell chords, inversions, substitutions, and the like. Strive for smooth voice-leading connections.

The I–vi–ii–V has been called the most pervasive harmonic formula in music. It is found in pop, rock, folk, country, and jazz. It is the basis of "Breezin'," "Blue Moon," "At Last," "I Got Rhythm," and hundreds of other tunes, and is often employed as a turnaround. This example can be played entirely with simple 7th chords or with extended forms like Dm9 and G13.

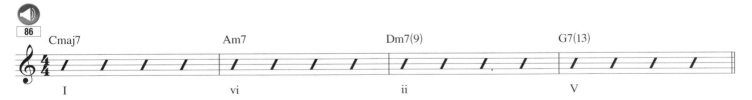

Often, the vi chord is played as a secondary dominant 7th VI and contains *alterations*—note the term "alt" placed next to the chord name as a prompt: A7alt. The alteration, in this case changing its quality from minor to altered dominant, directs motion to the minor chord, Dm7. Therefore, typical alterations such as A7♭9, A7♯5, and A7♯5♯9, which are indigenous to D minor, are appropriate. In the blues, this formula is sometimes played with only dominant 7th chords: C7–A7–D7–G7. (You can see this in action on the next page.)

The same formula is frequently reordered to produce a ii–V–I–vi (VI) progression. This example has a strong pull to Dm7 when an A7alt is played at the end of the four-bar phrase. Preparing Dm7 with its V chord in this way occurs in tunes like "Satin Doll," "Shiny Stockings," "Honeysuckle Rose," and many others that begin with a ii chord.

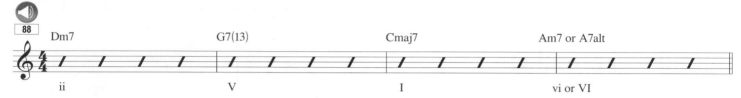

This is the classic turnaround formula used in countless tunes. It is a simple variation of Phrase 2 beginning on the iii chord, Em7, which functions as a substitute for Cmaj7 and sets up a cycle-of-4ths sequence: E–A–D–G. In the blues, this progression is also played with dominant 7th chords. Try using either of these phrases: E7#9–A7#5–D9–G13–C$^6_9$, with enriched and altered chords, or E7#9–Eb9–D9–Db7#9, its chromatic version.

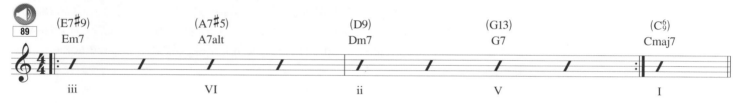

This phrase contains a chromatic move to emphasize the resolution to Cmaj7. It begins with a normal ii–V (Dm7–G7) and then shifts to a ii–V one half step above the destination (Cmaj7): Abm7–Db7. A similar progression is used in "Satin Doll," as well as several compositions by Wes Montgomery ("Four on Six" and "Road Song"). It has been a fixture of modern jazz harmony since the bebop era.

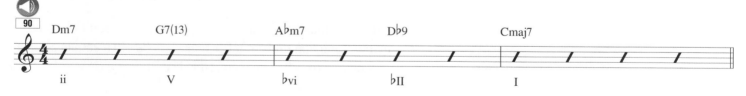

Sometimes, the resolution to C can be emphasized from below; this is a typical example. The Fm7–Bb7 (ii–V in the key of Eb, a 3rd away) generates motion upward to the tonic chord (Bb–C). It has a bluesy effect and is often used for that purpose. The formula has been heard in uptempo pieces like Tadd Dameron's "Lady Bird" and Clifford Brown's "Swingin'," as well as slow ballads such as Erroll Garner's "Misty" and Hoagy Carmichael's "Georgia on My Mind."

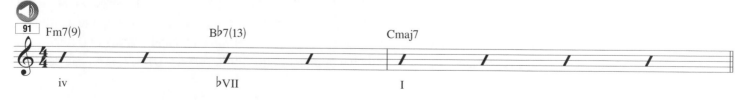

This phrase presents two variations of the common turnaround with chromaticism. Both have been heard in "Rhythm Changes" and similar tunes, where they are often interchangeable. Many players combine the two variations to produce a question-answer effect with the two phrases as shown. The first two bars depict a I–vi–ii–V formula altered with a diminished chord substituting for A7, adding a chromatic factor to the changes. Remember, C#°7 is a typical sub—a rootless A7♭9 chord in 1st inversion (A7♭9/C#), borrowed from the key of D minor (harmonic minor scale). Measures 3–4 contain a descending pattern with a flatted iii diminished (♭iii°) used to chromatically connect Em7 and Dm7. This idiomatic move is found in countless jazz standards, "Night and Day," "All the Things You Are," and "Embraceable You" chief among them.

Chromatic Progressions

Beyond basic progressions with only an occasional chromatic chord, generally used as a substitution, are more advanced phrases that rely heavily on chromaticism. These phrases represent the next step in your accumulation of harmonic formulas and the expansion of your vocabulary.

At this point, feel free to use any color or extension of the minor 7th or dominant 7th chords in a ii–V progression that suits the situation. Only a few voicings are specified, so use your ear and refer to chord forms and qualities in earlier chapters. Then, apply the Joe Pass approach. If a particular chord voicing doesn't sound right in the progression, try another form or another connection. This experimentation is a vital part of developing your personal harmonic sense and cannot be overstated.

This formula exploits a typical *side-slipping* pattern with a quick unprepared chromatic shift down from a half step above: E♭m7–A♭7 to Dm7–G7. The concept is based on movable ii–V phrases. Phrases like this are essential in the modern jazz lexicon.

In this phrase, a ii–V–I in C is approached from a half step below: C#m7–F#7 to Dm7–G7. It is a sort of "mirror image" of the last progression and another example of the movable ii–V pattern and its side-slipping effect in jazz. This formula and the previous one informed key harmonic moves in several John Coltrane hard-bop compositions, notably "Moment's Notice" and "Lazy Bird." Going beyond the concept of side slipping inevitably leads to playing "outside"—bitonality and atonality. If that's not your intention, use these patterns judiciously. Mix them with other more common accessible formulas.

This formula contains four chromatic chords in a row—five if you use E♭9 for A7alt as a tritone sub. The beginning chord is I, the tonic Cmaj7, and the next three are dominant 7ths: B7–B♭7–A7. The harmonic motion is to the ii chord, Dm7, in measure 4 via the A7 chord. The chromatic cycle is heard in countless jazz tunes; Benny Golson's bridge to "Stablemates" is a telling case. (Turn to the next page to see this shown.)

The previous progression can easily be transformed into a *cycle-of-4ths* formula, as in this phrase. With this transformation the chords move in perfect 4ths (or 5ths): C–F–Bb–Eb. The F7 and Eb7 are essentially tritone subs of the B7 and A7. The motion to the ii chord is from a half step above. This pattern has been applied to tunes like "There Is No Greater Love," "Yesterdays," "Come Rain or Come Shine," and many others.

This chromatic formula exploits several tritone subs. The Eb9 replaces A7, Ab7 replaces Dm7 (or D7), and Db9 is used instead of G7. It is basically a more harmonically active version of the I–vi–ii–V progression and as such, is a variation of a standard turnaround.

Another variation of the standard turnaround cadences on a dominant 7th. The formula involves mixing tritone subs with normal root-position chords. Note the chromatic motion in this phrase: Eb9–D9–Db9–C9. This sequence is frequently used as a blues turnaround.

Toggling between two chords of two different qualities a half step apart is an important and often-used maneuver in jazz harmony. Thelonius Monk's "Well, You Needn't" relies on this formula, which is repeated in its A sections. A common scenario is presented here: Cmaj7–Db9. Variations include "Lush Life" (C section), and "A Night in Tunisia" (A sections) where the minor mode is emphasized. A contemporary application is found in Snarky Puppy's "Bad Kids to the Back." Sometimes, both chords are of the same quality, as in "You Stepped Out of a Dream," where both are major 7th chords, or "Epistrophy," where both are dominant 7th chords.

This chromatic formula is a variation of Phrase 3. It is altered via a blues-based transformation. C7 is the presumed I chord, which is a direct reference to blues harmony. Also notable is the use of a II–V pattern in measure 3. There, D9, the dominant 9th chord, is an altered version of the diatonic Dm7. Sonny Rollins applied this progression to "Doxy."

Modulating Progressions

Mastering modulation, especially to remote keys, is a necessary skill in dealing with jazz harmony. To acquire this skill, a most effective preliminary technique requires placing a ii–V progression in the new key to prepare the modulation. This procedure works equally well for remote and closely related modulations. In these phrases, several common scenarios are depicted. Be aware of common tones as you play the formulas; they are often the key to a well-executed modulation.

Modulation from C major to the remote key of E♭ major, a minor 3rd away. An Fm7–B♭7 (ii–V in E♭) provides the preparation. Note that the F note is common to both keys. It is IV in C and ii of E♭. This common-tone linkage provides a pivot into the new key.

Modulation from C major to the even more remote key of E major, a major 3rd away. F♯m7–B7 is the preparation and is not based on a note in C. F♯ is a tritone away from C. This is an example of a major 3rds-related modulation straight out of the John Coltrane playbook, heard prominently in the second half of his "Giant Steps," and therefore is of great importance in modern jazz. It is an essential part of the Trane canon. The formula has its origins in "Have You Met Miss Jones?" bridge changes (see Chapter 4) and also appears as a chord change in "Summer Samba" and "I Remember You," where the tritone ii–V leads else-where—to the IV chord and back to the I, respectively. Note the final ii–V–I. This modulation from E back to C, Emaj7–Dm7–G7–Cmaj7, was a formula used by Trane in the last measure of "Giant Steps" as a turnaround to the beginning of the form.

Modulation from C major to F major, a 4th away. This is perhaps the most common and least remote modulation in jazz and standards. It is easily accomplished by using G and C, common to C and F, to produce a ii–V pivot into F: Gm7–C7–Fmaj7. You've heard this formula in tunes like "Misty," "Love Walked In," and "The Nearness of You." The phrase also presents another way to modulate from the new key of F into E♭ by using Fm7 as a pivot chord in measure 4. This sets in motion a chain of modulations or harmonic sequences in the phrase.

This variation of the previous formula contains a deceptive cadence. Note that in measure 4, the pivot chord to the expected E♭maj7 instead returns to C via a turnaround begun a half step lower: Fm7–B♭7–Em7–A7–Dm7–G7–C. This cadence occurs in "I Want to Talk About You," a tune made famous by John Coltrane. (Turn to the next page to see this shown.)

Modulation from C major to the remote key of A♭ major, a major 3rd lower or a minor 6th higher. This is the second of the tonal areas exploited by Coltrane in his major 3rds-related modulations of "Giant Steps." It is approached by B♭m7–E♭7, a ii–V a whole step lower: Cmaj7 to B♭m7–E♭7–A♭maj7. Note that this formula was used as turnaround back to the top of the form in "Giant Steps" (Phrase 2, measures 4–5). This formula was also used to modulate in several well-known standards, notably the bridges of "In a Sentimental Mood," "Smoke Gets in Your Eyes," and "Darn That Dream."

Modulation from C major to the remote key of A major, a minor 3rd or major 6th away, and then back to C. There are two modulations and, accordingly, two formulas in this phrase. Here, a ii–V is built on common tones B and E, which are present in both keys. The modulation is closely related when the tonal destination is A minor, the relative minor, as in "Seven Steps to Heaven," "Confirmation," or "Blues for Alice." However, in this case, the resolution is to A major. This is the tritone version of Phrase 1. The phrase returns to C major via another common tone, D, which provides a pivot for the progression: ii–V (Dm7–G7).

Modulation from C major to B♭ major, a whole step lower, and then from B♭ major to G major, a minor 3rd lower. There are also two modulations and formulas in this phrase. The first is achieved by simply *minorizing* the tonic, C, and making it into a ii–V (Cm7–F7) cadencing in B♭ major. From there, B♭ follows the formula of Phrase 6, pivoting on the common tones A and D (common to C major, B♭ major, and G major). B♭maj7 moves down a half step to Am7–D7 and finally cadences in G major, a closely related modulation, a 5th away from the original tonic, C. These formulas are prevalent in "I'll Remember April" and "All the Things You Are."

Modulation from C major to A minor, the relative minor. This is a very closely related modulation, as the key of C major shares the same notes as A minor. The phrase involves two common formulas: a ii–V–I in C (Dm7–G7–Cmaj7) followed by a ii–V–i in A minor (Bm7♭5–E7alt–Am7). Both have been applied to countless tunes in all periods of jazz.

Cycle Progressions

Cycle progressions abound in jazz. Two types of root movement are used with regularity: the cycle of 4ths (or 5ths) and the chromatic cycle. The formulas are often interchanged and act as substitutes for each other, regardless of root motion. Accomplished practitioners of jazz harmony treat these freely as related colors and modify them ad lib. To achieve a similar freedom in your own playing, learn these basic phrases and practice dropping them into your repertoire. It's a trial-and-error process; use your ear to determine which sounds best in a particular harmonic situation.

This first progression features a cycle of 4ths with major 7th chords. This four-chord phrase depicts root movement in perfect 4ths: C–F–Bb–Eb. It is a rudimentary formula but can be effective in modulating to Abmaj7 and then back to C with a ii–V–I pattern: Abmaj7–Dm7–G7–Cmaj7.

Next, we have a cycle of 4ths with dominant 7th chords. This is a tritone sub for the chromatic progressions heard earlier (Chromatic Progressions: Phrases 3 and 8). This formula has a fluid, bluesy sound. Notable examples from the repertoire are heard in the bridge of "Rhythm Changes" and the A section of Sonny Rollins' "Doxy," as well as John Lewis' "Django." Listen to the famous Joe Pass rendition of the latter on *For Django*. The basic formula occurs in measures 3–4 and 9–10 and is extended in measures 22–25 of the form.

Third is a cycle of 4ths with ii–V patterns. This formula is flexible and ubiquitous in jazz harmony, and can be used as modulating tool as well as a substitution. If begun on a major 7th chord a half step above, Gmaj7 in this case, it is the sequence used in "Blues for Alice" and "All God's Chillun Got Rhythm" to back-cycle within a I–IV chord change, G–C: Gmaj7–F#m7–B7–Em7–A7–Dm7–G7 to C7. If begun on Cmaj7, it can be used as a modern substitute for measures 1–4 of "Rhythm Changes": Cmaj7–F#m7–B7–Em7–A7–Dm7–G7 to C7. Try transposing this formula down a whole step to Bb and drop it into your "Rhythm Changes": Bbmaj7–Em7–A7–Dm7–G7–Cm7–F7–Bb7. You'll hear a modern effect with more active harmony.

On the next page, we have a vamp cycle. Sometimes, a I–IV progression with dominant 7th chords, a fragment of the cycle seen in Phrase 2, is used as a repeated pattern, known as a *vamp*. This phrase illustrates the idea. The C7–F7 is the fragment of the formula and is repeated freely as needed. It is often heard as an intro or outro figure for blues-based tunes like "When the Sun Comes Out" (check out the Stanley Turrentine version on *The Spoiler*) and "Willow Weep for Me" (à la Wes Montgomery on *Smokin' at the Half Note*).

The previous vamp cycle is often expanded with push chords on neighbor notes, mixing chromatic harmony with cycle-of-4ths movement. This example depicts that formula and its decorated motion. Gb7 approaches F7 from a half step above (upper neighbor) and B7 (lower neighbor) pushes upward to C7. This is a common embellishing practice in jazz harmony and is frequently seen in the chord-melody playing and comping of Joe Pass.

Here is a common cycle formula that involves stepwise descending motion. This example provides a characteristic progression in C moving down in whole steps to cadence on G7. Though begun on Cmaj7, the root motion: C–Bb–Ab–G changes suggest a different tonal or modal center. Possibilities include C minor, Ab major, or F minor. The chord qualities reflect that borrowing. Bbm, Abmaj7, and G7alt are chord colors associated with movement in those more remote keys, yet entail a strong resolution to G7, which begins the cycle again as the V of Cmaj7. This formula should also be learned as a variation beginning on Cm7.

The previous formula is often played as diatonic cycle in C minor. Ray Charles' "Hit the Road Jack" and Nina Simone's "Feeling Good" are familiar examples. In both cases, the progression is used in vamp-like manner as a repeating progression. In this formula, the cycle favors the minor key but contains dominant 7th chords on the Bb–Ab–G steps of the scale.

Here is a diatonic cycle of 4ths. This is arguably one of the most widely-used formulas in music. Here, it begins in the key of C major with a cycle of 4ths, however, the chord change in measures 4–5 (Fmaj7–Bm7b5) breaks the perfect-4th, root-movement pattern to remain diatonic, to stay in the tonal center. Fmaj7–Bm7b5 then pivots into A minor. In this formula every note is a common tone. The exact progression or variations of it have been used in many tunes including "Fly Me to the Moon," "All the Things You Are," "Autumn Leaves," "Only Trust Your Heart," "Weekend in L.A.," and "Manhã de Carnaval."

Coltrane Changes

John Coltrane's experiments with 3rds-related progressions resulted in a wealth of new harmonic possibilities and, with them, new chord formulas. Coltrane may have derived his formulas from tunes like "Have You Met Miss Jones?" but his application was broad, influential, and transformative. In his career, he used these changes in originals, contrafacts, and to stretch the existing harmony of standard tunes in the Great American Songbook.

The most pervasive harmonic formula in jazz is, arguably, the ii–V–I chord progression. Exploring how Coltrane reharmonized the ii–V–I with 3rds-related chord changes is an important first step in understanding, and ultimately applying, the transformations. This formula is an elaboration of a standard ii–V–I progression. It is a four-bar phrase: usually one bar of ii, one bar of V, and two bars of I. Trane added dominant 7th chords to the changes, modifying the harmonic pathway to create movement in and out of 3rds-related keys via modulatory V–I cadences. In C, this would mean movement in and out of A♭ major and E major, both a 3rd away from the tonic. Moving down a major 3rd takes you to A♭ and moving up a major 3rd to E. Those intervals outline an augmented chord and neatly divide the octave into three equal parts.

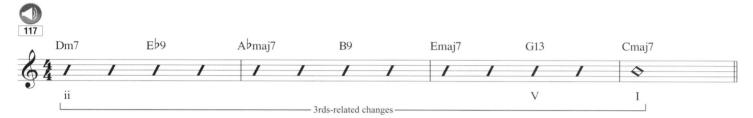

How does it work? Let's zoom in. Consider the ii chord, Dm7, as the starting point for the four-bar phrase. Next, cadence on A♭maj7 by placing E♭7 (its V chord) after Dm7, a half step above: Dm7–E♭7–A♭maj7. Then, move to Emaj7 via its V chord, B7: A♭maj7–B7–Emaj7. Finally, return to C by way of G7, its V chord: Emaj7–G7–Cmaj7. Stepping back, notice that the ii–V–I (Dm7–G7–Cmaj7) has been filled in with thirds-related changes. Each chord in measures 1–3 receives two beats, which results in faster harmonic rhythm. The additional harmony takes three bars to complete, so the final Cmaj7 chord is played for only one bar instead of two. This formula is heard throughout "Count Down" (contrafact on "Tune Up" changes) and in the bridge of "Fifth House" (contrafact on "What Is This Thing Called Love?").

Another important formula in the Coltrane canon is based on a major chord as the starting point, the presumed I chord, but otherwise follows similar guidelines. In C, movement is again to and through 3rds-related keys, A♭ major and E major, via their dominant 7th V chords. However, this four-bar phrase has a different harmonic rhythm. Note the Emaj7 chord, which occupies the whole bar in measure 3. The next phrase would typically begin the progression again in measure 5 with A♭maj7, a major 3rd higher. This formula is heard in Trane's "Giant Steps" and reharmonizations of "But Not for Me" and "Body and Soul." It was also used by Freddie Hubbard in his contrafact, "Dear John," based on the "Giant Steps" progression.

A variation of this formula is used to return to the I chord, C. In this case, the Emaj7 chord moves down a whole step to begin a ii–V–I to the tonic: Emaj7–Dm7–G7–Cmaj7. Coltrane used this pattern as a turnaround at the end of "Giant Steps" and "Exotica."

ii–V–I progressions can be applied to other 3rds-related sequences. A notable alternate is heard in Coltrane's "Central Park West." This formula is based on a diminished 7th chord and would therefore have four potential tonal centers, each a minor 3rd apart. In C, the possible keys would be C, E♭, A, and F♯. Each chord tone receives a ii–V–I progression. The exact symmetry, the most restrictive aspect of working with diminished harmony, is avoided by leaping a tritone, E♭ to A, for the third tonal center: A major, in the middle of the progression. That simple refinement lessens the predictability of four tonalities following an exact diminished arpeggio and groups the keys in this order: C–E♭–A–F♯.

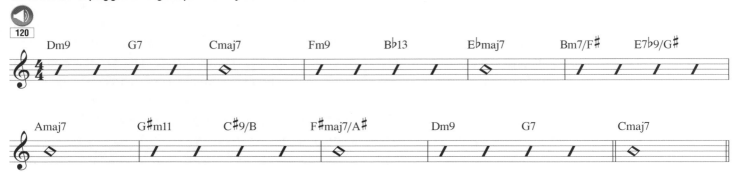

Another alternate 3rds-related Coltrane formula occurs in "Nita," which is based on the four notes of a major 7th chord in C: C–E–G–B, an asymmetric tone collection. Each chord tone demands its own ii–V–I progression and more unusual changes are naturally created in the process due to the unequal interval distances. Note the C♯m7♭5 in the progression—a harmonic gesture signifying a temporary minor tonality. Trane developed this sound more fully in "Satellite." The final four bars contain an abbreviated, 3rds-related pattern designed to resolve to the tonic sooner via a Gmaj7–G7 pivot.

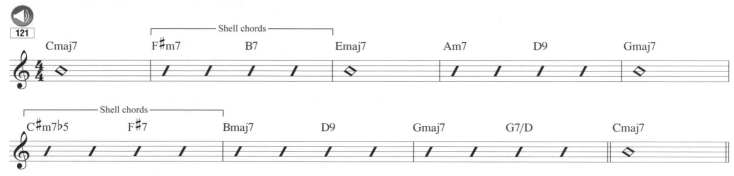

3rds-related formulas were stretched to their limit in Coltrane's contrafacts. "26-2" (based on the changes of Charlie Parker's "Confirmation") was exemplary. This progression contains a longer, more extensive formula with two four-bar phrases and modulating chord changes similar to "Count Down" and "Giant Steps." However, they are modified in measures 4 and 7–8 to address the original song's harmony, motion to the IV chord, via a ii–V–I progression: Gm7–C7–Fmaj7 in measures 4–5. A standard resolution phrase occurs in measures 7–9: Am7–D7–Dm7–G7–Cmaj7. Note the D7–G7–Cmaj7 progression is expanded with ii–V back-cycling patterns in this section: Am7–D7 and Dm7–G7.

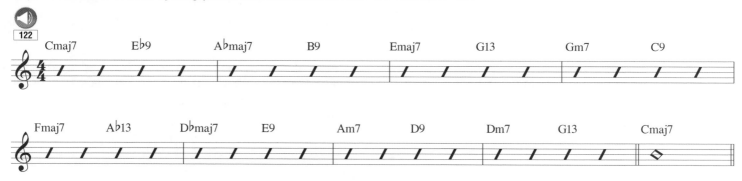

Coltrane's variations on this formula are heard in his second phrase of "26-2." The first four bars are identical to what was played in the previous example. In the second four bars, the same progression begins on Fmaj7 and cadences on Cmaj7, like an expanded IV–I progression: Fmaj7–E♭7–A♭maj7–B7–Emaj7–G7–Cmaj7.

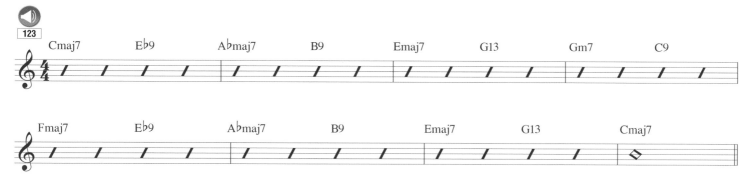

Compare Coltrane's changes in Phrases 6 and 7 with the original progression used by Charlie Parker in "Confirmation," shown here. Such investigation and comparison provide a telling, before-and-after look at his procedures and yield valuable insights into applying 3rds-related changes to standard progressions.

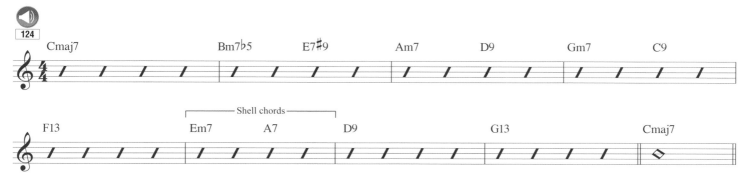

Minor Mode Progressions

Minor modes have unique qualities and colors. It stands to reason that harmonic formulas based on the minor mode would have similar attributes, and in fact, they do. Jazz composers and performers have for decades prized the minor tonality for its moody feeling and often exotic environment. Consequently, the repertoire is filled with notable minor-mode standards and original compositions. Among the most prominent are "In a Sentimental Mood," "Angel Eyes," "Summertime," "Alone Together," "Yesterdays," "Softly, As in a Morning Sunrise," "How Insensitive," "Airegin," "Soul Eyes," "Park Avenue Petite," "Nica's Dream," "Sugar," "Crescent," and "Blue in Green."

This is the standard formula for a i–vi–ii–V progression. It is often played as a vamp in an intro or outro of minor tunes, like "Softly, As in a Morning Sunrise" or "Yesterdays." In this context, the minor modes are mixed and the notes of different scales take on different roles in the harmony. Consider the flexible use of the sixth tone. It can be A or A♭, depending on whether you're drawing it from the harmonic minor, natural minor, or melodic minor scale, or the Dorian mode. The A is used as the root in Am7♭5 and also the 6th of Cm6. It is followed by Dm7♭5, which contains A♭ as its significant, flatted-5th chord tone. The seventh tone, which can be B or B♭, is similarly treated. It is the 7th in a Cm7 chord but can also be the ♯9 of a G7alt, which also contains B. In many cases, G7alt may also have E♭ scale tone, which sounds like a raised 5th (E♭ equals D♯ in a G7♯5), or A♭ (the flatted 9th) in its voicing.

A tonic C minor, i chord, is often played as a darker minor 6 chord, but can be a lighter minor 7 chord when a modal effect is desired. The combination of all these notes implies, at various points in the changes, harmonic minor and melodic minor scales, and Dorian and Aeolian modes. It is characteristic of the freer use of colors in minor keys. (This is demonstrated on the next page.)

This formula uses chromatic motion, D♭9 (a tritone sub for G7alt), as well as the standard ii–V–i: Dm7♭5–G7alt–Cm6. Sometimes the D♭9 is combined in the same measure with A♭m7, its ii chord: A♭m7–D♭9–Cm7. The formula was applied by Dizzy Gillespie in the A sections of "A Night in Tunisia."

A modulating formula is typically found in movement from i to the iv chord, here from Cm to Fm. The progression places a ii–V in the key of F minor (Gm7♭5–C7alt) to pivot into the iv chord, Fm7. The formula is heard in minor blues like "Birk's Works" and minor-mode jazz compositions such as "Airegin" and "Sugar," as well as the standard, "Alone Together."

A common variation of the previous formula entails movement to the iv and then back to the I. This can be particularly effective in minor blues, like "Birk's Works," where such motion is actually part of the structure. Here, the ii–Vs create additional harmonic activity and color.

Modulation from minor to major and back is presented in this cycle formula. The progression begins on Cm7, which becomes C7alt (think C7#5 here), and modulates to the *relative major* E♭ via a ii–V–I: Fm7–B♭7–E♭maj7. This is the most common modulation in a minor key. Why? These chords are closely related and require little alteration to modulate. Remember, C minor and E♭ major are essentially the same key, relative minor and major. Because of this close relation, every chord in the progression shares common tones with both keys. The return to the tonic C minor is typically accomplished with a ii–V–i pattern: Dm7♭5–G7alt–Cm6. This progression is heard in "Jordu" and "La Rue."

Modulation to the minor v chord and back is shown here. Note the passing tone in the inversion of Cm7, Cm/Bb. It generates this common sequence: Cm7–Cm/Bb (Cm7 in 3rd inversion or with the 7th in the bass) to Am7b5–D7–Gm7, a ii–V–i on the v chord, G minor. Listen for the passing-tone effect in the bass line: C–Bb–A. Note the first ending—here, a dominant V (G7alt) modulates back to Cm. Measures 1–3 of this formula can also be used as a iv–i progression in measures 5–7 of a minor blues. In the second ending, the G7 is enlarged with a ii–V change instead of G7. This motion is found in "I Hear a Rhapsody" and "Whisper Not."

Sometimes, a minor-mode progression, or a portion of it, is used to modulate to a *parallel major* key, for contrast or a harmonic surprise. This occurs in tunes like "Alone Together" (measures 11–14), "Once I Loved" (measures 13–15), "What's New?" (measures 6–7), and particularly in "What Is This Thing Called Love?," and its contrafact, "Hot House," in measures 5–8. This formula contains that harmonic motion. The Cmaj7 is established as the last chord in the phrase. It is reached after several chord changes in the minor mode.

This formula and its variants are heard in numerous minor-mode tunes. It is found verbatim in "Sunny," in measures 1–5. If the Abmaj7 is replaced with a dominant 7th chord, Ab7, it becomes a commonly used progression in a minor blues, in measures 7–11. This formula applies a ii–V–I progression to cadence on Ab (maj7 or 7) in measures 2–3: Bbm7–Eb7–Ab. The sequence then proceeds to a second ii–V–i in measures 4–5 to reestablish the tonic, Cm: Dm7–G7alt–Cm7.

A i–vi–ii–V formula can be reordered to generate a ii–V–iv–i pattern in the minor mode. This is the minor-mode equivalent of Phrase 3 in Basic Progressions, in the first section of this chapter. Here that procedure is used to create a variation of Minor-Mode Phrase 1 by beginning on the ii chord, Dm7b5.

CHAPTER 6

ADVANCED JAZZ HARMONY

Polychords

A *polychord* is defined as two or more chords sounded together, often stacked one on top of the other. This gets into the area of partial chords, fragmented voicings, and even the theory of "chordioid" harmony. But don't let exotic terms confound you. Save them for esoteric musical discussions into the wee hours with similarly inclined friends. The actual procedure is far less daunting.

Consider this simple demonstration. The extended dominant 7th chord, G13(9), is a diatonic structure based on the V chord in C major. It could be visualized as two fragments or *harmonic cells*, the combining of a G7 chord with an Fmaj7♭5, and written as Fmaj7♭5/G. That notation is similar to the slash-chord nomenclature introduced in Chapter 4 for writing inversions. In fact, at this point we may apply inversion thinking and labelling as steps toward understanding and utilizing polychords. With this approach it is useful to visualize two distinct shapes that make up the chord on the guitar. These isolated shapes are its components, or *partial chords*.

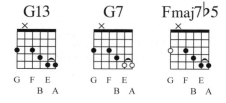

On piano, the sounding of two chords simultaneously is a common procedure; playing one chord with the left hand and a different one with the right hand at the same time is idiomatic to a keyboard. However, since two full four-note chords played together would contain more than six notes, a *shorthand* system for guitar is required to name and realize polychords.

On guitar, we use abbreviated forms or partial chords with fewer tones to convey the harmonic implications of larger polychords comprised of six or more notes. Looking back at G13, or Fmaj7♭5/G, we take *common tones* into account shared by the chords. These commonalities remove redundancy and result in fewer notes and a more compact chord. F is in both G7 and Fmaj7, B is the 3rd of G7 and flatted 5th of Fmaj7, A is the 9th and 3rd, and so on.

Common 7th chords have polytonal possibilities. While not true polychords, they are useful in visualizing the *chord-on-chord* relationship, vital to understanding polychords, with simple triad shapes. It is valuable to isolate and recognize *triads* in the top voices or *upper structure* of these chords. Note that Cmaj7 has an Em triad and Dm7 has an F major triad on top of their respective bass note. For more background on this important harmonic relationship review Chapter 2.

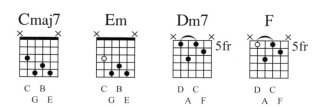

So far, we've seen several diatonic examples. What about more complex chords with chromatic alterations that are not diatonic? This basic example reveals that the same principle of isolating triad shapes holds with altered chords, in this case a Dm7♭5. Note that its upper structure contains an F minor triad above a D bass note. That's why many jazz musicians play F minor melodies on a Dm7♭5 chord. Put another way, Dm7♭5 is simply an inversion of Fm6 with the 6th in the bass. Pat Martino has alluded to the idea as *minor conversion*—a principle heard in his improvisations over half-diminished chords in the last four measures of "Along Came Betty."

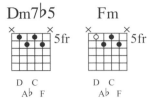

Shorthand Polychords

The following five forms are typical *shorthand polychords* frequently played on guitar.

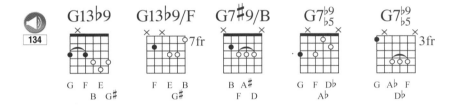

G13♭9 is is an altered chord (see Chapter 1). Note that it has an E major triad over a G bass note: E/G7. G13♭9 chord acts like an alteration and an extension, but it is also a shorthand polychord. The B note in E major is a common tone; G♯ is both the flatted 9th of G7 and the 3rd of E major (G♯=A♭ enharmonically). This root-position form in the third position is facilitated by *thumb fretting* of the G bass note. The sonority is often used as the fourth chord in the verse of Stevie Wonder's "You Are the Sunshine of My Life," where it is an A13♭9. In that progression the upper structure generates characteristic voice leading: its F♯ major triad in the upper structure moving down chromatically to an F major triad over Dm, or Dm7.

The rootless G13♭9/F in the seventh position is another abbreviated form. It simply places an F note (the 7th of G7) in the bass under an E major triad: E/F. That's the compact version of a 3rd-inversion altered dominant 7th chord. This shape is minimal but has a powerful pull toward resolution typical of 3rd-inversion dominants.

The sonority has also been used as a stand-alone polychord in modern jazz, notably in several versions of Thelonious Monk's "'Round Midnight." There it is written as D/E♭, a highly enriched substitution for E♭maj7. It functions as a dissonant tonic chord sometimes labelled a cumbersome "E♭maj9#11#9." That spelling underscores the utility of naming such complex chords as simple slash forms. D/E♭ or E♭maj9#11#9? Your choice. To hear the sound in context listen to the music at its source. Check out its usage by Monk, Miles Davis (*'Round About Midnight*), and Kenny Burrell (*Blue Muse*) in their renditions of "'Round Midnight."

The rootless G7#9/B presents a characteristic guitar form of an abbreviated polychord. It is essentially a *revoicing* of the previous form, moved to another position on the fingerboard to produce G7#9. Note the B♭ triad above a B bass note in the voicing. D and F are common tones in the chord. So what gives it that dissonant quality? The B note must be used in the voicing in conjunction with B♭, to combine B and B♭ in the same chord. There's the rub. Note that B♭ is enharmonic with A♯ and therefore becomes the raised 9th in the spelling. This shape was used as a 1st-inversion voicing of a C7#9 chord by Kenny Burrell in "Chitlins Con Carne" during the second theme statement. If the shape is moved to the eighth position it would still be a G7 chord, but would become G13♭9/F, a 3rd-inversion form. Many polychords share this *plural-use* attribute.

G7♭9♭5 is a root-position polychord that contains the tritone substitution, D♭, and its parent chord, G7, in the same form. This shape places a D♭ major triad above the G bass note. Note that F is common to both chords. This polychord is found as the second chord of McCoy Tyner's accompaniment in "Say It (Over and Over Again)" (John Coltrane, *Ballads*), where it was used as a dominant VI (V of ii) in the I–VI–ii–V progression. The previous chord, G7#9/B, becomes a closely related form when moved to the fifth position. In that transformation it is a rootless partial polychord: D♭/D, a D♭ major triad over a D bass note.

G7♭9♭5 voiced with a D♭ triad over G is a typical polychord. This form contains a D♭ triad spelled A♭–D♭–F, instead of F–A♭–D♭ as in the previous shape. The sonority was used to good effect by Horace Silver in the coda of "Nica's Dream." There it was played a whole step lower, B/F, and toggled from B/F to Cm7♭5 just before the final phrase of the tune. Listen and make an effort to identify the sound.

Polychords and Diminished Harmony

The polychord forms of the previous section lend themselves to *diminished harmony*. Diminished harmony refers to chords and arpeggios based on division of the octave into four equal parts, each a minor 3rd (three half steps) apart. When operating within the diminished harmony system, dominant chords with alterations based on notes of the *diminished scale*—here, F–G–A♭(G#)–A#(B♭)–B–C#(D♭)–D–E can be treated like diminished 7th chords.

The diminished scale has eight tones and is comprised of only whole steps and half steps, alternating in sequence. It is like adding a leading tone one half step below each note of a diminished arpeggio. The pattern is *symmetrical*, repeating on every other step of the scale or on every note of a diminished arpeggio. That reality opens up a world of possibilities for both altered chords and polychords.

Let's imagine a diminished chord built on F, the 7th tone of G7: F–A♭–B–D. Now consider the upper structure of the G13♭9, voiced F–B–E–G#(A♭) as an F diminished chord with a "suspension": D replaced by E. This shape can be moved up or down in minor 3rds to produce different voicings and spellings of an altered dominant chord. It functions exactly like a diminished chord. Note the variety of altered colors created with the procedure: G13♭9, G7♭9, G7#9, and G7♭9♭5. Every one of these chords has its commonality in shared notes of the F diminished scale. They are members of the same family. Compare the notes in the chords with the scale notes above.

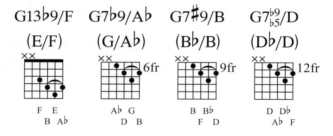

The simple G major triad (G–B–D), also available in the diminished scale, can be voiced with an A♭ in the bass to achieve a polychordal effect. Though no F note is present in the voicing, a dominant 7th chord sound is strongly implied, indicated by the 7th in parentheses, G(7)/A♭, seen often in notation. Lowering the G note to F in any of these forms automatically creates an A♭°7 chord or rootless G7♭9.

These forms illustrate the basic sounds in a number of idiomatic fingerings. Some of them will look and sound familiar to you; they are indeed shapes you've already played. This realization underscores the value of diminished harmony as the basis for a wide range of altered chords and polychords. A telling example of diminished harmony blended with tertian harmony is found in the standard "Poor Butterfly" (measures 3 and 19). Check out the version by Cannonball Adderley on *Cannonball Takes Charge* with Wynton Kelly on piano, and listen for the pull of A♭°7 to A♭maj9 in measures 3–4 of the tune.

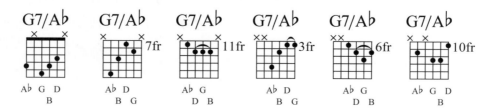

Polychord Progressions

As it was with basic chord sounds, shell chords, and inversions, it is essential to put polychords to work in changes as soon as possible. In this way, the chords have a functional context in your repertoire. The *turnaround* progression of iii (or I)–VI–ii–V–I is ideal for this purpose. Combining shorthand polychords with extended chords in this harmonic situation adds considerable color and unique motion to a standard pattern. These phrases exemplify several typical progressions. Play the polychord forms while relating to the basic changes as simply Em7–A7–Dm7–G7 and C.

On the C chord, play either a 6/9 or maj7 voicing. You are adding the color to the basic progression. Note the abundant *chromaticism* and *parallelism* in the first, third, and fourth phrases. The second phrase has a *pedal point* in the top voice; G is maintained through the changes.

Play these phrases with different rates of chord change and in various rhythm grooves: swing or Latin with two chords per bar, bossa nova or funk with one chord per bar, or other variations. Experiment and make up your own renditions. Apply different types of articulation. Strum the chords in quarter-note rhythm, comp with rhythmic variety using space and syncopation, pluck the chords with the fingers for Latin or Brazilian variations, or arpeggiate freely with the fingers in a rubato, slow-ballad feel.

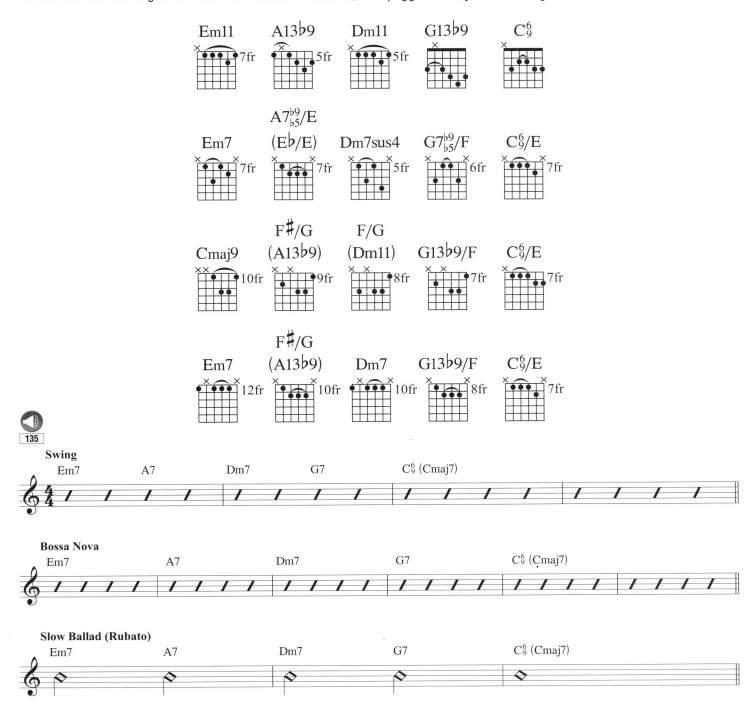

These alternative forms present other types of voice leading, movement, and connections characteristic of polychords. Note greater inner-voice activity and varied melodic lines in the upper part of the chords. Apply similar varied grooves, comping approaches, different harmonic rhythm, and articulations. Try them with the prevous turnaround progressions.

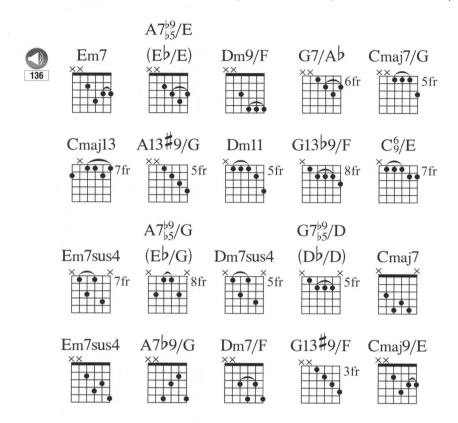

Pedal Point

Pedal point refers to a tone, usually in the bass, which is sustained through chord changes. The term originates from the Baroque period (circa 1600–1750) of European classical music, when a sustained note activated by the foot pedal of an organ was a common sound in composition and performance. Today, pedal point is a fundamental procedure in many forms of music—classical, rock, pop, country, and jazz, virtually any style that uses chords. Typically, the pedal-point effect is established with a chord having a consonant relationship to the bass note. It then becomes increasingly dissonant as other chords are sounded over the bass in a progression.

In jazz, chords changing over a single sustained bass note, or bass riff, frequently result in polychords and dissonance, and that's the goal. They are often played to create tension or to supply variety in a section, as in the practice of applying a pedal point to the bridge of a tune. A telling example is John Coltrane's treatment of the bridge in "Say It (Over and Over Again)." Listen for Jimmy Garrison's repeated bass note sounded under McCoy Tyner's freer modal accompaniment.

Pedal points are prevalent in modal and post-bop jazz styles but are also found in arrangements of standards. "On Green Dolphin Street" is a well-known example, as are Duke Ellington's "Satin Doll" (intro), Kenny Barron's arrangement of "Spring Is Here" and Miles Davis' version of "Someday My Prince Will Come" (intro). Other noteworthy pieces in the repertoire exploiting pedal point include Herbie Hancock's "Dolphin Dance," John Coltrane's "Naima," Stevie Wonder's "Too High," Bill Evans' intro to "So What," and Wayne Shorter's "Children of the Night."

A pedal point is often played in the first seven measures of "On Green Dolphin Street," the A section, particularly when a Latin groove is used as a contrast to the tune's B and C sections set in a swing rhythm. In this example, the idea is depicted with a series of triads descending over a sustained C pedal point. Note the mixture of whole-step and half-step motion, as well as the strong pull to the final tonic C chord via its dissonant upper neighbor, Db/C.

John Coltrane used pedal point effectively in "Spiral." His main theme was harmonized with six triads descending chromatically over a sustained D bass note. In this phrase, the sequence is begun on a 2nd-inversion chord, G/D. Typically, pedal-point phrases are begun on the tonic, as in "Green Dolphin Street," or the fifth tone, as in "Spiral." From there, G/D continues with Gb, F, E, Eb, and D triads before cadencing on a surprising Ebmaj7 3rds relation.

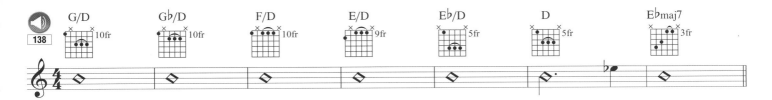

Antônio Carlos Jobim harnessed the power of pedal point in the Brazilian jazz classic, "Triste." His intro is a quintessentially guitar-friendly moment in the genre. Clearly composed on the guitar, this figure poses extended and altered chords over an A pedal bass note, the open fifth string. The voicings employ open high-E and B strings in conjunction with fretted notes on the third and fourth strings to produce unique, guitar-istic sonorities. Note the arrow designations in the example suggesting up and down strokes to capture the flavor of the syncopated rhythm. You can play this progression with conventional plectrum strumming or fingertip strumming, or apply fingerstyle plucking articulation as was heard on the original recording.

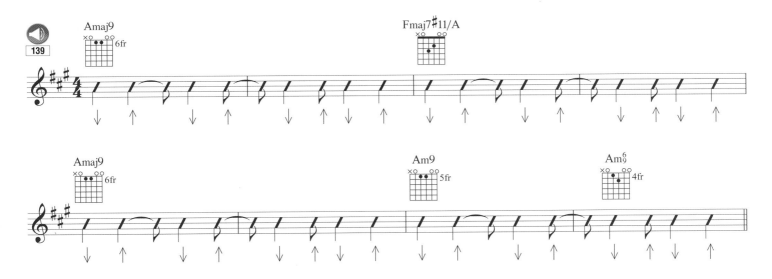

Pedal point has been used to impart a mysterious, unresolved effect to tunes. The standard "Angel Eyes" is a case in point. Its minor modality is enhanced by a pedal-point treatment in the first two bars of verses. Listen to Barney Kessel's version on *Poll Winners Ride Again!* Barney plays the piece in A minor to facilitate use of the open fifth string as the pedal tone, which strengthens the sustaining impression on guitar. However, the phrase can easily be played in the standard keys of Dm or Cm as shown.

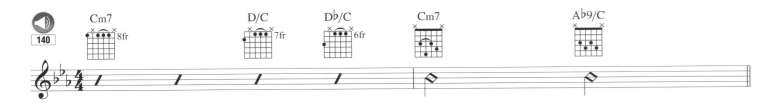

Wes Montgomery produced a different modal but similarly haunting effect in his intro to "I've Grown Accustomed to Her Face." He used triads from mixed major modes posed over a low-E pedal point to create E, D/E, and F/E in the first two measures. Note the F(#4)/E in the phrase and the overall "Spanish" mood. The closely related Dm6/E in the third phrase heightens this impression. The final chord, E6/9, is made of stacked 4ths beginning with G# (G#–C#–F#–B–E) over an E bass note. It provides an ideal segue into the subject of *quartal harmony*.

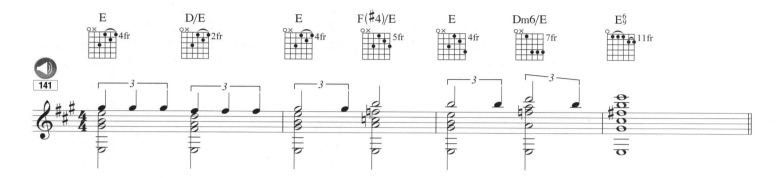

Quartal Harmony

Chords built on 4th intervals are called *quartal*. We've already seen chords based on standard *tertian harmony*, built on diatonic 3rds, and chords based on the diminished scale with its symmetrical, minor-3rd intervals and whole-step/half-step structure. Quartal harmony is a familiar—indeed, idiomatic—sound in modern jazz and fusion. It is a system based on 4th intervals, and by inversion, 5th intervals, instead of 3rds. For example, instead of a typical 7th chord, like C7: C–E–G–Bb, made of consecutive 3rds, we would have a chord built on 4th intervals, like C–F–Bb–Eb or C–F#–B–E. In jazz, quartal harmony came into regular usage among musicians of the late 1950s and early 1960s as an outgrowth of experimenting with modes, intervals and impressionistic music, and remains a favored approach for generating modern extended chords and melodies in compositions and improvisation. Jazz guitarists known for their use of quartal harmony include Jim Hall, Joe Diorio, Ed Bickert, Kurt Rosenwinkel, and George Benson.

The following example depicts a scale of quartal chords in C minor. Every form is made of consecutive 4th intervals. Here, as befits modal music, the Dorian mode is the source scale: C–D–Eb–G–A–Bb (same as Bb major). The root tones are on the fifth string. The sonorities can be thought of as arising from Cm or Bb major, or even Gm or Eb major, depending on the changes in a piece of music. Composers like McCoy Tyner, Bill Evans, Chick Corea, Wayne Shorter, and Herbie Hancock tend to apply these sounds freely, guided by intuition and imagination.

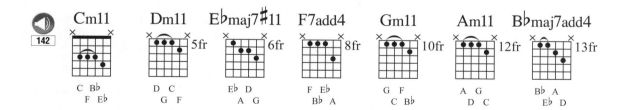

Several shapes will seem familiar. Indeed, they are. The quartal form for Cm11, Dm11, Gm11, and Am11 chords was introduced in the first chapter as an extended chord of minor quality. It was seen again in relation to inversions, in Chapter 4, where it was the upper partial of a rootless major 6/9 chord. And Ebmaj7#11 was in the altered chord section of Chapter 1. But what about unusual and dissonant chords like F7add4 and Bbmaj7add4?

Quartal harmony, like tertian harmony, is not symmetrical. In diatonic harmony, there are major and minor 3rds, based on half and whole steps in a major scale. In quartal harmony, there is a similar asymmetric group of intervals stacked in 4ths. This initial understanding leads to a clear perception of quartal chords. The qualities of 4ths (and 5ths) are perfect, diminished, and augmented. The perfect 4th is two and half steps apart, C–F, F–B♭, B♭–E♭, and so on. The tritone, seen in E♭maj7#11, is an augmented 4th interval: E♭–A. Three successive perfect 4th intervals comprise the minor 11th chords. F7add4 has two perfect 4ths (F–B♭–E♭) and one augmented 4th: E♭–A. B♭maj7add4 has a perfect 4th (B♭–E♭) followed by an augmented 4th (E♭–A) and then a perfect 4th (A–D). These asymmetric intervals produce greater harmonic complexity and more exotic chord types in the quartal family. Play the forms and listen to the various colors.

It is valuable to learn equivalent quartal forms with fourth-string roots. This is the same chord scale in Em, based again on the Dorian mode. Note other familiar shapes. Here, Gmaj7#11 is equivalent to the upper partial of an A13(9) chord.

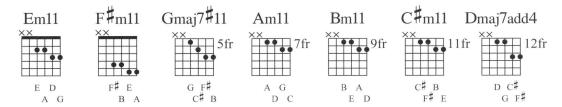

Virtually any progression can be subjected to quartal harmony with satisfying albeit modernistic results. Begin to explore common situations and make substitutions. This figure applies quartal chords to a Cm scenario. In a standard chart, the chords would be written as Cm7, Dm7, and E♭maj7. However, you can voice them as quartal forms shown in the grids below the music to *modernize* the harmony. The progression borrows its rhythm from the intro of "Stolen Moments" but generates a progression quite different from the Oliver Nelson minor blues. George Benson used numerous variations of quartal-chord movement in his comping behind the organ solo of "So What" (*Beyond the Blue Horizon*).

The basic rhythm figure in Herbie Hancock's "Maiden Voyage" can also be expanded with quartal harmony. In this example, a simple, one-finger barred shape produces the chord, D9sus4, and its bass line: A–D–A. The figure is moved in parallel motion: a minor 3rd higher and back, F9sus4 to D9sus4. While the fingering may be simple the resulting modal effect is hardly simplistic.

Parallelism and quartal harmony are compatible and often used together in a progression. Consider this telling phrase from Barney Kessel, one of the earliest traditional jazz guitarists to embrace quartal harmony. Though he played these forms in standard songs like "Misty," the result is modern and impressionistic. The quartal chords, voiced as consecutive perfect 4ths in a parallel progression, follow the diatonic bass notes A–G–F–E in the key of F major. This phrase epitomizes the plural thinking possible with quartal chords. The first chord in the sequence can be seen as an F6/9/A (1st inversion) or a B♭maj13/A (3rd inversion), and the last chord as a rootless major 13th, Fmaj13/E (3rd inversion) or C6/9/E (1st inversion). What's important is the sound, the motion and its function, not the label.

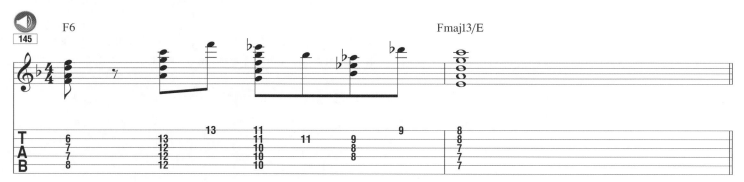

Kenny Burrell is another innovative jazz guitarist whose playing and musical evolution span several styles and epochs. His application of quartal harmony enlivened countless chord passages in the repertoire. This figure from "Tenderly" (*Lucky So and So*) presents a classic standard updated with parallelism, chromatic movement and quartal harmony. Note the use of perfect 4th shapes alternating with a second closely-related form that includes a perfect 5th interval in the top voice of the minor 11 chords. That procedure emphasizes the connection between 4ths and 5ths in quartal harmony.

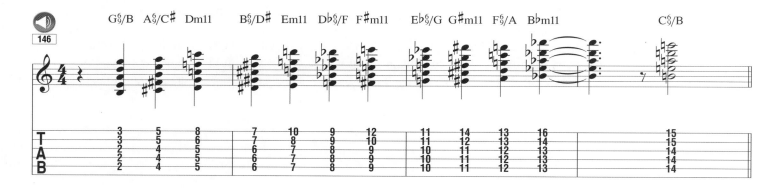

Quartal harmony and parallelism reach a high point when factoring in the diminished scale. Consider a C7#9 as a starting chord. This form naturally occurs in the eight-tone D♭ diminished scale: D♭–E♭–E–G♭–G–A–B♭–C. Note the alternate respelling of E as F♭, a theoretical note name, that makes it a *diminished 4th*. Though theoretical, it serves a useful purpose in applying the diminished scale and symmetry to quartal chords.

This series of chords illustrates quartal forms based on the diminished scale. It combines symmetry with intervals of different quality 4ths: perfect 4ths, augmented 4ths, and diminished 4ths. Remember, a diminished 4th is enharmonic with a major 3rd. Allowing chords based on the diminished scale, like C7#9, to generate a quartal family opens up possibilities for a modern sound and unique parallelism over an altered C7 chord.

Consider the following respellings. In C7#9, C–E is C–Fb, a diminished 4th. Fb–Bb is an augmented 4th and Bb–Eb is a perfect 4th, however they are heard as the 3rd, 7th, and raised 9th tones of a C7 chord. In the second form, a less common voicing which we could call C7b5b9, the intervals are Db–Gb (a perfect 4th), Gb–C (an augmented 4th) and C–Fb (a diminished 4th). In a C7 chord, that's the flatted 9th, flatted 5th, root, and 3rd. The same shapes repeat in the diminished family as Eb7, F#7, and A7.

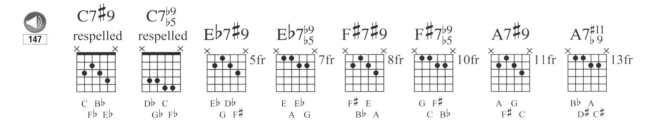

In modern jazz, these shapes can replace traditional diminished chords moving in half-step/whole-step motion or in minor 3rds. Quartal respelling, in conjunction with the diminished scale, allows these chords to function in four different keys, shown in the previous example, or to function within the same key as substitutions. The forms here are respelled altered C7 chords; several are rootless voicings.

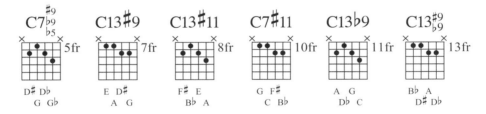

These respellings can get pretty far afield in theory and overly complicated in labelling. Keep it simple and don't let it become a "name game." Use your ear and be open to new sounds. Listen to each shape for its dissonance, notice its movement as you practice, and consider its possible function as an altered dominant, in this case some kind of C7 chord.

A parting shot and word to the wise: John Coltrane used the idea of stacking dominant 7th chords built on minor 3rds in the development of his "sheets of sound" concept in improvisation. In "Coltrane on Coltrane," he stated his desire to apply a "three-on-one chord approach" melodically. "On C7, I sometimes superimposed an Eb7, up to an F#7 resolving to an F. That way, I could play three chords on one."

Reharmonization

Any tune can enjoy different interpretations. In jazz, reharmonization is a regularly pursued practice that automatically creates new interpretations on the chordal level. Reharmonization means using different chords, substitutions and even alternate progressions in place of what might be found in lead sheets and fakebooks. In fact, some players are recognized by their personal choices of alternate chords. We've seen reharmonizations of 12-bar blues in Charlie Parker's "Blues for Alice" and Bud Powell's "Dance of the Infidels." Countless standards have been subjected to similar refinements. Reharmonization is also used as a strategy to develop more advanced melodic improvisations.

Reharmonization is a vast topic, worthy of volumes on its own. However, some basics should be initially understood and applied within the broad category of advanced jazz harmony. Consider this familiar progression. It is a standard chord sequence heard in the last eight measures of "Stella by Starlight" as well as "Woody'n You" and other tunes.

When reharmonizing, start with the most basic form of the original chord changes. This chart depicts the standard changes. Play the progression using established chord fingerings from previous chapters.

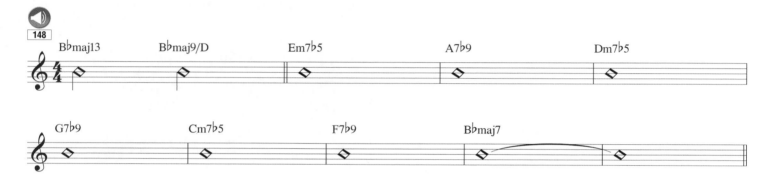

This example is a typical jazz reharmonization of the changes. Play the chords. Listen and compare. You'll hear the harmony moving into unexpected but musically satisfying areas.

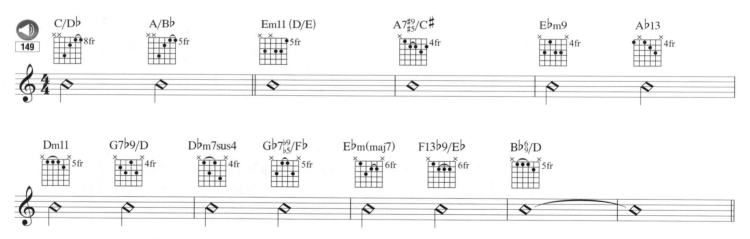

Several points are noteworthy. This reharmonized progression brings together plural chords, inversions, rootless chords, polychords, diminished harmony, and quartal harmony. The following observations are offered to emphasize and expound upon material already learned and now applied in a different real-world context.

- The B♭maj9 chord with the ninth tone, C, in the top voice can always be reharmonized with a C triad combined with a D♭ diminished triad, C/D♭. The polychord essentially applies diminished scale harmony to a major 7th chord. Here, the C/D♭ is connected to a similar chord, A/B♭. It is the same shape a minor 3rd lower and functions like a diminished chord. This form is a reharmonization of the B♭maj7 chord. A similar assumption can be drawn: the major-7th tone, A, can be reharmonized with A/B♭ from the diminished scale.

- Em7♭5 and A7♭9 are reharmonized with polychords containing triads on the top three strings. Em11 has a D major triad on an E bass note and A7#9#5/C# has an F major triad on top of a quartal voicing.

- The most active reharmonization takes place in the next four measures. The harmonic rhythm is increased to two chords per bar. It is begun with E♭m9–A♭13 replacing Dm7♭5. The common tone F in the top voice of the two chords connects both to Dm7. It is essentially a simple ii–V progression, played a half step higher, replacing a single chord—the chordal version of side-slipping.

- G7♭9 is reharmonized with a back-cycling procedure. Dm11, a quartal chord, and D°7, a rootless altered chord (G7♭9/D), replace the single dominant 7th chord. Note the voice leading in the middle voices of these two forms.

- Cm7♭5 is reharmonized with another ii–V a half step above. Here, a more sophisticated progression is used: D♭m7sus4 and G♭7♭9♭5/F♭. This harmonizes the common tone G♭ in the top voice. G♭ links the reharmonized changes to the original Cm7♭5 chord.

- F7♭9 is replaced with E♭m(maj7) and F13♭9/E♭. Note the common tone in the bass. Above the bass, the voice leading spells out a D+ triad moving to a D major triad. The use of E♭ minor as a reharmonization of F7 is a typical maneuver in modern jazz. It is also an inversion/extension of the previous Cm7♭5 and a characteristic minor conversion.

- The final tonic chord B♭6/9/D is a quartal form. It is also plural chord. B♭6/9/D is identical with Dm11 in measure 5.

This cycle progression is one of the most pervasive in jazz. It is found in standards and jazz originals as well as bossa novas like "Corcovado." Moreover, it is the basis for the most common turnaround: iii–VI–ii–V–I. A similar reharmonization procedure can be used to expand the changes. In this chart there are two staves. The top line shows the standard changes. The bottom line is its reharmonization. Note the use of half-step movement throughout, which creates a steady descending chromatic sequence of ii–V progressions. Play both and compare the sound of the standard and reharmonized chords.

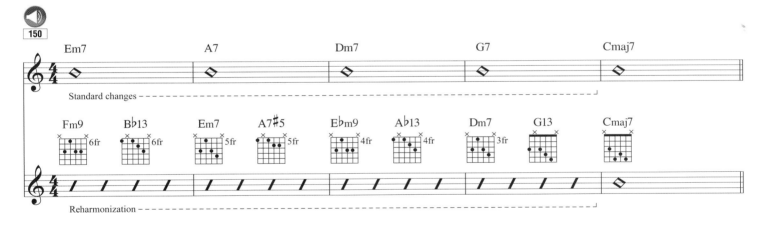

Shorter progressions invite a deeper look into reharmonization. This is like placing the reharmonized move under a sonic microscope. Duke Ellington's "In a Sentimental Mood" provides a look at several options. This is the basic progression. It is approached from a simple pentatonic melody to Dm. The original progression is the common pattern often used with a minor mode: Dm–Dm(maj7)–Dm7. See Chapter 1. What is different is the sustained G tone in the top voice, which adds an 11th tone to the harmony starting with Dmsus4. Play the example and listen for a suspended quality in the progression.

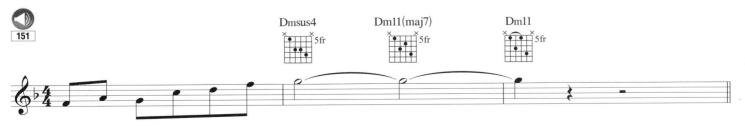

A common reharmonization entails substituting a Bm7(add ♭6) chord for Dm7sus4, followed by B♭m13 and Am11, for the minor-mode changes. (See this in action on the next page.)

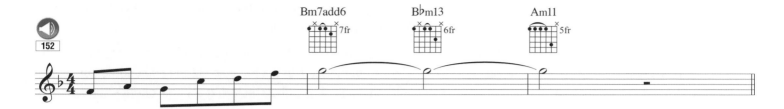

Kenny Burrell reharmonized the same line in two different ways in the coda of his rendition. The first replaces the expected Dmsus4 destination chord with an altered dominant 7th in a quartal voicing: E13#9. The second applies a polychord from the diminished scale: G/Ab.

An investigation of Henry Mancini's "Dreamsville" as played by Pat Martino and Gil Goldstein (*We'll Be Together Again*) reveals another useful reharmonization. This maneuver is so common it has become an unofficial "rule" of reharmonization: whenever a melody cadences on the 9th of a major 9th chord reharmonize that tone with a 7#9 a half step lower. Horace Silver applied the same principle in the bridge of "Nica's Dream" (measure 7).

In this example, Cmaj9 is replaced with B7#9. D is the common tone that links the chromatic chords and acts as a pivot. Note two options. Either can be the final chord. Martino ended his entire arrangement on this reharmonization. Play both. Compare and listen to the contrasting effect.

Sometimes both forms are used together to create a "secondary" progression—a "progression within a progression"—with B7#9 resolving to Cmaj9. Play this pattern and listen to the upward half-step "pull" of the chord change.

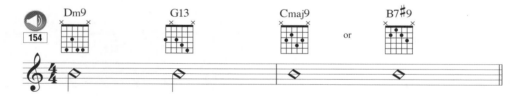

Pianist Bill Evans was a master of reharmonization. His version of "Spring Is Here" demonstrates several significant possibilities in the first four bars. The top staff presents the standard changes while the bottom staff shows the alternate progression Evans created through reharmonization. Note that the Ab°7 chord is reharmonized as an altered chord, E7#9, and as a tritone substitution, Dm11. The common tone linking the three chords is G.

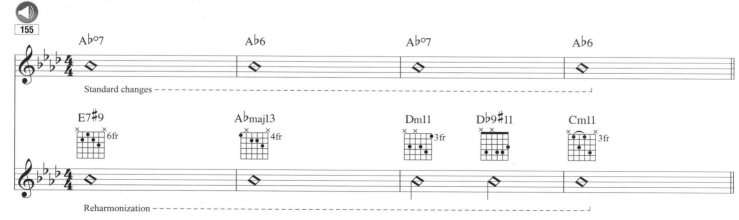

94

Another related "rule" of reharmonization arises from the previous example. It is commonly found in tunes like "Misty," where a progression cadences on a major chord with the major 7th tone in the top voice. That chord, a tonic major, receives a m11 chord a tritone away. For example, in "Misty," Ebmaj7 is reharmonized with Am11. In this example, notice the parallel polychords used over Bb7alt, a maneuver I first saw played by Joe Pass when he began "Misty" in concert. These forms are members of the diminished scale family and are used symmetrically to harmonize the Bb–G melody. In the next measure, Am11 reharmonizes Ebmaj7 by pivoting on the common tone D. The common tone prevails through Ab7b5 and the resolution to Ebmaj7, which acts as another progression within a progression.

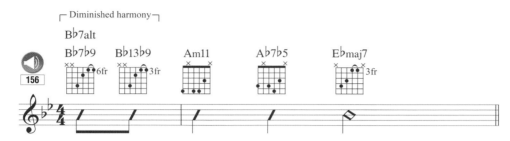

Variations of this harmonic move are found in standards like "I Remember You," "Summer Samba," and "Little Boat (O Barquino)," where they are part of the actual progression. In these examples from the tunes, the destination chord following the change is different; which tells you much about the flexibility of alternate harmony. In the first, the motion is a return to the I chord, Fmaj7. In the second, it is to the IV chord, Bbmaj7. And in the third, it is to Ebmaj7, a new tonic, one whole step lower.

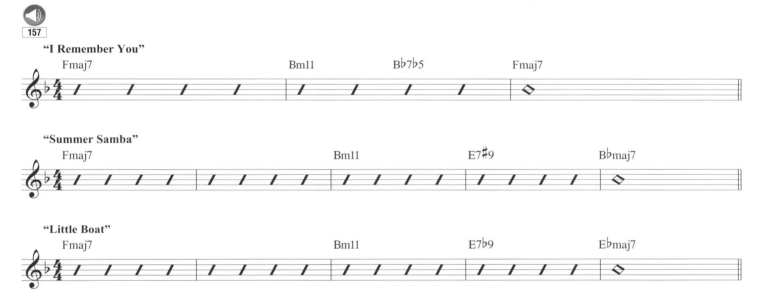

Reharmonization relies on common-tone strategies, extant in several of the previous examples. A typical scenario found in many standard songs occurs when a ii–V progression harmonizes a melody note on the fourth step of the scale, as in measures 15–16 of "There Will Never Be Another You." This phrase illustrates the procedure within a comping figure that could also be applied to a chord-melody treatment.

The first example is the phrase played without reharmonization. Note the Ab tone in measures 3–4 in the top voice of Fm7 and Bb7b9. Ab is the fourth step of an Eb major scale: Eb–F–G–Ab–Bb–C–D.

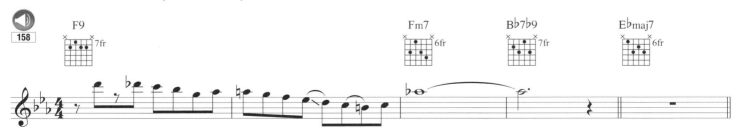

This example contains reharmonization of the same phrase. Here, the important A♭ tone becomes part of a chromatic cycle that adds two chords, G♭m9 and C♭13, to the progression. The A♭ common tone unites four chords: G♭m9–C♭13–Fm7–B♭7♭9. This technique is especially effective when the original ii–V occupies two measures allowing for two shorter ii–Vs in sequence, one in each bar, essentially doubling the rate of chord change. A strategy emerges: The common tone and its connection with the standard ii–V, Fm7–B♭7, allows for reharmonization and an alternate set of changes.

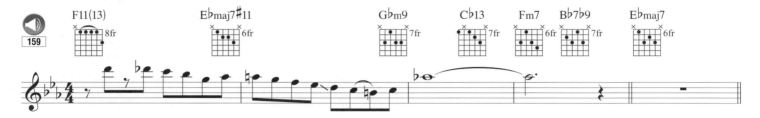

The next time you look at a fakebook such as *The Real Book*, notice how many melodies in standard songs end on the tonic note of the key. For example, C in the key of C. This is usually the top voice of a tonic chord (I) and is generally preceded by a ii–V progression. For example, Dm7–G7 to C major. The tonic melody note is typically harmonized with a consonant major 6th or 6/9 chord. However, the practice of always harmonizing the tonic in this way produces monotony, predictability and blandness. Many musicians have sought harmonic variety with substitute progressions, particularly at the end of a main section or in the coda of an arrangement.

One of the most common tactics for reharmonizing in this situation entails replacing the tonic with a 6-chord substitute progression that begins on a "surprise chord," essentially a deceptive cadence, and cycles back to the final I chord. This phrase in E♭, based on the common standard "Misty," typifies the situation.

Now compare that basic progression with these substitutions. This pattern is played on strings 6 through 2.

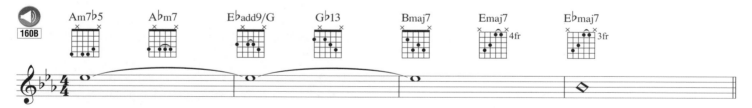

The E♭ tone is reharmonized with Am7♭5, similar to the Am11 in Track 152, a half step below B♭7. It commences a 6-chord progression that pivots on a sustained E♭ tone and cadences on E♭maj7 in measure 4. Note the smooth voice leading and visiting of remote tonalities in the chord changes. Am7♭5 is followed by three chromatically descending chords: A♭m7, E♭add9/G, and G♭13. Each could be in a different key center. G♭13 begins a cycle-of-4ths progression, G♭13 (F♯13)–Bmaj7–Emaj7, that sounds like it's temporarily in B major, yielding a 3rds-related modulation—B is a major 3rd below E♭ (D♯). The final E♭maj7 resolves out of the Emaj7 in that sequence and produces a strong ending sonority with its downward pull from an upper neighbor.

Comparable forms should be learned as a progression on the next set of strings: strings 5 through 1. This phrase, based on the changes of "I Can't Get Started" in C, exemplifies a stock situation.

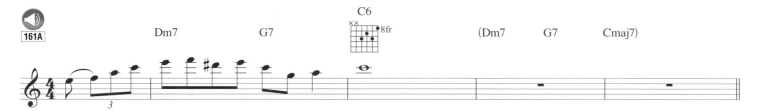

This variation is a 6-chord substitute progression with slightly different voicings, all pivoting on a sustained C note. Note the use of quartal harmony in Fm11, C6/9/E, and B♭m11/E♭ chords. These sonorities modernize the chord colors considerably.

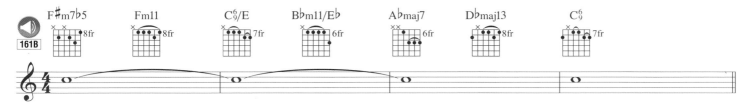

Augmented Harmony

Augmented harmony has been part of jazz since its earliest days. In ragtime music, Tin Pan Alley repertoire (the genesis of the Great American Songbook) and the classic jazz period, it was heard often as a conventional enrichment of the I chord. Nearly 100 years later, augmented harmony is ubiquitous and appears in many forms with various functions. Consider its use in Stevie Wonder's "You Are the Sunshine of My Life" (intro), Chuck Berry's opening fanfare of "School Days," or numerous Beatles tunes like, "Oh! Darling."

In jazz, augmented harmony has lent expressive colors to countless pieces. Billy Strayhorn explored numerous augmented chords in one of the most monumental of jazz art songs, "Lush Life" (written between 1933–1936, first recorded in 1948). Thelonious Monk applied augmented sonorities regularly in his bebop compositions; "Four in One" (1952) and "Trinkle Tinkle" (1954) are salient examples. In the post-bop milieu, Wayne Shorter's "JuJu" (1965) reveals that augmented harmony transcends style and era.

The augmented chord is most commonly used in ii–V–I progressions as an alteration of the V7 chord: a dominant 7th with an augmented 5th, written 7#5. G7#5 is spelled G–B–D#–F. Play these typical V–I cadences. Listen to the function and voice leading of the augmented chord tone: the D# (raised or "sharped" 5th) in G7#5. It moves logically upward to the 3rd, E, of Cmaj7 and C7 chords. The latter is also a common progression in the blues, typically found in bars 4–5 of the 12-bar form. This progression was first seen in Chapter 1.

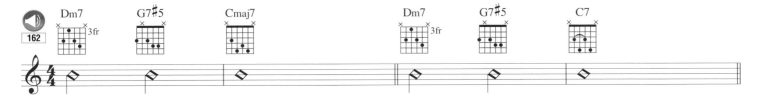

The V7 augmented chord is diatonic in melodic minor (*ascending form*, colloquially called the "jazz minor scale") and harmonic minor scales, two characteristic *tonal* environments in jazz harmony. These scales illustrate the point. E♭ in both scales is enharmonic with D#. The notes that comprise G7#5 also exist in both scales: G–B–E♭/D#–F. This progression is invaluable when a common tone in the melody of the two chords is desired. (Turn to the next page to see this shown.)

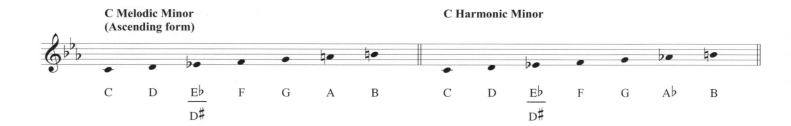

This V–i progression in C minor reveals the E♭ common-tone connection in both chords. The E♭/D# tone inflects the G7#5 and is the minor 3rd of Cm(maj7).

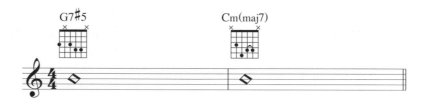

We saw this type of diatonic connection earlier in Chapter 1, detailing the use of Dm7♭5 as an "altered" chord in a minor mode. Review that section for more clarification.

In jazz harmony, many progressions utilize the enharmonic attribute to generate an alternate and decidedly more sophisticated function for a 7#5 chord. When viewed as a ♭6 (E♭ in C minor) the tone descends stepwise to the 9th of the next chord. This naturally produces smooth voice leading. Though it is considered a ♭6 in the scale the nomenclature in chord charts typically names the chord G7#5 to describe its augmented quality and function. In these progressions, motion to the 9th of three chords of different quality (major, dominant, and minor) is the goal. The conclusion is that the G7#5 can go to any chord a 4th above (with a C root) and is particularly strong when the chord contains a 9th tone in the top voice. Play these cadences and listen to the directional downward pull and contrasting colors.

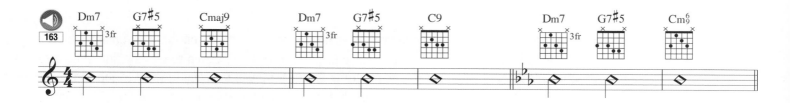

These examples from the repertoire depict this movement in real-world scenarios. The first is based on the opening phrase of "Tangerine." Note the use of an augmented chord, D7#5, to harmonize D–B♭ melody notes in measure 2 and its resolution to a Gm9 chord in 3.

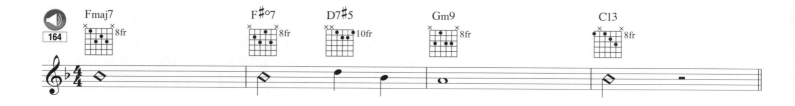

The second example addresses the cycle progression in Henry Mancini's "Mr. Lucky." There are several examples of augmented harmony in this sequence. Check out the augmented chords G7#5 and F7#5 in measures 2 and 4. Both are preceded by their 13th chord, G13 and F13, respectively. Both resolve to Cm9 and B♭maj9, respectively, to harmonize the 9th tone. A 3rds-related and typical application is heard in measure 6. Here, an E9#11, a member of the *augmented family*, is used as a neighbor chord, a half step above E♭maj7, for a chromatic resolution. It functions as a tritone substitute for a B♭maj9 chord.

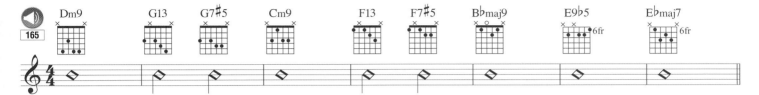

The 7#5 chord (G7#5) is often paired with iim9 (Dm9) to produce a Dm9–G7#5–Cmaj9 progression and harmonize the passing-note melody E–E♭–D. Check out bars 11–13 of Benny Golson's "Stablemates" for another telling example.

Augmented harmony is closely related to the *whole-tone scale*. This is a six-note *synthetic scale* made entirely of whole steps. In G, it is spelled G–A–B–C#–D#–F. Note that, like melodic and harmonic minor scales, it contains the notes of a dominant 7th chord with an augmented 5th, G7#5: G–B–D#–F. As in the case of the minor modes, the D# is heard enharmonically as E♭. Moreover, the C# is heard as a D♭, which allows for both flatted-5th and augmented-11th spellings in chord charts. This is seen where G7♭5 is alternatively written as G7#11, or more typically, G9#11.

The 7#5 can occur on any step of the whole-tone scale, which makes it function symmetrically like diminished chords in a diminished scale. Unlike the diminished scale, the whole-tone scale has no half steps and therefore no leading tones or chromatic neighbors. This produces an attractive harmonic vagueness that was ingeniously exploited by Stevie Wonder and Wayne Shorter.

Chords in the whole-tone scale family include G7#5, G7♭5, G9#5, and G9♭5. These upper-string forms are frequently used to facilitate symmetrical motion in augmented chord passages, typical of jazz-guitar application. They can be played on any step of the whole-tone scale.

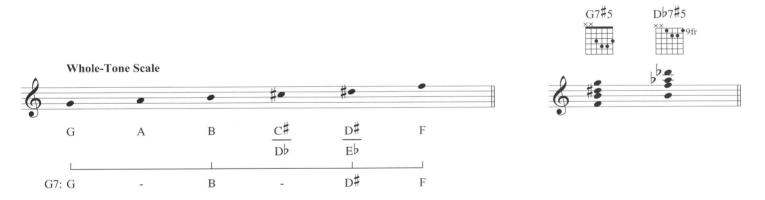

Another intriguing asset in the whole-tone scale family entails its organic tritone possibilities. On the guitar this makes a strong visual/aural result. Note the symmetry and exact fingering of G7#5 and D♭7#5 forms at the third and ninth positions, respectively. These shapes are inherent in the whole-tone scale and occur as a result of the scale's symmetry. We can use this attribute to create a parallel-motion effect, applying the form to tritone substitution. Following are some other augmented harmony shapes.

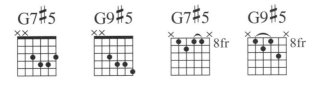

Wes Montgomery employed augmented harmony and parallel whole-tone scale movement in the blues. It has since become part of the jazz guitar canon. Wes typically used the augmented sound to lend color and generate activity from I to IV7 in the crucial fourth bar of a 12-bar blues form where greater dissonance is desired. In these instances, he applied 7#5 forms in key phrases, especially when improvising block-chord passages or comping. This chord fill from "West Coast Blues" (solo chorus 9: bars 4–5) uses a single 7#5 form played at the sixth, third, first, and fifth positions. It demonstrates his typical use of symmetry and parallelism in whole tones.

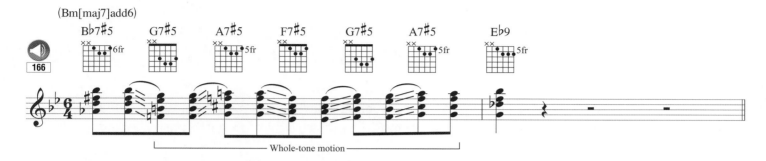

Variations of Wes' augmented-harmony figures in the blues, generally occurring in measure 4, are also found in "Missile Blues" (eighth chorus), "Sun Down" (fifth chorus), "Naptown Blues" (fourth chorus), and "Movin' Wes" (third chorus).

The melodic minor scale (ascending form) is a common source for altered harmony. It contains both augmented and diminished sounds in its structure; sharing the advantages of both without the limitations of either. Used as a harmonic substitution it provides all the alterations of a dominant 7th: ♭5, #5, ♭9, and #9.

This example presents a two-octave melodic minor scale in C: C–D–E♭–F–G–A–B–C, etc. Note the five-note, whole-tone augmented series beginning on the E♭ tone: E♭–F–G–A–B. Next, check out the whole-step/half-step diminished scale portion, a six-note series, beginning on A: A–B–C–D–E♭–F. Both are partial scales that overlap, and they share common tones and symmetry. Together, they produce the "fully altered" scale typically applied to dominant 7th chords with altered 5ths and 9ths.

C Melodic Minor Scale

When played in conjunction with a fully altered chord a half step below, the melodic minor scale clearly sounds like a go-to choice. This phrase is instructive. Play the ascending, stepwise C melodic minor melody and conclude on a B7#9#5. The two sound like they belong together. This sort of minor conversion is an essential element of the bebop language when coloring dominant 7th chords.

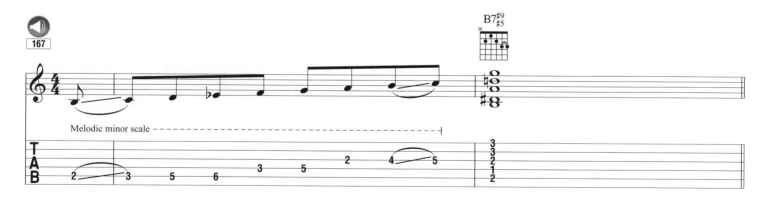

Why does this seemingly remote relationship work? Note the common tones uniting C minor and B7: C–D–Eb/D#–F–G–A–B and B–D#–A–D–G. The plural application of the melodic minor scale as a harmonic substitution for a dominant 7th chord makes for more interesting and varied sounds than a strictly symmetrical, six-note whole-tone scale. This is due to the half steps in the scale.

Consider the use of this dominant 7th chord as a strong dissonance in the blues. There it often functions as an enriched tonic-dominant chord (I7) that resolves to a IV7 chord. This phrase illustrates a familiar application heard in measures 1–5 of a blues chorus in G.

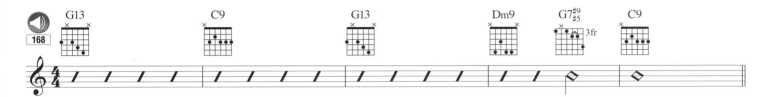

The harmonic minor scale has its own inherent advantages as regards augmented harmony. The spelling of C harmonic minor is G–Ab–B–C–D–Eb–F. This scale yields two augmented chords of different quality, on steps V and III, respectively: G7#5, often with a flatted 9th, Ab (G7#5b9), and Ebmaj7#5. In this instance, the Eb of the key is considered part of the augmented harmony enriching a G7#5 chord. Many jazz musicians use the plural attribute (Eb=D#) when working with augmented harmony.

The B note in the scale produces Ebmaj7#5. This chord has both mainstream and modern applications. It is found as an enrichment of a tonic major 7th chord in standards, an inversion of a rootless tonic minor chord: Cm(maj9)/Eb, or even an atypical V chord with the augmented 5th in the bass: G+/D#. In the latter case, the atypical voicing contains both an unaltered 5th (D) and altered 5th (Eb=D#).

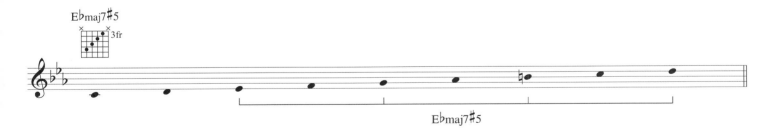

It is useful to acquaint the ear with the possibilities for augmented harmony in the harmonic minor scale as soon as possible. This simple exercise presents a useful practice approach learned from Joe Pass. Play the scale stepwise beginning on a chord tone and conclude with its related chord. Here, begin the C harmonic minor scale on B (the 3rd of G7) and ascend stepwise to Eb (the #5/b6). Then play the G7#5 chord. Give your ear time to process the aural connection. (This is shown on the next page.)

This related exercise pertains to Ebmaj7#5 in the C harmonic minor scale. Play the ascending line beginning on D (the major 7th of Ebmaj7#5), ascend to G (the 3rd), and then sound an Ebmaj7#5 chord. Listen for a similar musical result with a different augmented color.

The value of linking scales, and ultimately melody from the jazz language, with chords is exponential. The more you hear the two sounds as shades of one color, the more your harmonic acumen grows.

In the repertoire, examples of augmented harmony derived from the aforementioned minor scales are abundant. A typical scenario involves the function of a 7#5 chord as a III chord, often resolving to IVmaj7, almost like an enriched form of the iii minor substitution for a tonic chord. This progression from "Someday My Prince Will Come" depicts this usage plus the standard application as a V7 chord in a minor mode. It contains two typical applications of augmented harmony, D7#5 resolving to Ebmaj7, a "disguised" Gm, and G7#5 resolving to Cm, the ii chord of the key.

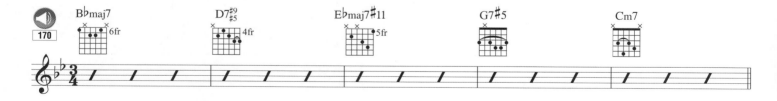

Two other noteworthy examples from the repertoire include the use of the 7#5 as an enriched III chord in the changes of Fats Waller's "Ain't Misbehavin'," in bars 3–4: Ebmaj7–G7#5–Abmaj7–Db9, and Benny Golson's "I Remember Clifford," second chord of A sections: Ebmaj7–G7#5–Abmaj7–A°7–Bb7. Note the different progressions that follow the G7#5–Abmaj7 connection.

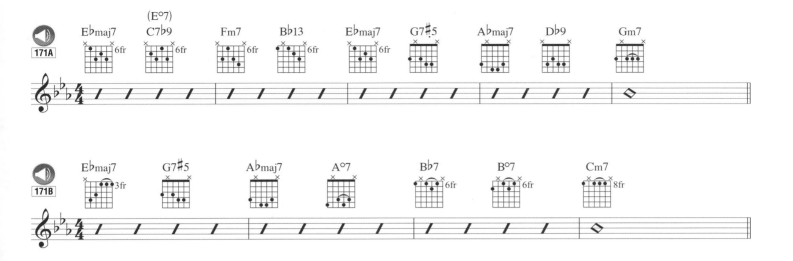

The maj7#5 sonority can be used as substitute for the I in tunes like "Misty" where the final chord of a phrase has the major seventh tone in the melody. This characteristic B♭7–E♭maj7 progression cadences on a colorful E♭maj7#5 and continues with a polychord Bm/E♭–E♭maj7 sequence that resolves the dissonance.

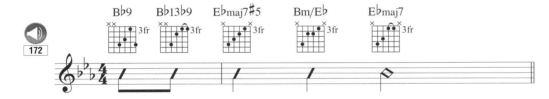

The maj7#5 chord is sometimes found as part of static set of changes sharing the same bass note, similar to a pedal-point. This progression comprised of E♭maj7, E♭maj7#5, and E♭maj7(add6) chords contains chromatic (B♭–B–C) inner-voice motion. It was made emblematic in jazz with Miles Davis' arrangement of "It Never Entered My Mind."

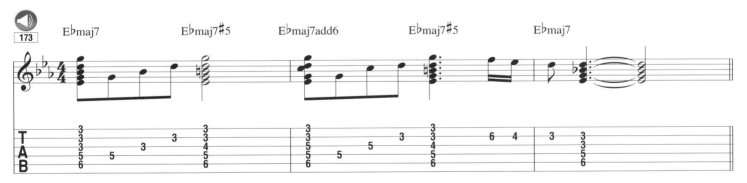

Along similar lines is the familiar progression in which a m6 or m#5 sonority functions as an augmented chord in a minor tonality. Heard frequently as an expansion of static minor harmony, it is a product of chromatic voice leading and acts as a passing chord or extension. It is invariably played over a sustained root tone in the bass, akin to a pedal point. The sound is so prevalent that it transcends category, uniting disparate genres like hard bop, rock, classical, and popular musics. Consider the use in minor-mode jazz tunes as well as the "James Bond Theme." The Beatles applied the m#5 augmented chord in progressions of several compositions such as "Hey Bulldog," "Savoy Truffle," and "Fool on the Hill."

This example is in G minor. Note that Gm and Gm6 are connected with a Gm♭6 (or Gm#5). Check out the chromatic motion within the chords: D–D#–E–E♭. This is a case of mixing minor modes within a short progression or phrase. The Gm triad exists in every G minor mode, the Gm (#5 or ♭6) is from the natural minor or harmonic minor scale, and Gm6 is from the Dorian mode and melodic minor scale. A plural chord, it can also be viewed as Gm♭6/Gm#5 specific to the key of G minor tonality or as the 1st-inversion triad, E♭/G. The E♭ indigenous to the minor mode is enharmonic with D#.

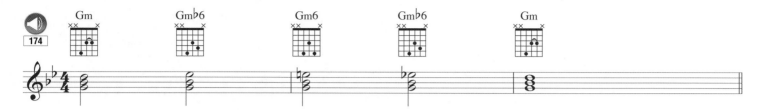

Grant Green played a sequence containing the m#5 and its characteristic voice-leading progression in his intro to "Airegin" on *The Complete Quartets with Sonny Clark*. This phrase depicts a similar, riff-like melody built on the Gm–Gm#5–Gm6 progression. It exemplifies the close connection between harmony and melody in jazz. The D–D#–E–E♭ chord tones are emphasized, indeed outlined, in the melody. Note the labelling of the operative chord as both a Gm#5 and Gm♭6. Why the seeming contradiction? The names reflect the function and direction of the passing tone in the chord: Gm#5 in ascent to Gm6 and Gm♭6 in descent to Gm. Pianist Wynton Kelly used a variation of the same idea in his "Four on Six" solo with Wes Montgomery (3:50) as did saxophonist Vincent Herring during his improvisations in the coda of "Come Rain or Come Shine" (4:02).

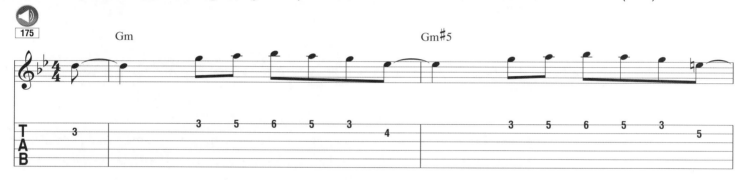

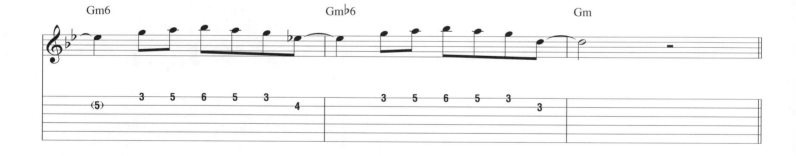

CHAPTER 7

CHORD-MELODY

Chord-melody is exactly that: chord and melody occurring simultaneously. In jazz guitar, there are many different approaches to the subject. Simple homophonic playing where each melody note receives a chord is a given. You'll find numerous examples of this sound in preceding chapters—particularly in the block-chord phrases of Chapter 4. There are various forms of chord-melody that involve *polyphony*. Consider the independent voices, multiple parts and embellishing lines, and extremely intricate passages, often involving counterpoint, in the music of Segovia, Chet Atkins, and Joe Pass.

Many jazz guitarists use the term "chord-melody" broadly to describe their treatment of a tune. Some players create chord-melody arrangements that rival the piano in complexity and activity. Others freely weave chord-melody phrases into single-note solos to provide contrasting textures. Still, others punch chords rhythmically ad lib in opportune spots for an accompa-nimental effect or to produce call-and-response phrases. Bottom line: There are practically as many individual chord-melody styles as there are players.

In devising a chord-melody strategy, a few basic points deserve mention at the outset. Position the melody to be harmonized on the upper strings. It's logical; this leaves room for chords below the melody. Select a melody to be harmonized and listen to instrumentalists and singers who have recorded a version. This leads to internalizing the music. Be open to employing and combining various sounds learned thus far: basic chords, extensions, alterations, substitutions, inversions, shell chords, partial chords, parallelism, quartal harmony, diminished harmony, pedal point, polychords, etc. Use both homophonic and polyphonic textures. Some phrases will need two or more single notes per chord. In this regard, consider space to be your friend. Often a more interesting and varied sound is created by alternating chord textures and single notes judiciously. As regards articulation, play the same phrases with a pick, pick and fingers, fingerstyle, or with the thumb. Experiment with arpeggiating the chords or sounding the melody note(s) and bass notes apart from the chord. And, last but certainly not least, *listen* to great chord-melody players.

Chord Phrases

ii–V–I Progressions

It is useful to harmonize characteristic jazz melodies that typify the jazz language and involve ii–V–I progressions. These phrases demonstrate several typical chord-melody scenarios in and around ii–V–I progressions, and are generally suitable for comping and chord–melody playing. Listen for the sound of homophony versus polyphony and varied textures.

The "Honeysuckle Rose" motif is one of the most pervasive melodies in jazz. It is found in the lines of countless instrumen-talists and is a staple of the bebop language. This example subjects the "Honey" motive to chord-melody treatment. It is first stated as a short ii–V progression in G: Am7–D7. Note the suspensions in the melody: D–C over Am7 and B–A over D7. The motive is imitated a tritone away as E♭m7–A♭7, where the progression acts like a two-chord substitution for D7. Consequently, the motive is played in two keys before it resolves to the original tonic. That's an idea I heard Dexter Gordon play on sax. Here, the progression is Am7–D13 and E♭m7–A♭13 resolving to Gmaj7. Note that the motive's melody is contained within the chord shapes and is articulated by arpeggiating the forms. This type of arpeggiation is also found in the melody of Monk's "Ask Me Now." The texture is varied, with both single notes and chords, and the overall impression is legato and sustaining. (This is shown on the next page.)

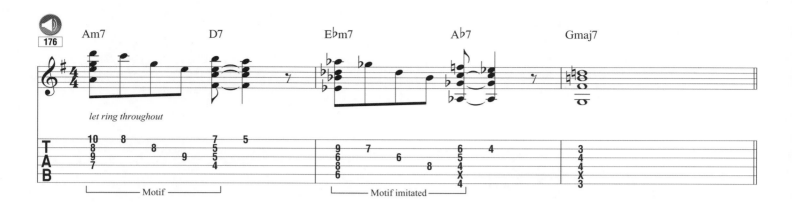

This phrase is based on the changes of "Autumn Leaves." It exemplifies the use of space, fills between chords, alternation of textures, and rhythmic devices. The cycle progression is essentially a series of 4th steps diatonic to G major and E minor. It provides a different harmonic environment containing two ii–V–I progressions, in G major and E minor, and an opportunity for sequential chord-melody phrases. In contrast to the previous example, which emphasized legato movement within sustained chords, the music employs independent single-note lines and punctuating chords with more active rhythms and syncopation.

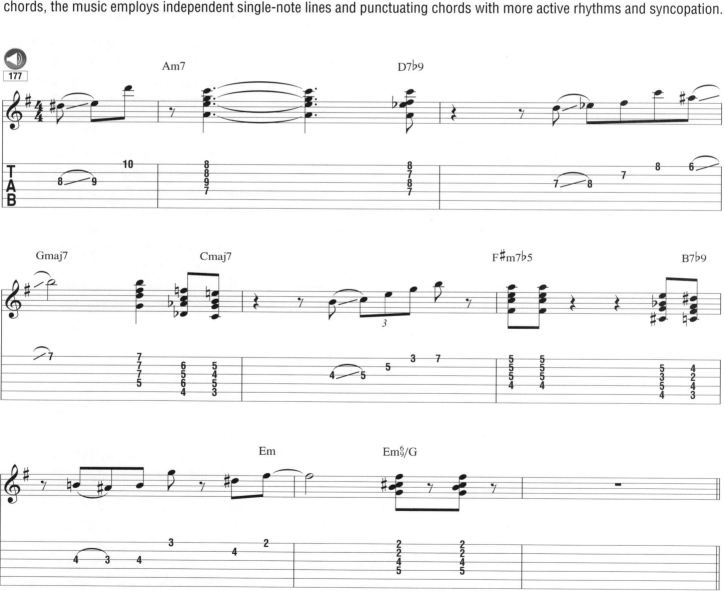

This ii–V–I phrase in A♭ employs a sustained legato approach. It combines an ascending arpeggio, the bebop scale, and altered-chord harmony. Note the "push-chord" slur from below (Am7–B♭m7) to harmonize C and D♭ in the line. The D♭–F–A♭–C notes outline a B♭m9 chord in the melody and are built on two inversions. The B♭m9 arpeggio is answered with a chromatic line (E♭–D–D♭) from the bebop scale. The descending wide-interval leap from D♭ to E emphasizes the flatted-9th dissonance in the altered chord, E♭13(♭9). The resolution depicts quartal harmonization of a standard bebop phrase ending.

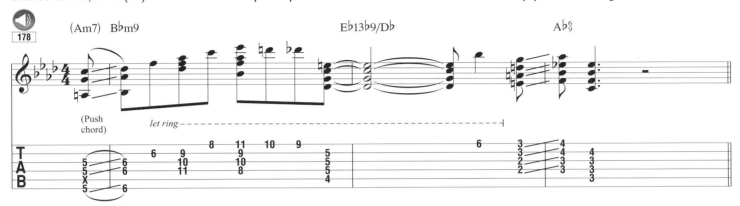

This figure alludes to the chord style of Howard Roberts and conveys the impression of a big-band figure à la Count Basie. The feeling is big, spacious, and rhythmically tight, like a horn section's "shout chorus" phrase. Larger chord forms and a homophonic approach are used throughout. The melody in measure 1 is harmonized with a single Dm7 on the first five strings while the remaining bars use wide-spread divided voicings spanning the lower five strings. G7 is defined by a ii–V progression, Dm9–G13♭9. Note the chromatic bass line, A–A♭–G, in the changes. A reharmonized "Basie tag" lick (F6/9–A♭/G♭–C6/G) ends the phrase. The voicings are a direct reference to Mr. Roberts.

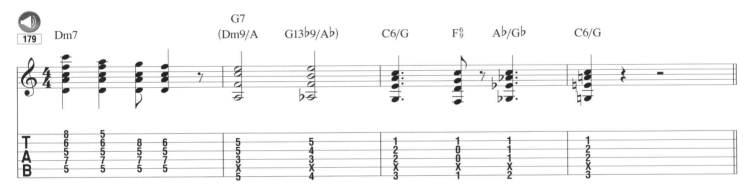

This ii–V–I phrase in G combines diatonic, chromatic and altered-chord harmony. Note the "push chord" passage, G#m7–Am7, harmonizing the B–C melody with its lower neighbor. The F–E♭ melody over D7 defines the idiomatic #9–♭9 motion resolving to D, the 5th of a G chord—here, a G6/9. This is a common phrase ending used throughout the jazz genre in chordal and single-note form.

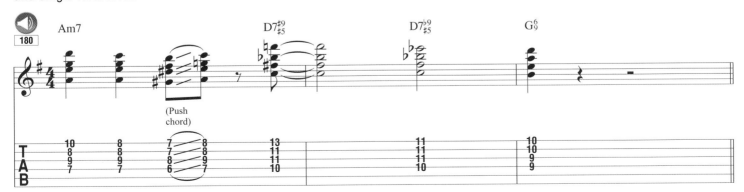

Barney Kessel, one of the early chord-melody masters of the bebop era, was fond of using *parallel 3rd dyads* to outline chords and harmonize arpeggios—the technique and texture became an identifier of his style. This ii–V–I phrase demonstrates the use of parallel minor and major thirds to approach the D7, V chord. Note the smooth voice-leading connection and transition from 3rd dyads to a four-note D13♭9.

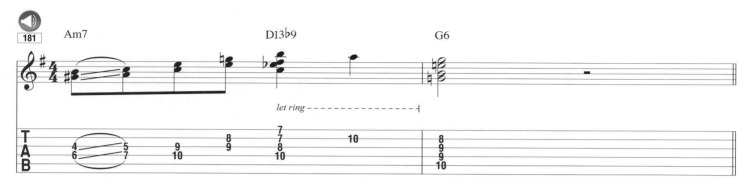

The same phrase can function a 3rd lower, also as a ii–V–I in E, using the identical melody, positions and fingering with only a slight modification of the ending chord to Emaj7. Why does this plural progression work? The 3rds and altered dominant are harmonically open enough to imply both keys: in the key of E as an F#m7♭5–B7♭9 progression or the key of G as an Am7–D13♭9. The B7♭9, part of the diminished family, can be moved in minor 3rd intervals and therefore named with either label: B7♭9 or D13♭9. This perception produces a useful and practical tactic for tunes that contain modulation(s) to a 3rds-related key, as in the bridges of "All the Things You Are" and "I'll Remember April."

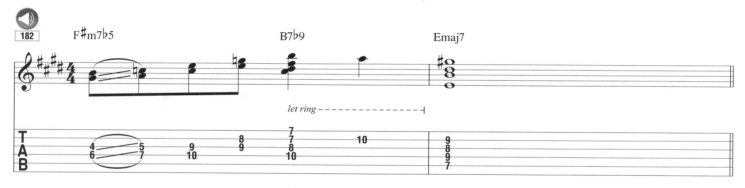

With practice and the continued accumulation of vocabulary, varied chord-melody phrases can be created spontaneously as you build up your resources. Let yourself be creative. This example demonstrates what can happen with just a little effort. The parallel 3rds passage from Track 181 is shifted rhythmically to produce a pickup and extended with two additional 3rd dyads. The resolution is borrowed from Track 180. It is changed to D7#5#9 followed by a single note. The ending chord is Gmaj9. These small subtleties of addition, combination, and rhythmic and harmonic variety yield effective results.

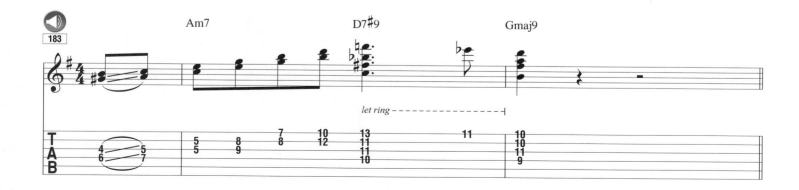

Wes Montgomery harnessed diminished chords regularly as passing chords and altered-dominant substitutions. This phrase depicts the type of parallel motion found in his approach. Here, a ii–V–I in G, Am7–D7–G, is preceded by a chain of parallel diminished chords: D°7–F°7–A♭°7–B°7. These inversions function as substitutions for E7♭9. Note the targeting effect of the B♭m7–A♭m7 figure on the last beat to *enclose* the destination chord, Am7. That is a bebop melody in chord form. Am7 is played as several common inversions and partial chords, and contains a push-chord pattern: C#9–D9. The D7 is made of mixed altered chords. Note use of D7#5 and D13 sounds in the same passage. The resolution to Gmaj9 is similar to the melody of Track 180. The final progression contains a I7–IV7 cadence that conveys a bluesy feeling. Parallel diminished chords are used as a substitute for G7♭9, resolving to C7 via a G7♭9 back-cycling maneuver. Try playing this example with your thumb like Wes Montgomery.

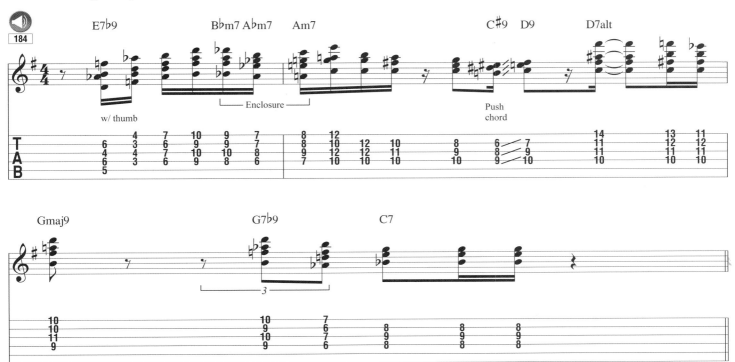

Turnaround Phrases

The I–VI–ii–V turnaround progression is a ubiquitous chord pattern in jazz, found in blues tunes and countless standards. Mastering variations of turnaround changes is an important step in developing chord-melody facility.

The following phrases present a number of approaches to harmonizing the turnaround. Note the use of various extensions, alterations, substitutions, inversions, quartal, and rootless forms. Though there are many options for analysis, keep it simple. Follow Joe Pass' example. Boil the harmony down to essential basic sounds: G major, E7, Am7, and D7. Consider the added or altered tones to be decorations of the basic chords. Only two characteristic rhythm patterns and slight variations are used throughout the phrases.

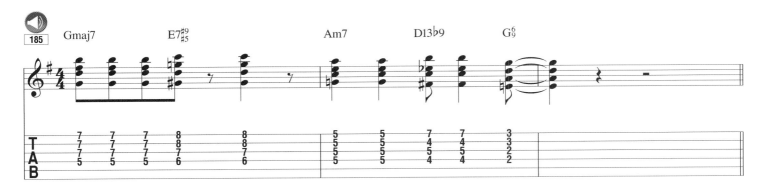

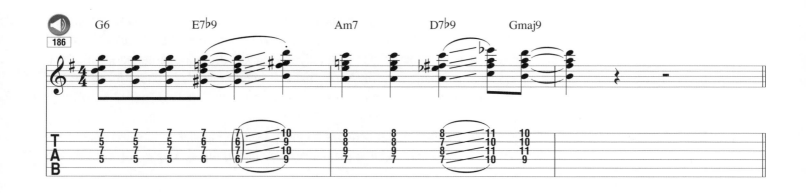

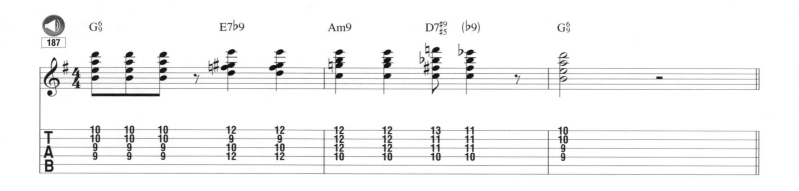

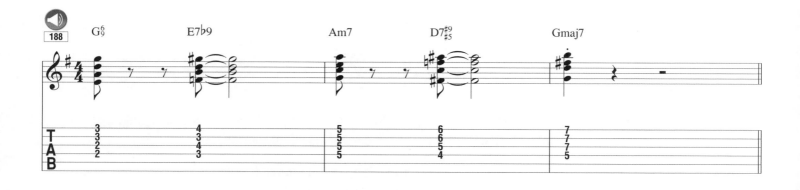

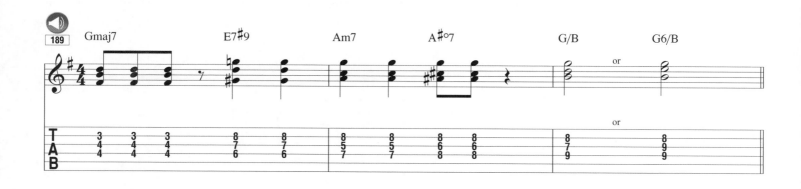

This phrase exploits a sequential approach. Note the same figure played a whole step apart as Gmaj7(9)–E7♭9 and Am7–D7♭9 in the first two measures. This approach creates a thematic feeling in the progression. Two possible chords are offered in the final bar as a resolution. Play either or both, and listen.

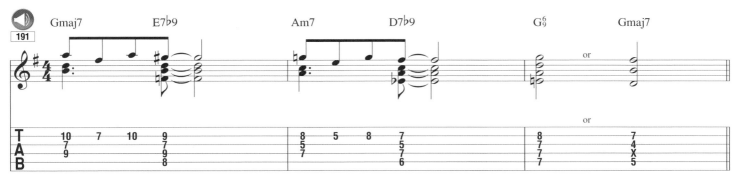

The pedal point in chord-melody is typified by this phrase. A D note in the top voice is maintained through the changes. Note the changing identity of the pedal-point melody as it is held above the chords. It is the 5th of G6/9, the 7th of E7#9, the 11th of Am7, and the root of D7♭5♭9.

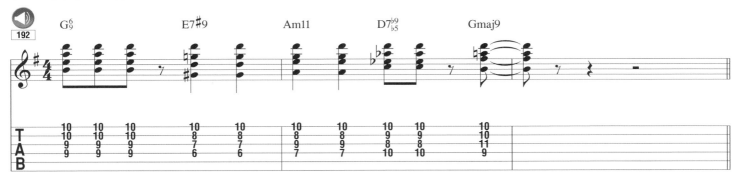

There are various combinations in this phrase. Note the push chord, diminished substitutions for E7, inversions of Am7–Am9, and chord-and-single-note texture on D7.

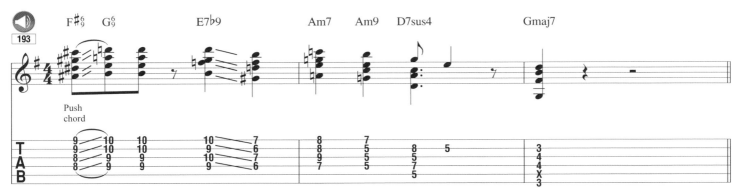

This sequential phrase, like Track 191, has a thematic imitative quality. Note the common tones that link the highest and lowest notes of the chords: D and B in Gmaj9 and E7♭9. This type of shared harmonic content results in particularly smooth voice leading and makes the parallel movement in the inner voices more interesting.

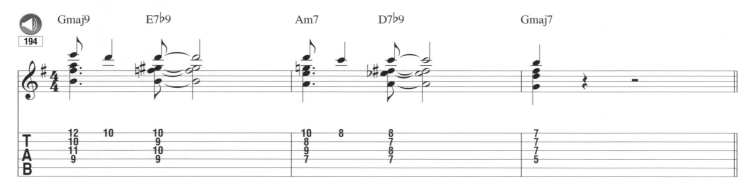

Clusters have a lush pianistic quality and are associated with guitarist Johnny Smith's chord-melody style. Check out his famed version of "Moonlight in Vermont." The name "cluster" signifies a chord with notes that are positioned close together or clustered, like grapes in a cluster on a vine. On a keyboard, these are usually comprised of at least three adjacent tones of a diatonic or chromatic scale—for example, steps 1, 2, and 3 in a row producing a sonority. The adjacent 2nd intervals create a dissonant but beautiful and sophisticated sound.

On the guitar, cluster chords are frequently made into three-note shorthand forms with 3rd and 2nd intervals in the voicing. They typically necessitate wider stretches to span the intervals in the voicing. Jazz guitarists who have used clusters include the aforementioned Johnny Smith, Jim Hall, Kenny Burrell, Barney Kessel, Sonny Sharrock, Allan Holdsworth, and Kurt Rosenwinkel.

This practice phrase subjects turnaround changes to a cluster treatment. Have a look at the notes on the staff in the Gadd9 and Am7 chords. You'll see that the adjacent B and A tones in Gadd9 and the A and G in Am7 appear to be bunched together. Those major 2nd intervals give the cluster chords their distinctive color. Note that Gmaj7 contains an even closer minor 2nd interval, G–F#, in the voicing. Play the chords initially in half-note rhythms and listen.

Caveat: Be careful to avoid over-stretching. Don't hold a cluster chord for too long. If a chord is difficult to reach, play it in a higher position where the frets are closer together. With practice, the ability to stretch increases and becomes more comfortable. When you are comfortable, apply the rhythm patterns from Tracks 185–190 to the clusters.

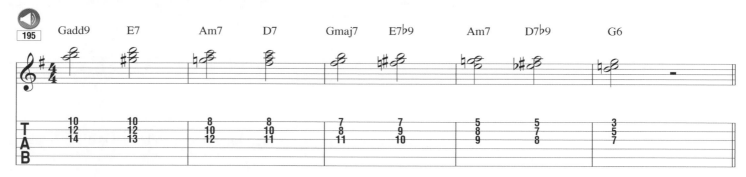

Clusters can be combined successfully with other more common chord forms to create textural variety or produce a call-and-response effect. This example applies cluster chords in the first two measures, that's the antecedent or "call" phrase. It is answered by more conventional chords in the consequent phrase or "response" of measures 3–4. The overall impression is of two texturally different turnaround phrases repeated in a vamped sequence. The practice of vamping turnarounds became a regular feature of many bebop arrangements, used to lengthen a tune's form during solos, usually in the last chorus. Consider the Miles Davis Quintet's application of the procedure in "If I Were a Bell" and "I Could Write a Book" on *Relaxin'*.

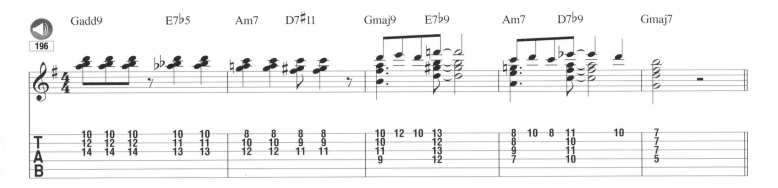

Coltrane Changes

Chord-melody strategies are useful in negotiating modulatory 3rds-related progressions. "Giant Steps" was John Coltrane's iconic tune that set new standards for jazz harmony and navigating these challenging sequences. This phrase applies chordal elements to his changes and melodic outlines. Note the use of both basic three-note and four-note forms as well as common tones connecting ii–V–Is in E♭ and G.

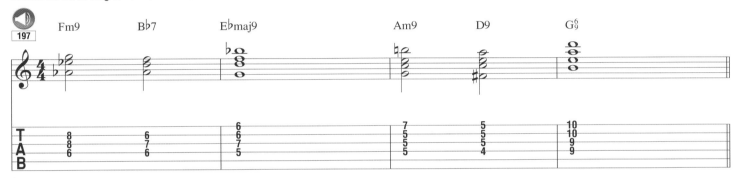

"Central Park West" was another important Trane tune that employed 3rds-related harmony. This example depicts common chord-melody shapes and movement through four tonal centers: B, D, A♭, and F. Note the varied dominant colors applied and mixture of basic chords, extensions, and altered sounds: F#7, A13, E♭7(9), and C7♭5♭9.

Chord-Melody Harmonization and Variations

Most of the forms in the preceding sections were played as block chords. This initially presents a simple, concise realization of the shapes and their movement through chord changes. However, after learning the progressions and connections, feel free to experiment with different textural possibilities and combinations—consider block chords versus partial chords, single notes, or dyads. Add passing tones in the bass line. Try different approaches to a chord's color—change a minor 7th chord to a dominant 7th chord and the like. Mix basic, extended, altered, and substitute chord sounds. Play the phrases with different types of articulation. Apply arpeggiations and varied attacks, such as strumming versus plucking. Bottom line: Use your ear.

This reinterpretation of Track 185 demonstrates several typical variations. Note the fingerstyle articulation. This produces a polyphonic harp-like sound reminiscent of Joe Pass, Ted Greene, Jimmy Bruno, or Martin Taylor. The Gmaj7 is plucked. E7#9#5 contains an additional chromatic passing tone, C#, that leads to D in the Am7(11) chord, which is rendered as an arpeggiation. The V chord is a different form of D13♭9 and has an added D note in the melody. The final chord is Gmaj9 with the 9th in the melody.

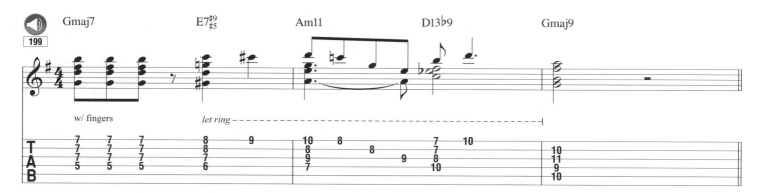

This variation also applies a fingerstyle approach. It is made of cluster chords spelling out the turnaround progression. The rhythms are slight modifications of Track 185. Note the voice leading and different types of movement in the cluster chords and connections. The E7♭9, Am7, and D7#5 are partial chords that have chord/single-note textures. Played with a pick, this section has the "music box" effect heard in Johnny Smith's style. The final chord is rendered as *broken dyads*: outside two notes followed by inner two notes. The final G note is sounded by tapping with the pick hand on the low E string at the third fret. Barney Kessel applied this type of two-handed playing in the early 1950s. Check out his intro to "Tenderly" on *Easy Like: Barney Kessel, Vol. 1*. For variety, play this phrase with a mix of plectrum strumming and hybrid picking.

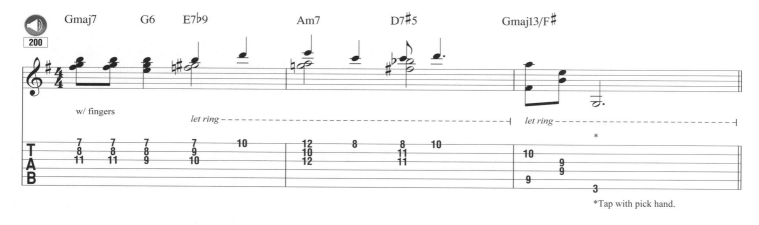

This variation is played with the thumb and reflects Wes Montgomery's block-chord approach and articulation. The harmony is based on a bebop melody and contains many aspects of the genre. Consider the neighbor-tone slides on G6, the use of diminished harmony and parallelism on E7♭9, and extended and altered chord sounds through Am7–D7–G. The ornament of D7#5#9 is a familiar bop phrase ending played in chord form.

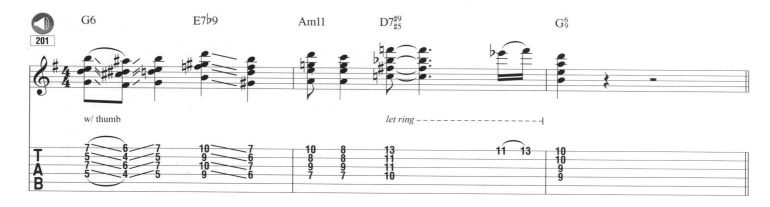

Blues and Chord-Melody

Blues melodies, like bebop melodies, are prime candidates for harmonization. Linking chords with blues lines deepens a player's understanding, imparts soulfulness to chord-melody work, and increases the range of options within the 12-bar form. This phrase in G harmonizes a standard blues melody in quartal chords. (See *Quartal Harmony* in Chapter 6.) Here, a common lick in the G *blues scale* (G–Bb–C–Db–D–F) is rendered as a series of three-note quartal chords, each built on a step of the scale. A particularly bluesy feeling is created by sliding to and from the *blue note*, Db—the flatted 5th. Kenny Burrell, the master of blues in jazz, used this idea to good effect in the opening of "K.B. Blues" and in the final chorus of his solo in "Bluescape." The cadence figure to follow is an idiomatic resolution: G13–G7#5–C9 and emphasizes the important I–IV chord change in measures 4–5 of the 12-bar progression (see *Blues,* Chapter 3). Note the common tone in the melody, smooth voice leading, and inversions in the progression.

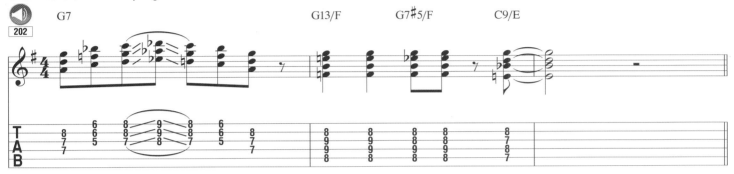

This variation in G harmonizes a descending blues scale melody with quartal chords. Note the slur at the beginning and characteristic syncopation throughout. The chromatic motion to the tonic chord, F13–F#13–G13, from a whole step below is a familiar maneuver in blues harmony. Through repetition of the pattern and its rhythms an effective chordal riff can be created. Riff-based conception is part and parcel of the blues. That idea is demonstrated in measures 2–4. Note the simple variations in the figure: F13–F#13–G13 and G13–F#13–G13.

Blues harmony is enlivened and expanded with back-cycling. The procedure was used consistently in the chord-melody playing of Joe Pass. Check out "Joe's Blues" on *Intercontinental* for telling examples. This phrase in F is made more interesting by additional C7alt and Db7 chords, essentially providing more color and generating harmonic motion through a static F7. The melody is based on the *F minor pentatonic scale* (F–Ab–Bb–C–Eb). The minor pentatonic scale is closely related to the blues scale and is a default sound in the blues vernacular. Note the harmonizing of Eb and Ab tones of the scale with C7#5#9, and the Bb tone with Db13. Every chord in the phrase is an inversion and the added dominants are rootless. Because they are rootless, the C7#5#9 and Db13 are extremely flexible and can be heard as tritone substitutes: Gb13 and G7#5#9.

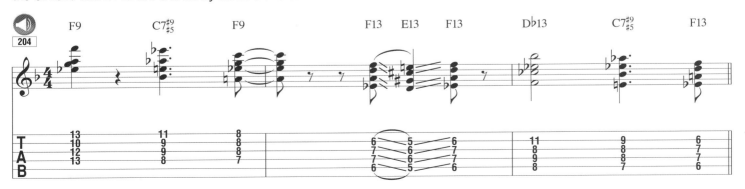

115

This example presents one full-length chorus of a 12-bar swing blues in G arranged as a chord-melody piece. It combines and applies many of elements from previous sections in this chapter. Note blues-riff phrases, quartal chords harmonizing the blues scale, diminished substitutions, altered chords, rootless chords, push chords, parallelism, back-cycling, the ii–V progression in bars 9–10 of the form, and reharmonized 3rds-related changes in the final turnaround. Compare these refinements with the basic 12-bar blues progression in Chapter 3. You'll hear borrowings and repurposing of material gleaned from many influences, including guitarists Kenny Burrell, Joe Pass, Herb Ellis, Wes Montgomery, Howard Roberts, and Barney Kessel as well as piano players Hampton Hawes and Red Garland in the mix. Experiment with plectrum-style strumming, thumb strumming, and fingerstyle plucking for contrasting effects.

Standards and Chord-Melody

Standard songs from the Great American Songbook have long served as superb vehicles for chord-melody playing and arranging. This example demonstrates a typical rendering of the first eight bars (A section) of "On Green Dolphin Street," one of the most evergreen of standards. It can be played as written, with only slight timing adjustments, in a moderate swing feel or a Latin groove. The piece is in C major, the most common key, and contains numerous chord-melody devices. These are notated in parentheses below the basic chords. Note the harmonizing of the opening phrase in the first four bars. This demonstrates a characteristic way of handling a parallel major/minor situation: introducing a theme in C major and then imitating it in C minor with similar motifs. It particularly suits the spirit of the tune and its original melody. The second phrase contains quartal and tertian chords. Check out the parallel motion and inversions played over Db and C. A big-band flavor is implied in the syncopation and chromatic figure (Dm11–D#m11–Em11), a back-cycling progression, leading to Em7.

Realizing a chord-melody arrangement from scratch is a worthy goal in applying jazz harmony. Once you've learned and gotten comfortable with Track 206, compare the variety of chords above with the most rudimentary form of the tune found below. Only basic chord types are notated, typical of old-school sheet music. That's all that existed when players like Joe Pass and Wes Montgomery were coming up. Jazz musicians simply had to create their own realizations of the harmony by ear, guided by experience gained on the bandstand or from careful listening. In fact, the original "fake books" were nothing more than abbreviated charts compiled directly from piano-vocal sheet music and sold "under the counter" with titles like *Golden Standards of the 1900s*. This seeming limitation, however, has hidden benefits. It is arguably the closest to what the composer originally wrote. Moreover, referring to and elaborating on the most basic changes allows you to hear and ultimately realize the varied sounds in the broadest context and prompts you to be creative.

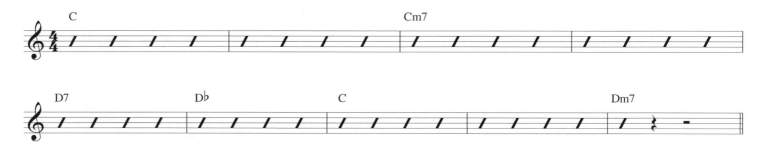

This chord chart depicts the sort of basic changes found in fakebooks, like *The Real Book*, and others. Note that chord colors and progressions are notated with more specificity; Cmaj7 and Dbmaj7 instead of just C and Db, and A7 indicating the V of ii chord motion. These are characteristic jazz refinements that are in use by experienced players.

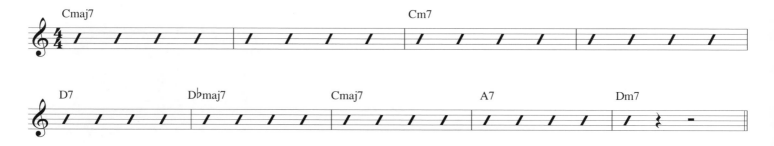

The slow tempo, *rubato*-elastic feeling and resulting increased space for harmonic movement makes ballads even more open to chord-melody embellishing. "Darn That Dream" is a beautiful ballad, and a favorite in the jazz repertoire, with interesting progressions and deviations from typical diatonic harmony, lush sonorities, and a compelling melody, including extension and alteration tones. This arrangement of the first eight bars (A section) presents a number of possibilities but only scratches the surface. Check out the moving lines incorporated into the question-and-answer chord phrases: Gmaj7–Bbm7–Eb7 and Am7–B7b5. The first chord contains a descending moving voice and is answered by an ascending voice, resulting in a contrapuntal, oblique-motion sound—all played on the 4th string and sounded with the basic chord.

This was a favorite tactic of Barney Kessel and many others. The ascending figure used over A7 in measure 3 exploits a dissonant polychord moving in and out of the basic harmony in parallel motion, an effect heard often in the piano playing of Herbie Hancock and McCoy Tyner. The imitative pattern used over E7alt in measure 4 employs a sequence of altered chords and mixes diminished and augmented harmony. In the second half, different articulations and rhythms are pursued for contrast. Note more sustained arpeggios and chords in measures 5–6 as well as melodic fills, based on the diminished scale, added to Am7 and D7 chords in measure 7. The turnaround in 8 contains greater activity toward movement into the second A section and alludes to Joe Pass, Howard Roberts, Johnny Smith, and Kenny Burrell. This progression is played more legato. Let the chords and melody notes sustain to maximum duration.

This simple chord chart on the next page presents the traditional sheet-music changes of "Darn That Dream." Several chords are indicated in "old-school" terms, notably the Dm6 that is interchangeable with Bm7♭5, the G major without a particular color specified, and the G°7 that is an inversion of the ♭iii°, later written as B♭°7 to chromatically connect B and A bass notes.

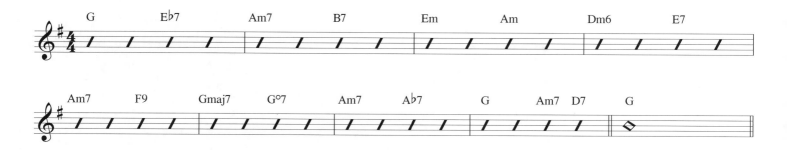

These modified changes are found in *The Real Book* (6th edition) and modern piano-vocal sheets. Note the greater specificity and concessions to contemporary jazz practices: Gmaj7, B♭m7–E♭7 (a ii–V in A♭), Bm7♭5, and Bm7 substituting for an extended Gmaj7. Reharmonization includes A7/C♯ and Cm6 instead of Am (a completely different progression), B♭m7 instead of B♭°7, and the cycle-of-4ths turnaround: Bm7–E7–Am7–D7 to Gmaj7.

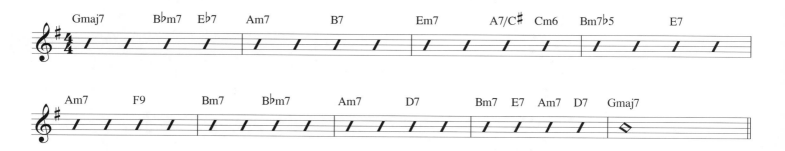

More possibilities are found in other sources. This chart combines elements from *The Colorado Book* and *The New Real Book*. Note the optional D7 or A/C♯ in measure 3. My realization joins the two sounds with parallelism. G6 and B7 are labelled B7♭5 for greater specificity. The turnaround contains a ♭5 substitution, B♭7 for E7. This option is accommodated with a shared diminished chord: B° can be either E7♭9 or B♭7♭9. That solution underscores the utility of diminished harmony for dominant 7th chords.

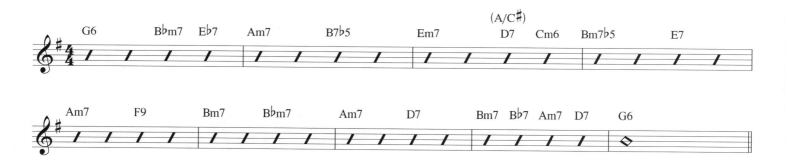

The specificity presented in fake books may be helpful in initially crafting an arrangement, however it is advisable to rely on your ear and emulate the practices of the masters. This is gained by listening to their takes on harmonizing standards. In this regard, the following versions of "Darn That Dream" by instrumentalists and singers are suggested: Dexter Gordon, Sonny Rollins, Bill Evans and Jim Hall, Chet Baker, Billie Holiday, Sarah Vaughan (with Count Basie), Ella Fitzgerald (with Nelson Riddle), Tony Bennett, Miles Davis, Joe Pass, Howard Roberts, Johnny Smith, Wes Montgomery (*Echoes of Indiana Avenue*), Corey Christiansen, Eric Alexander, Kurt Rosenwinkel, Julian Lage, and Cyrus Chestnut.

Walking Bass Lines and Stride-Guitar Style

In this chapter, we've seen chord-melody in many forms. Most of the examples have addressed the most common situations: harmonizing a melody in the highest voice with accompaniment chords or using inner-voice movement within particular shapes. Chord-melody playing also involves bass-line movement. This specialty is evident in the walking bass phrases of Joe Pass, George Van Eps, Martin Taylor, Jimmy Bruno, Tuck Andress, and other harmonically astute guitarists. Many refer to this approach as "stride guitar," a play on the term "stride piano." Stride piano was a style that evolved out of ragtime and defined early jazz pianists like Fats Waller, Art Tatum, Duke Ellington, and Earl Hines in the 1920s and '30s. It is generally described as a single-note, bass-register melody in a quarter-note pulse alternating with a chord on the second and fourth beats. The stride-piano approach is well suited to guitar because it was streamlined and played with the left hand on the keyboard.

Turnarounds provide an ideal starting point for acquiring the stride-guitar technique. This example subjects a blues turnaround in F to the approach and is played fingerstyle. The cliché "oom-pah" sound of alternating bass note and chord every other beat is lessened by avoiding a chord attack on beat four. This also facilitates melodic motion into the next chord tone on the first beat of the following bar. Note the half-step approach into chord tones throughout. This is idiomatic to the stride-guitar approach. Note also that each measure begins with a broken shell-chord figure: root and two-note chord partial of 3rd and 7th tones.

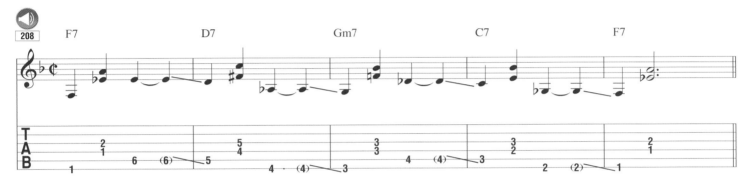

This variation is a similar turnaround phrase in the major mode. The chords are all diatonic to the key center, but the sound, melodic motion and articulation are nearly identical to the previous blues progression.

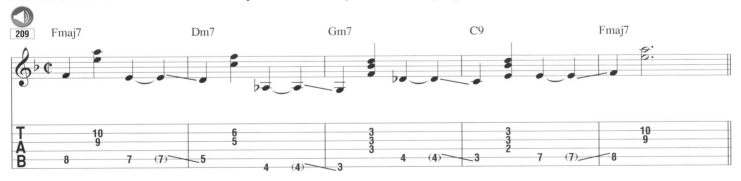

Chromaticism and secondary dominants, D7 and G7, provide an alternate harmonic scheme for diatonic colors.

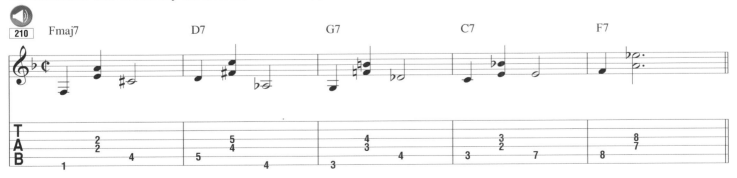

Stride guitar is particularly effective for rendering cycle-of-4ths movement in common jazz progressions. The example on the next page demonstrates the idea in chord form to the changes of "Django," as played by Joe Pass in his solo, measures 3–5.

121

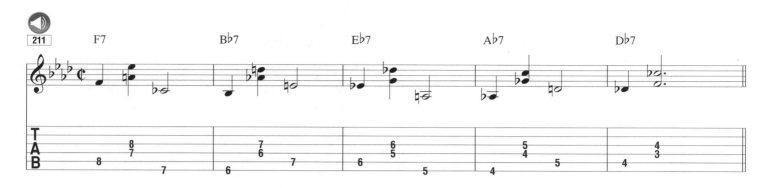

"Cherokee" is an important standard that unites disparate styles in the jazz repertoire. In your listening, be sure to explore versions by Charlie Parker, Clifford Brown, Count Basie, Bud Powell, Sonny Stitt, Johnny Griffin, Ahmad Jamal, Phineas Newborn, Joey DeFrancesco, Wynton Marsalis, Kamasi Washington, and guitarists Joe Pass, Tal Farlow, Johnny Smith—even Brian Setzer has a bebop version. This stride-guitar example is built on the progression in the A sections of "Cherokee." Note the secondary chords used as extended inversions in the changes. Dm7 functions as Bb/D, Cm7 as Eb/C, and Gm7 as Bb/G. Similarly, Eb6 and D°7 are simple substitutions for Cm7 and G7. What binds them all together is the walking-bass melody.

PART II:

MELODY

CHAPTER 8

ESSENTIAL ELEMENTS OF MELODY

Basics of Melody

Melody—what is it and how does it work in jazz? Melody is generally defined as a succession of tones moving through time. We are apt to elaborate with adjectives like memorable, effective, attractive, or ear-catching to further make a point of how melody affects the listener subjectively. Melody is the combination of pitch and rhythm; that's self-evident. However, the selection and organization of specific pitches and rhythms that produce an idiomatic or memorable melody are less obvious. These tend to spring organically from the *language* of the music.

A word about rhythm: From this chapter onward, aforementioned organic jazz melodies will have both pitch-oriented and rhythmic considerations. At this stage, begin to see the two aspects as inseparable and, indeed symbiotic, elements of the music. Listen and appreciate both characteristics at work in a melody, whether it's a stream of straight eighth notes, a florid double-timed passage, a highly syncopated line, or a lyrical phrase with long notes, ties, rests, and pauses.

For decades, guitarists have acquired the melodic language of jazz from wind players (trumpet, saxophone, flute, trombone, etc.) and applied it to their fingerboards. Its single-note nature allows any melody from these sources to be applied to the guitar. In fact, the way guitarists like Charlie Christian, Wes Montgomery, Joe Pass, George Benson, and Pat Martino have manifested this transformation is what distinguishes their use of the language. The same holds true today for a new or aspiring jazz guitarist.

To acquire the jazz language from predecessors is a prerequisite. As Cannonball Adderley put it, "There's no future without the past, and anybody who doesn't really understand where jazz has come from has no right to direct where it's going." Through the processes of *acquisition* and *assimilation* (involving study and practice), the past of jazz, and where it came from, can be understood and, better still, internalized. After assimilation the experienced player can direct their sense of where the music is going and tell a story with a message. Therein lies the final stage, *innovation*—opening the door of imagination, the creation of a personal statement with infinite possibilities.

Stepwise Motion and Scales

Scales are often taught as a route to learning jazz melody; however, a scale is but one and, arguably the most mundane, melody configuration. The term "scale" (*scala*, Greek) means "ladder-like," as in scaling a wall, is generally confined to specific descending and ascending motion. It has its place in a rudimentary training phase of a player's technical development. But scalar thinking and scale-based playing confined to the ladder conception has limited use in jazz performance and melody. Let's instead substitute the word *stepwise* to redefine the typical ascending/descending motion of scales and consider it a *sound*. Stepwise activity versus strict scalar thinking effectively simplifies and reconciles the perception of this type of *horizontal motion* in jazz melody.

In making music with stepwise motion, scales are repurposed to produce melodies. Consider a simple but instructive example. This melody contains an ascending, one-octave stepwise line in D major played over two chords, G/A and Dmaj9. A purely diatonic line in D, it begins and ends on A. That tone is not the tonic or keynote, D, of scale construction yet its motion is scalar or, more specifically, stepwise. Note the harmonic implications. In context over the changes, A is a *common tone*: the root of A7 and the 5th of D, the overall key center or tonality. Once the octave is reached, a contrasting melody completes the phrase. That drives home a central point: A stepwise melody is the most obvious form of horizontal movement and often acts as a means of reaching a destination or *melodic goal*.

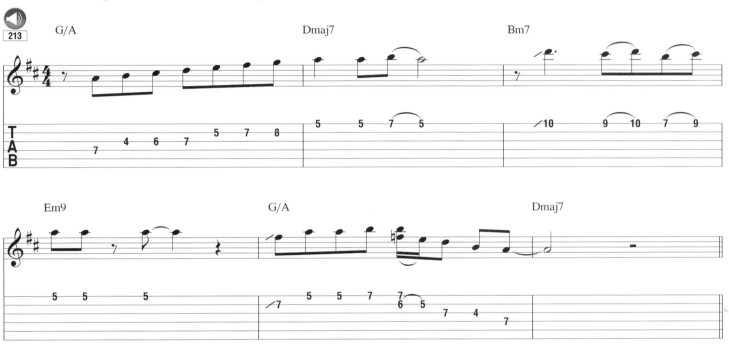

You've heard this stepwise sound in "Breezin'," a cross-over R&B instrumental played by jazz guitarists Gabor Szabo and George Benson, as well as Freddie Hubbard's "Philly Mignon."

This Sonny Rollins line in G has a similar horizontal structure. It begins on D, the 5th of the key, and ascends stepwise for one octave to a syncopated rhythmic *motive*, which completes the phrase. That's the goal. A motive (or *motif*) is a short melodic or rhythmic formula from which longer passages are formed. Rollins' "Pent-Up House" exploits the idea thematically. By viewing this situation as stepwise melody, cumbersome and inaccurate labels like Mixolydian mode are avoided. It is simply a stepwise melody beginning on D.

Rhythmic variety makes stepwise melody more interesting and musical, as in "Breezin'" and "Pent-Up House," as well as "The Dolphin," "Quiet Now" (meas. 5), and "What Are You Doing the Rest of Your Life," all of which begin after a rest on beat 1. This acts as a *pickup* to the rest of the phrase. The most effective use of stepwise melody generates movement toward a goal. This can mean the crammed flurry up to a sustained melody note in John Coltrane's improvisations or deliberate theme melodies in compositions like "Chelsea Bridge," "Blue in Green," "Someone to Watch Over Me," "In a Sentimental Mood," or "Bluesette." The example on the next page is in 3/4 meter and ascends in Bb major from F to Eb, a 7th. The melodic goal is Eb, which signals arrival at an Am7b5 chord.

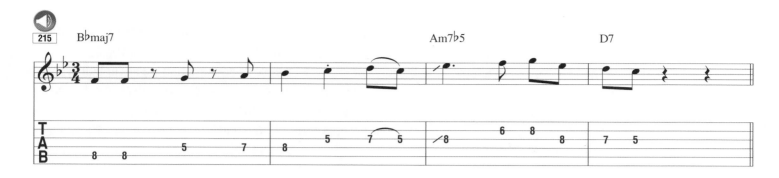

Stepwise motion can be applied to any tonality. This improvised line is similar to Donald Byrd's trumpet solo in "Nica's Dream" and is in the minor mode. It contains material that was later used by John Coltrane as his theme for "Mr. P. C." Note the ascending stepwise diatonic motion in Bb minor with repeated notes answered by descending pentatonic motion.

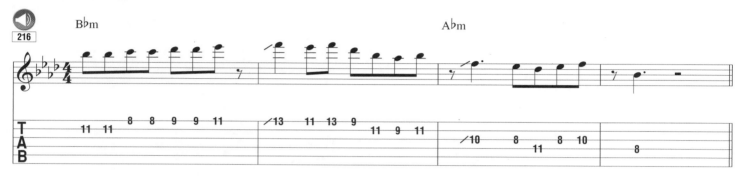

Another stepwise melody in the minor mode with rhythmic variations is found in "Dear Old Stockholm," a Swedish song reinterpreted by Miles Davis, Stan Getz, John Coltrane, and others. This phrase contains ascending motion in the first bar answered by a descending stepwise line with syncopated rhythms in the third measure.

Stepwise melody can move in ascending or descending direction within the same phrase. When combined, changes of direction create the line's shape, or *melodic contour*. The impression of the shape can be smooth and even like rolling hills or a sine wave, or jagged and angular like a sawtooth shape, depending on the melody. Check out the A sections of "I'll Remember April," "You Are Too Beautiful," and "You Don't Know What Love Is" (meas. 3 and 5), or the bridge of "One Note Samba." Listen to the melodies in these pieces to develop a feeling for and an aural recognition of stepwise contours.

In jazz improvisation, stepwise melodies are often punctuated with skips in 3rds, 4ths, or other larger intervals, and expanded and decorated with chromatic passing tones. In longer lines, they are replete with changes of direction resulting in varied melodic contours. These elements are idiomatic to jazz melody.

This characteristic bebop phrase is played over Gm–Am7b5–D7b9–Gm, a i–ii–V–i progression in G minor. The melody contains stepwise motion and changes of direction with a variety of contours. Note the chromatic passing tones in measures 2–3 and skips in 3–4 that emphasize chord tones. No particular scale explains this typical line. Depending on where it is in time, it could be labelled melodic minor, harmonic minor, or diminished. However, for our purposes let's simply consider it a melody reflecting the underlying harmony. Note the C–Bb tones in measure 4, beat 2, at the phrase ending.

126

The same melody can be made into a bluesier variation with a few simple modifications at the phrase ending. It has new rhythmic material but still ends on C–B♭ tones at the same point in time. The *enclosure* is a type of melodic cell used to surround or approach chord tones in a melody by enclosing them in a group. It is played in measures 3–4 to target D, the 5th of Gm, and establish the blues melody.

Changing the register and range of a melody creates another variation. This modified phrase is played an octave higher and contains a different ending. The melody is extended to measure 5, beat 1 and is expanded with a John Coltrane motive from "Trane's Blues" (3:41) on *Workin' with the Miles Davis Quintet*.

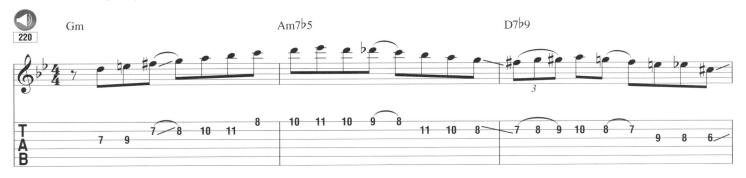

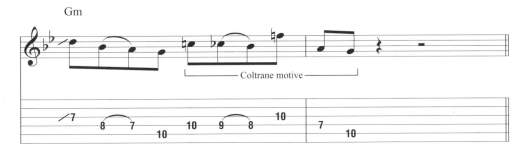

As jazz musicians grow, they collect and learn to modify and manipulate elements of the melodic language. (More on this in an upcoming section, Improvisation: Themes and Variations.)

There are countless examples of stepwise melody in the jazz repertoire. Listen to recordings of the greats and examine lead sheets of standards to find other applications. Make a point of recognizing stepwise melodies and their variations by ear.

Arpeggios and Chord Tones

Much of jazz is harmonic in nature—that is, chord-based. It follows that it is important to consider note-to-chord relationships in melody. This brings harmony into the world of melody and rhythm. Arpeggios illustrate the most fundamental form of note-chord relationships and have been a staple of jazz melody since its inception. The awareness of chord tones within a melody facilitates improvisation over changes. The greatest jazz players make you feel like you are hearing chord progressions moving in their melodies. This is the *vertical* aspect of melody, spelling the chord of the moment to make music.

Like stepwise melody, which is a succession of tones in a key, arpeggios are a succession of tones in a chord. Arpeggios are readily understood by playing the tones of a given chord as single notes. Consider a G7 chord, the dominant or V chord of C major. Its notes are, in succession from the root: G–B–D–F—the triad plus a 7th tone. This is akin to melodic skips of the previous section. However, these skips define chord tones. If one was to continue skipping or arpeggiating in order, the remaining notes in the key of C would be A–C–E, the 9th, 11th, and 13th tones. These are extensions of the chord, reflecting G9, G11, and G13 sonorities. (Review Harmony, Chapter 1, for more details.)

It is useful to perceive extension tones as upper parts of the basic, root-position chord. Remember Charlie "Bird" Parker's assertion that his style was informed by playing the "higher intervals of chords as a melody line." It starts with the full, seven-tone arpeggio as a source of melody content. Play this arpeggio and end on G13.

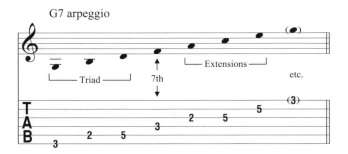

Think of the F-tone, the 7th, as the junction of lower and upper parts of a chord. In many jazz melodies, that's what creates a particular color or mood. For example, typical blues lines are based on the lower part of chord (triad plus the 7th tone), while more sophisticated and impressionistic melodies exploit the upper part, consisting of 9ths, 11ths, and 13ths, plus the 7th.

When viewing upper parts as four-note groups above the root tone, several familiar forms appear. Playing from the B note produces the arpeggio of Bm7♭5, from the D note, Dm7, and from F, Fmaj7, and so on.

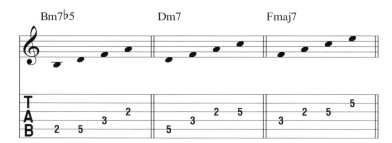

Are these arpeggios applicable to G7? Yes, indeed they are desirable. Most jazz musicians play them regularly in improvisations and memorialize them in compositions. Charlie Parker applied two exemplary arpeggio melodies as cells in "Donna Lee." Both, one dominant and the other major in quality, are built from the 3rd of the chord and arpeggiated to the 9th.

This example depicts Bird's use of arpeggios to navigate a ii–V–I progression. Note the stepwise approach to the E♭m9 arpeggio, chromatic descent into E, the #5 of an A♭7 chord, and then E♭, the 9th of D♭maj7—that's the bebop targeting effect based on extensions, and it reflects the chord changes E♭m9–A♭7#5–D♭maj9.

The all-important ii–V–I progression in jazz demands a player be able to address the changes with a number of idiomatic melodic formulas. These two patterns contain four-note arpeggios in typical combinations that are ubiquitous. They function as interlocking cells and form the basis for melodic connection of chord sounds. The C–B connection reflects the voice leading in a Dm7–G7 progression. Check out the inclusion of a C# leading tone as a pickup for Dm7 and the larger skip of A–D in C6/9. Notice the triplet rhythm over Gm7 and a diminished arpeggio (E–G–B♭–D♭) as a substitution for C7. The Fmaj7 contains two neighbor notes. E is a lower neighbor approached by leap and is the major 7th, but here sounds like its goal is the F note. B♭ is an upper neighbor, a non-chord tone approached by leap resolving to A. Listen for the targeting effect of placing chord tones on strong beats to emphasize *melodic spelling* of the chord changes.

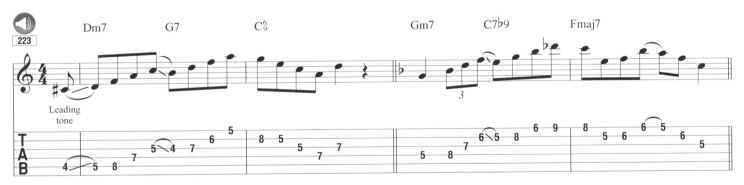

Arpeggio figures are often combined with leaps and stepwise motion. When wider leaps are played the melody usually returns in the opposite direction by step and sometimes by skip, either diatonically or chromatically. These lines depict typical motion and contours. Notice the stepwise descent after a wider E–D♭ leap in the first figure. In the second, a wide leap of E–B♭ is resolved from below with an enclosure to A, the 3rd of Fmaj7, via chromatic tones. Turn to the next page to see this in action.

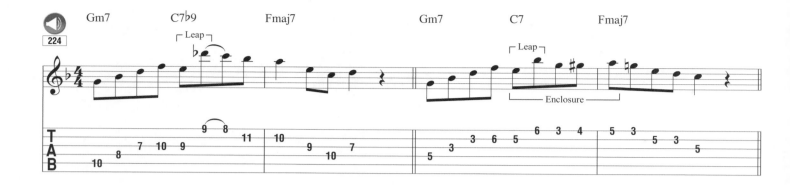

This Sonny Stitt phrase played in many solos exemplifies the combination of chord-tone leaps, stepwise motion, changes of direction—here, creating more jagged contours and chromatic passing tones. In measure 3, an Fm7 arpeggio is superimposed over Bb7 to produce an extended sound.

One of John Coltrane's favorite arpeggio formulas involved making a three-note triad shape into a four-note group. This phrase demonstrates the motion heard in many classic Trane solos of the 1950s. Each triad arpeggio in measure 2 is a cell begun with a chromatic lower neighbor note, acting as a leading tone. These patterns tend to descend diatonically and form a sequence. Listen to the mixture of stepwise and arpeggio contours. Visualizing triads in arpeggio melodies opens the door to polytonal perceptions indigenous to jazz.

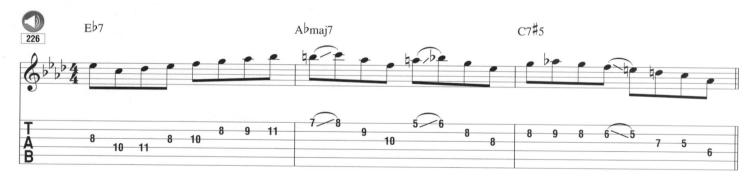

Wes Montgomery employed a similar strategy in his improvisations. In this passage from "West Coast Blues," a four-note arpeggio is expanded with a lower neighbor tone to create a six-note group. Like Trane, he moved these cells diatonically in descending motion to produce a sequence. The melody in measure 3–4 depicts Wes' use of arpeggios over a modern turnaround: Bbmaj7–Db7–Gbmaj7–B7. Note standard arpeggio outlines over Bbmaj7 and Gbmaj7 contrasted by leaps, chromaticism, and stepwise motion over Db7.

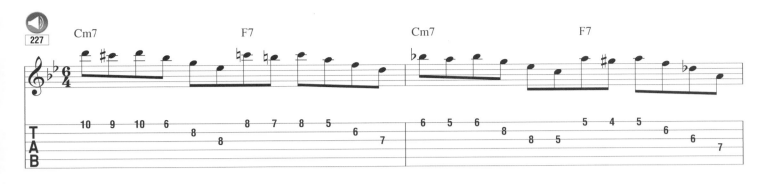

Charlie Christian, the father of electric jazz guitar, was a regular exploiter of arpeggios. This example from "Gone With 'What' Wind," a blues in C, contains a mixture of characteristic sounds. Note the use of a riff-based figure and stepwise motion to begin the phrase. A Cm6 arpeggio ascends in measure 2 and descends as C6 arpeggio in the same line. A Dm6 arpeggio is mixed with chromatic passing tones over G7 in measures 5–6. Chromaticism is found again in the C6 arpeggio in measures 7–8. This phrase reconciles the two common aspects of melody: horizontal and vertical motion.

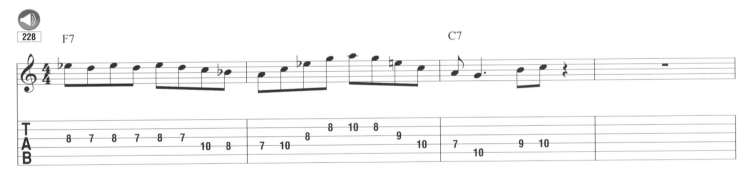

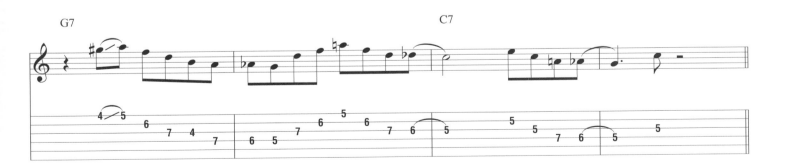

Horizontal and Vertical Melodic Motion

Horizontal and vertical motion in jazz melody are combined freely to address the musical situation. If the tune has a number of chord changes and the harmonic rhythm is faster, vertical motion and the spelling of the harmony with arpeggios is a requisite strategy. If the chord changes are minimal or static, as in a vamp or simple modal tune, horizontal movement is effective, especially as melodic contrast to chord outlining and repeated patterns. (Check out Miles Davis' solo in "So What.") In the work of jazz greats, a balance of horizontal and vertical movement is expected and normal, and borne out by a deeper examination of their lines.

This Bird phrase over "Rhythm Changes" is particularly well balanced. It has a mixture of elements: stepwise motion—diatonic and chromatic, leaps and skips, changes of direction, and characteristic bebop chord outlining that splits the difference between horizontal and vertical motion.

This Coltrane line over the 3rds-related changes of "26-2" is more intricate and deliberately vertical. In response to the complex and harmonically active progression the melody is made entirely of arpeggio or partial arpeggio figures in measures 1–3. Only the final cadence, C7–F7 in measures 3–4, has a horizontal contour.

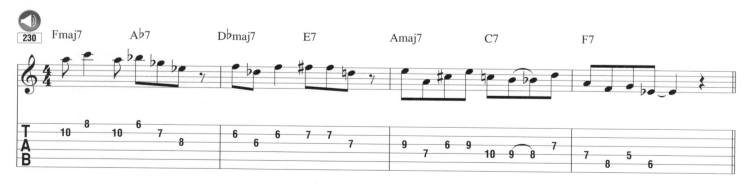

Horizontal motion and motivic development are often pursued in a static modal context. This Cannonball Adderley phrase from "Milestones" is exemplary and offers solutions to the potential monotony of a persistent Gm7 chord. The stepwise patterns in measures 1–3 are thematic and establish a motive sequenced on different chord tones: E, G, and B♭, implying Gm6. The melody segment that answers the sequence in measure 4 is also thematic and contains shorter, four-note cells, having step-wise motion and skips inside the tonal center. It leads to a final side-slipping gesture in E♭ minor—often described as playing "outside" (the key center)—that bends the tonality in measure 6.

By contrast, this Wes Montgomery phrase from "Four on Six" emphasizes vertical chord spelling with ascending arpeggios over a repeating Gm7–C7 progression, functioning like a typical vamp. Note the combination of extensions (Gm9) and triad (Gm) forms in measure 1. The arpeggio line in measures 2–3 poses a Dm arpeggio over a Gm7 tonality. This extension is a favorite tactic among modern jazz musicians.

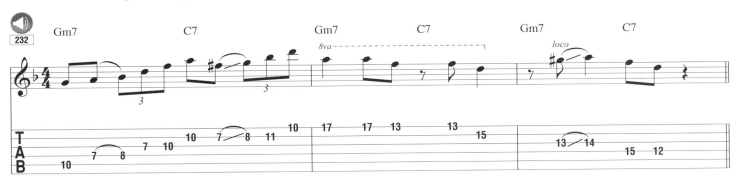

Parting shot: Arpeggios are malleable and open to unlimited creative applications. They can be constructed from any diatonic or chromatic scale, and played in infinite combinations over any conceivable background. In his *Thesaurus of Scales and Melodic Patterns*, Nicolas Slonimsky devoted a chapter to Heptatonic Arpeggios (page 155). These are seven-note arpeggios built on every type of scale and mode. His patterns spell diatonic, extended, and altered chords in melody form, and many are well suited to jazz. According to Quincy Jones, John Coltrane studied from the book extensively, as have many other jazz artists and contemporary composers. Maybe it should be in your woodshed.

CHAPTER 9

FOUR ESSENTIAL JAZZ SOUNDS, PART I: THE HEXATONIC SCALE

While there is no shortage of scale nomenclature attributed to jazz in academic volumes devoted to the subject, many are theoretical constructs without a verifiable language pedigree. In the context of this course, based on the practices of jazz performers in the real world and substantiated by transcribing and analyzing improvisations and compositions, we find there is actually a small handful of idiomatic melody sounds. These are ubiquitous; recurring with such frequency that they are inescapable components of the lexicon. They are deemed essential because they enjoy myriad applications and spawn seemingly infinite variations. As an entry into the world of jazz language four essential jazz sounds are offered for your study.

As stated in Chapter 8, scales are repurposed to become melodies or sounds. Once a scale is introduced in these chapters as a *pitch collection*, it is followed immediately by idiomatic lines that demonstrate melodic aspects of its sound in context. For our purposes, consider a scale to be a sound and more a container of available pitches than a method of performance.

Hexatonic Basics

A hexatonic "scale" can be considered from two perspectives. It can be seen as a pentatonic scale with an added tone. Five plus one equals six, *penta*-tonic becomes *hexa*-tonic. That possibility would be accessible to blues and rock musicians. Or, it can be seen as a traditional, seven-note diatonic scale, like a major scale, with a missing tone. Seven minus one equals six, *dia*-tonic becomes *hexa*-tonic. Classically trained musicians and those with theory backgrounds may relate more to this view. The great pianist and jazz scholar, Mark Levine, in *The Jazz Theory Book*, referred to the hexatonic perception as a diatonic scale with an "avoid note" when played over a maj7 chord. In either case, you wind up with six tones. Hexatonic melodies became prevalent in the hard bop era and are found in the playing of countless jazz artists from Sonny Rollins, John Coltrane, and Cannonball Adderley to Wes Montgomery, Pat Martino, and Joe Pass.

This is a G major hexatonic scale in the second position. Note that it is a six-note pitch collection: G–A–B–D–E–F#, corresponding to steps 1–2–3–5–6–7 of a G major scale without a fourth step.

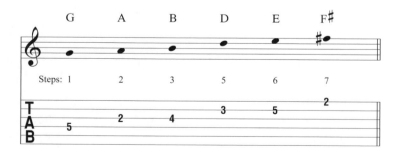

The G major hexatonic sound can be played over a number of major chords: Gmaj7, Gmaj9, Gmaj13, G6, and G6/9. Because it lacks a fourth step, it could also be used over a Gmaj7♭5 or Gmaj7#11—that's the "avoid note" principle in action. Play this hexatonic melody and relate it to any and all major chords in the Harmony section.

Here are four possible chord forms that relate to hexatonic melody in the second position. Follow this procedure to train your ear. Play a chord, play the melody, and then play the chord again. Add more major chords in the process. Listen for note-to-chord relationships.

The hexatonic sound has myriad possibilities beyond a major chord. Therein lies its flexibility and utility. The sound played over Gmaj7 can be applied with little or no modification to a minor 7th and/or dominant 7th chord. In these examples the previous melody is "reassigned" to Em9, A13, or A11(13) chords, and is re-fingered in a higher position. Make re-fingering a habit with useful melodies—play them in different fingerings and positions. Note that Em9–A13 is a ii–V progression in D. Conclusion: Hexatonic melodies are useful as melodies over ii–V changes as an "inside" sound.

The hexatonic sound can generate strong dissonance when applied to altered chords. Play this variation over Cmaj7#11 and C#m7♭5. Over Cmaj7#11, you'll hear a more abstract extended sound suitable for post-bop settings. Modern jazz musicians like Joe Henderson, Wayne Shorter, Herbie Hancock, and Pat Metheny have made extensive use of the maj7#11 sonority in their music. When applying the G hexatonic to Cmaj7#11, notice that the pitch collection has no root (C), as a result it emphasizes extensions and color tones. C#m7♭5, in relation to G hexatonic, also has no root (C#) and produces a similar effect. However, by thinking of C#m7♭5 as an E minor chord (Em6), a connection is easily made. Pat Martino, a master of minor conversion, has used this application throughout his improvisations.

These widely used hexatonic phrases are jazz-language applications containing motives found in the playing of great improvisers. They are so prevalent in the genre that they can be ascribed to many performers and not one in particular. Play these six melodies and listen for chord tones on strong beats.

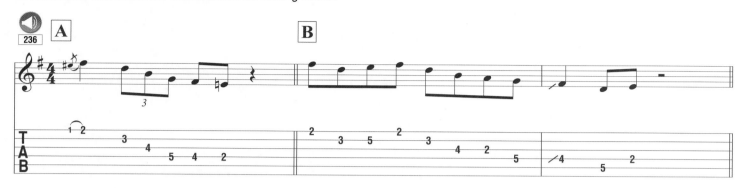

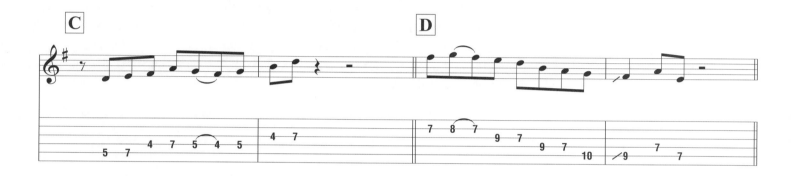

Check out the varied contours and combinations of stepwise and arpeggio-based melody. Track 236, figure A is a straight descending arpeggio with a stepwise ending. Figure B descends but has a winding stepwise contour with some skips. Figure C is almost a "mirror image," an ascending melody with skips and a winding contour. Figure D is a variation combining elements of the previous two. Figure E is an elongated variation mixing elements of the previous three. Note the phrase ending is the same melody cell as the beginning of Figure B. Figure F is a decorated phrase containing arpeggio outlines and chromatic passing tones. When you have acquired and assimilated these melodies, play them over Gmaj7, Em9, A13, Cmaj7#11, and C#m7♭5 chords. Use your ear and make slight adjustments if needed to emphasize alternate chord tones.

Hexatonic sounds are like a melodic/harmonic kaleidoscope. Twist them just a little and you'll create something else—often something surprising. The F#7sus4♭9 is a more exotic post-bop voicing for an altered chord. It is also the polychord, Gmaj7/F#. This colorful sonority was used by John Coltrane in the bridge of "Naima." Try playing G hexatonic melodies over this unusual chord as a substitution. Listen for the realignment of chord tones to a new tonic and the resulting modern dissonance produced by the simple repurposing of a hexatonic melody.

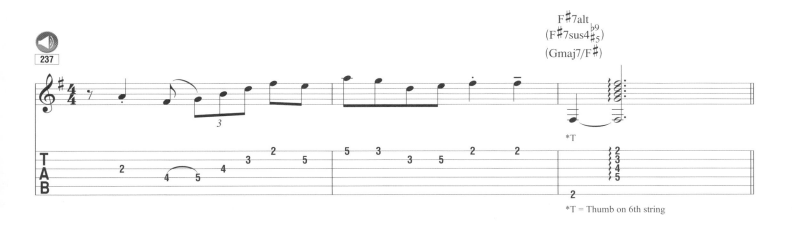

*T = Thumb on 6th string

Hexatonic Vocabulary

The hexatonic sound is an essential element in jazz. The following phrases depict its varied usage by the great masters.

This Vincent Herring line from his "Body and Soul" solo illustrates a typical use of the hexatonic sound as an *arrival* melody in a ii–V–I progression. The D♭maj7, I chord, receives a pure hexatonic stepwise line as a resolution and contrast to the E♭m7 arpeggio and blues melody played over A♭7. Note the melodic targeting of the E♭ tone, the major 9th of D♭.

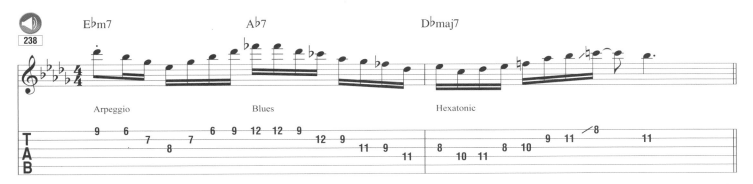

Cannonball Adderley used the hexatonic as a resolution frequently in his improvisations. This phrase from "Once I Loved" is also played over a ii–V–I progression, here in C. After chromaticism and altered-chord sounds, Adderley applied a common hexatonic melody over Cmaj7, approached stepwise from a diminished substitution line. Notice the cell on beat 2 of measure 2. It's the same figure Herring used to begin his hexatonic melody. Here it occurs in the middle of the line. Conclusion: That figure is played on a strong beat. As long as it remains the same in beat orientation, that hexatonic cell can be moved along the time span to any part of a phrase or any other strong beat in a phrase. That's another rewarding aspect of working with melodies in the jazz language. Its rhythmic placement is not strictly assigned to a particular beat. It can and does vary at the discretion of the player along a time span, depending on connection to and from other melodic cells.

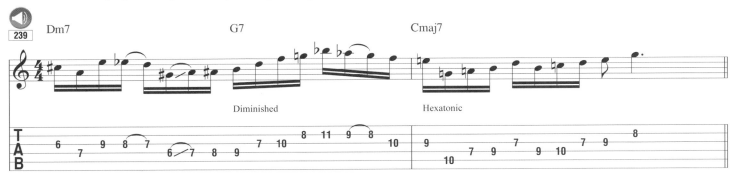

This Cannonball phrase, also from "Once I Loved," over a ii–V–I in Bb reveals his use of the hexatonic as both a minor and major sound. He plays a Cm hexatonic over Cm7, the ii chord, to approach F7#5 arpeggio with upper and lower neighbor-note targeting (indicated by the bracket). Adderley plays an arpeggio-based ascending figure in the resolution. Note the motive in the closing line on beats 3–4. It's a fixture of the jazz language.

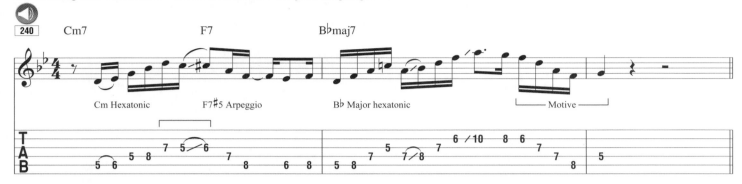

Sonny Rollins used a variation of the same motive in his solo on "Tune Up." His hexatonic phrase begins on F7, the V chord in Bb, and continues to the resolution in measure 2, where the motive is played over the I chord, Bbmaj7. It leads directly to a characteristic bebop line over the A7alt chord.

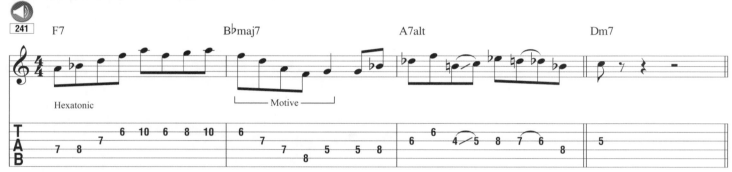

Dexter Gordon played a simple hexatonic melody on Dbmaj7 after repeating arpeggio figures through Ebm7–Ab7 in this ii–V–I phrase from "Blue Bossa."

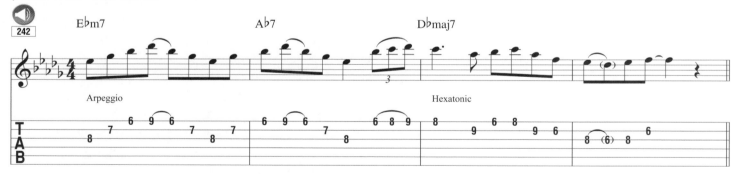

Pat Martino also applied the hexatonic as a resolution sound in ii–V–I changes. This phrase from "Opus De Don" (*Opus De Don*, Don Patterson) illustrates a typical usage in the hard-bop context. Like Herring's, Adderley's, and Rollins' lines, Pat's melody ends on the sixth tone—here, F of an Abmaj7 chord. This is a familiar voice-leading sound that is often chosen when playing a hexatonic over a major chord. It connotes an Abmaj7–Ab6 chord change melodically.

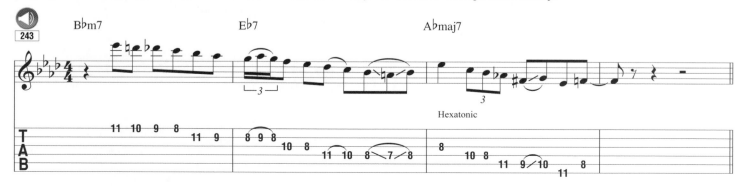

This Wes Montgomery phrase from "Days of Wine and Roses" contains extensive use of the hexatonic sound over two minor chords a 3rd apart, Gm7 and B♭m7. Aside from an occasional targeting by a lower neighbor note, this lengthy, double-timed line is based exclusively on hexatonic melody.

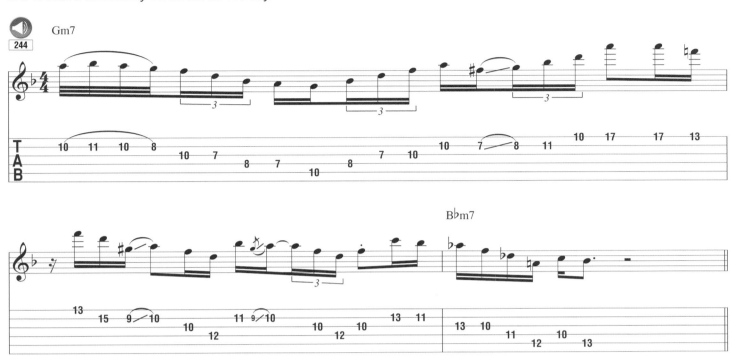

Grant Green decorated the hexatonic and the major arpeggio with chromatic neighbor notes in this double-timed ii–V–I phrase from "Little Girl Blue." The figure on the and-of beat 1 in measure 3 is a common motive combining the hexatonic with a major 7th arpeggio.

The Pat Martino phrase (on the next page) from "It's You or No One" (*Funk You*, Don Patterson) contains two examples of the hexatonic sound used over different chords—in this case, Gm7 and Fmaj7, the ii and I chords of a ii–V–I in F. Note the rising Gm7 hexatonic in measures 1–2, the deliberate targeting of a diminished arpeggio for C7♭9 in 2, and the F hexatonic played over a major seventh chord in 3–4. This phrase illustrates an ideal balance of stepwise melody, arpeggio chord outlining, and the winding contours of horizontal motion.

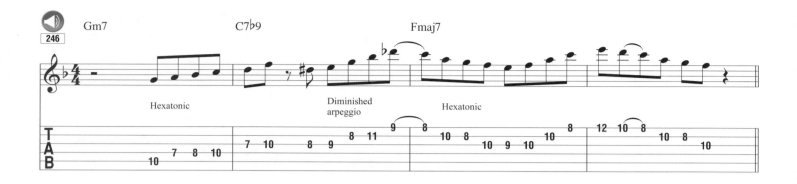

Joe Pass used the hexatonic sound modally to play over minor chords in the bridge of "C.E.D." (*Sound of Synanon*). This passage is an instructive example of the jazz language's call-and-response phraseology. The melody over Fm7 provides the question, and the answer is heard when the chord changes to A♭m7. Both phrases contain purely hexatonic content in the minor mode. Both begin with a pickup. Each could be played as a separate melody. To develop a longer line in the same key, simply transpose the A♭m7 phrase down a minor 3rd to F minor. Next, transpose both to D minor and try playing the melodies while improvising over "So What" or "Impressions."

John Coltrane was a master of harmonic innovation, and his application of the hexatonic sound was second to none. This group of phrases is from "Goldsboro Express," a contrafact of the "Donna Lee" ("Indiana") changes, recorded at the height of his hard bop period in 1958 when he was working out many ideas for improvising over various progressions. It is illuminating and instructive to examine Trane's use of hexatonic melody over the tune's fast-moving changes. In the first phrase, over F7– B♭maj7 (V–I), he approaches the hexatonic with a descending stepwise melody to target B♭, the root of B♭maj7. The melody then ascends smoothly through the hexatonic. The chromatic passing tones (G–G♭–F) at the phrase ending are characteristic of the major-bebop sound.

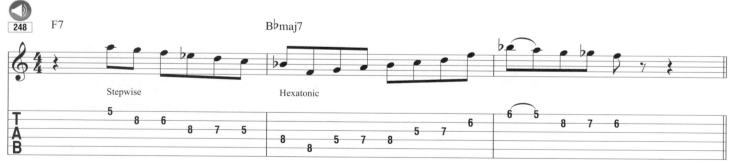

The second "Goldsboro Express" phrase has two examples of the major hexatonic sound in different contexts. It is played over a IV–iv–I progression: A♭maj7–A♭m7–E♭maj7, one of the most common patterns in jazz standards. Consider tunes like "There Will Never Be Another You," "I Thought About You," or "Misty." The structure of Trane's phrase is noteworthy for its elegance and symmetry: hexatonic–arpeggio–hexatonic presents a well-defined harmonic roadmap. The line over A♭maj7 is a typical arching line with chromatic passing tones (B♭–A–A♭) at the end. The melody over E♭maj7 is begun on the 3rd of the chord, G, and continues with winding, even contours. In between is a simple descending arpeggio figure for A♭m7. This phrase could also be played over a typical variation of the changes: A♭maj7–D♭9–E♭maj7.

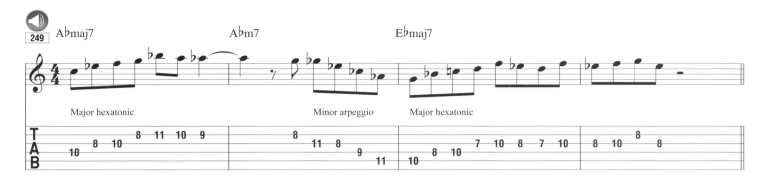

The third "Goldsboro Express" phrase is played over B♭7–E♭maj7, a V–I cadence in E♭. This time, Trane targets the 5th of E♭maj7, B♭, with a stepwise, dominant-bebop melody and begins a trademark ascending sequence pattern that he exploited often in his improvisations. This pattern consists of two four-note melodic cells, B♭–C–D–F and E♭–F–G–B♭, representing the 5th (B♭) and tonic (E♭) of the chord. The cells played in succession produce the familiar sequence melody. Note that both are in the hexatonic pitch collection and share the same tones. The closing motive, B♭–C–B♭, is a simple fragmented theme excerpt Trane drew from the melody of "All This and Heaven Too." It was used often as a phrase ending and has been quoted in turn by players like George Benson, Vincent Herring, and Cannonball Adderley.

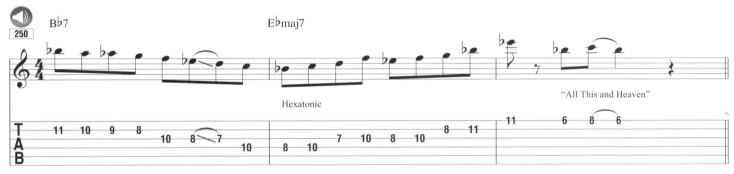

Sometimes, the hexatonic is used as an arrival sound in unusual, often chromatic chord changes. That seems logical, as the hexatonic is both a well-grounded and fluid sound with plural applications. In this example, from Wes Montgomery's solo in "Hymn for Carl," it is a point of resolution in an unconventional chord change that begins in F minor, prepares a move to the expected B♭ minor via an F7♭9 chord, but then suddenly cadences on an unprepared Bmaj7. Wes handles the situation by pivoting on a common tone, C♯, enharmonically the D♭ in the expected B♭ minor chord. He uses that tone to begin as straight a hexatonic descent as exists. This line is textbook.

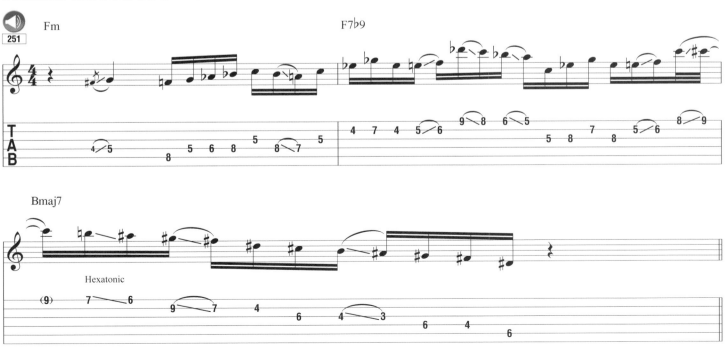

The hexatonic can be expanded by minorizing. Changing one tone in the pitch collection not only doubles the possibilities but allows for a number of colorful and modern substitutions. This example shows the simple transformation made by lowering the 3rd of the "scale."

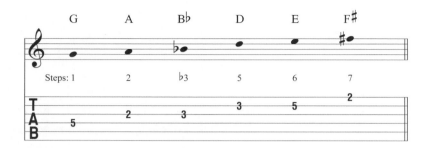

Apply the minorized hexatonic sound to a harmonic setting. The following line is a transformed version of Figure B of Track 236. Play this melody and listen for the effect of the transformation over these three chords: C9#11, Gm(maj13), and Em7♭5.

Feed the creative impulse. Take it one step further by playing the minorized melody over F#7#5#9 and A13♭9.

CHAPTER 10

FOUR ESSENTIAL SOUNDS, PART II: THE BEBOP SCALE

Bebop Scale Basics

The bebop scale, deemed essential by esteemed jazz educators David Baker and Barry Harris, is ubiquitous and vital to the jazz language. The concept is simple but effective. It is the expansion of a seven-note diatonic scale with one additional note—but that note changes the function and intent of the melody dramatically. The bebop scale has the effect of producing an eight-note scale with a chromatic passing tone in its structure. Like the hexatonic scale, bebop scales yield an additional benefit of transforming an odd number of notes into an even number of notes, ideal for most jazz rhythmically. You can play the simplest stepwise form of a bebop scale in steady eighth notes, neatly occupy one bar of music and place a chord tone on every strong beat.

The Dominant Bebop Scale

The primary bebop scale is generally associated with a dominant 7th chord. Consider G7: The chord tones are G–B–D–F. The eight tones in its bebop scale are G–A–B–C–D–E–F and F♯ or G♭. In the most common application, the G♭ acts as a passing tone descending from the root, G, to the minor 7th tone, F. This motion often occurs as a three-note series or cell and defines the G7 sound. It places melodic emphasis on a strong beat, rhythmically, indicated by the bracket in this example. Note the important chord tones on strong beats: G–F–D–B and G—outlining the G major triad and F, the seventh tone.

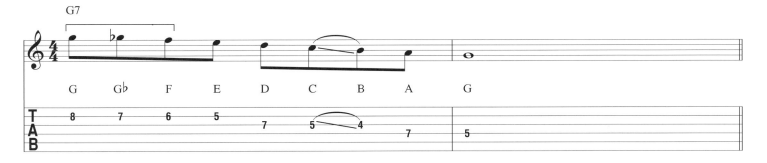

These melodies are common forms of the G7 bebop scale sound in context. They are V–I cadence lines: G7 to Cmaj7. Play and listen for the resolution to a C major sound in the phrases.

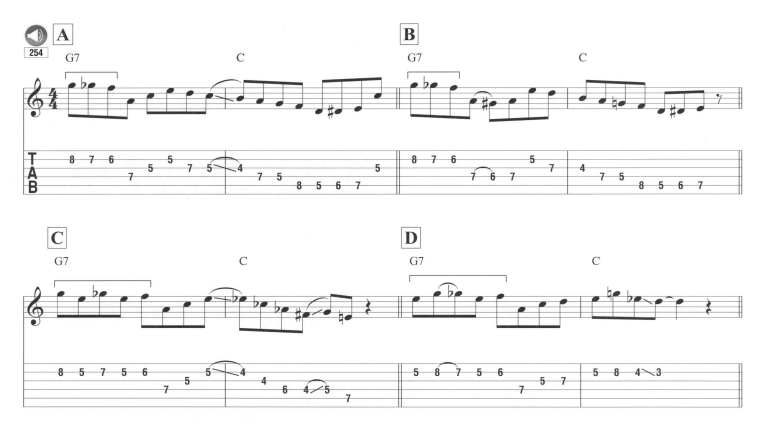

Part of the assimilation process is understanding what you're playing. Note the characteristic elements in the melody. If internalized in the practice phase during assimilation these elements foster an intuitive response in improvisation. As Charlie Parker aptly put it, "Master your instrument, master the music, and then forget all that bulls#&! and just play."

In Track 254, figure A the bebop scale cell (G–Gb–F) is combined with a leap (F–A), a superimposed arpeggio (Am), some stepwise motion (E–D–C–B–A–G–F) and an *enclosure* (F–D–D#–E) that targets E, the third of C major.

Figure B is a variation with a leap down (F–A) to a *neighbor-tone* cell (A–G#–A) and then a leap up to continue stepwise descent (A–E–D) into a favorite John Coltrane pentatonic pattern (E–D–B–A–G). It ends with an enclosure of E.

Figure C contains a zigzagging approach to playing the bebop scale cell. Note the toggling motion of the pedal-tone contour (E is the repeated pedal tone): G–*E*–Gb–*E*–F. The melody still targets F on a strong beat, but a beat later, and lengthens the cell metrically. The triad arpeggios in the phrase, Am and Abm, are also cells. They comprise a common bebop device of using Am diatonically followed by Abm chromatically as an in-out-in tension into a resolution—here, a *delayed resolution*. The resolution to C doesn't occur until beat 3—it's delayed. Delaying resolution is a common tactic in playing changes; it creates unpredictability and adds greater dissonance to a line. (Check out Charlie Parker's solo in "Thrivin' From a Riff," in the bridge, second chorus, for an example in the repertoire.) Here, note the enclosure of G, the 5th of C major, at the ending. The final, two-note cell is a short motive used by Dizzy Gillespie in "Groovin' High" and is a bebop staple.

Figure D presents a different enclosure targeting the F tone: E–G–Gb–E–F. Again, it increases the metric space. After a leap down (F–A), the melody ascends with a pentatonic cell (A–C–D–E) and concludes with a favorite Charle Parker phrase ending emphasizing the 9th of the Cmaj7(9) chord, D.

The Bebop Scale and Minor Conversion

The dominant bebop scale is frequently played as a *plural melody* over a related minor 7th chord. Consider a ii–V progression in C: Dm7–G7. The notes in a G7 bebop scale are G–Gb–F–E–D–C–B–A–G. The important G–Gb–F cell can also target the minor 3rd of Dm7. This is the most basic and serviceable form of minor conversion (G7=Dm7) and works seamlessly when using the jazz language as a basis for melody. Many players, including John Coltrane, Wes Montgomery, Cannonball Adderley, Pat Martino, George Benson, and Grant Green use the dominant bebop scale as a minor sound in a tonic minor, modal, or vamp context.

These two phrases illustrate the minor-conversion possibilities of a Dm7 bebop scale. Note the rhythmic placement of the bebop scale cells at different points in the melodies. Also notice the elements of arpeggio, melodic skips, leaps, and neighbor-tone activity.

These six variations present other possibilities of converting, combining and repurposing bebop scale elements in varied harmonic settings. Note the exploration of different fingerings and positions on the fingerboard. Re-fingering and relocating lines are essential steps to mastering the instrument and the music.

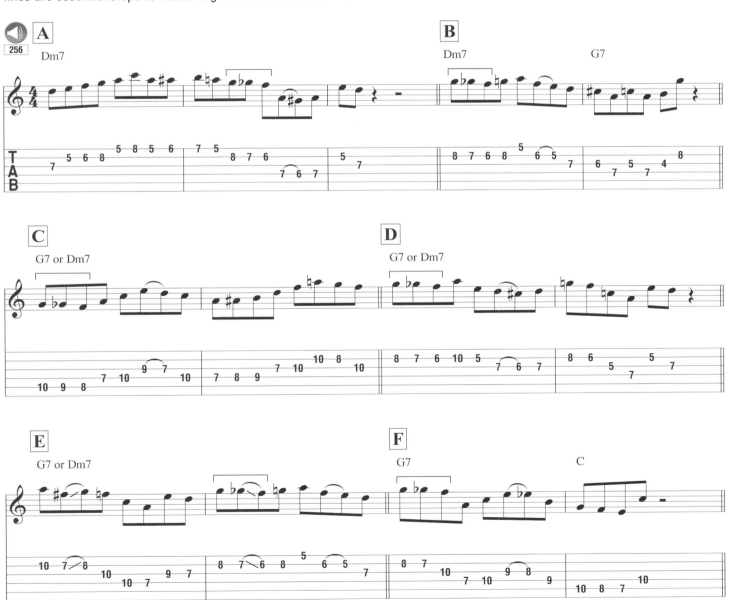

This phrase expands the bebop scale idea into a longer, more complex pattern. Three-note cells indigenous to the bebop scale are used to create a series of motives in a chromatic scale in the first two measures. Here, a chromatic scale is divided and made thematic with the use of the cell and a skip, resulting in a recurring four-note motive. Check out the repeating pattern of three chromatic notes and an upward skip in the first half: G–Gb–F–A, E–Eb–D–F, and Db–C–B–Db. They are similar to figures used in improvisation by Cannonball Adderley to approach chord tones in a "spiral" motion. Through this descent the Db bebop scale is reached in measure 2. The navigation naturally produces the tritone substitute for G7, Db7. The first two measures can be played over ii–V, ii–bII, or as a side-slipping melody in modal tunes and vamps.

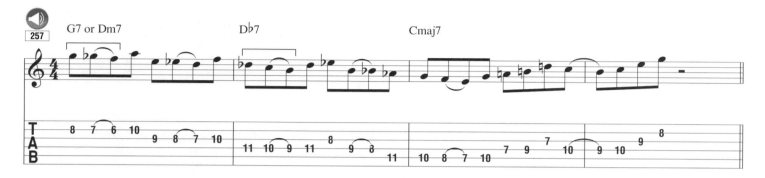

The Major Bebop Scale

The major bebop scale is used over—you guessed it—major chords. The diatonic major scale contains seven tones. In a major bebop scale a chromatic note is added between the fifth and sixth degrees. In C: C–D–E–F–G–G# or Ab–A–B, marked by the brackets. Like the dominant bebop scale, it produces an even, eight-tone pitch collection and is valuable for targeting operative tones in a melody. The sixth tone, significant in swing and major blues, is emphasized in the major bebop scale.

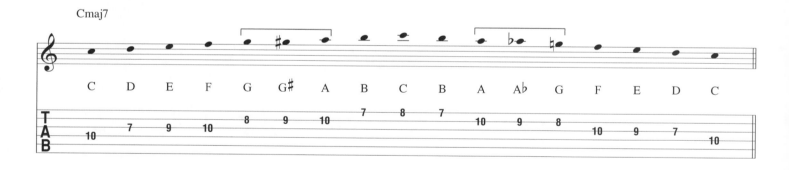

These characteristic phrases illustrate idiomatic use of the major bebop scale in improvised jazz lines over a Cmaj7 chord.

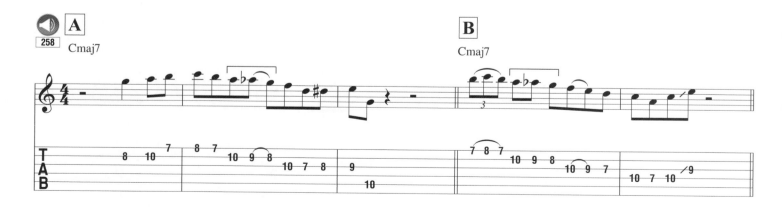

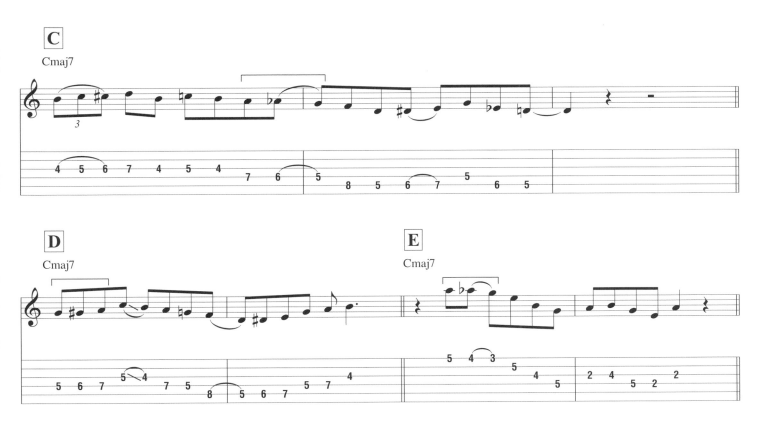

The chromaticism in the major bebop scale is also useful in navigating through chord changes. This pair of phrases shares a common rising line in measure 1 and depicts two typical ways a bebop scale melody can function harmonically. It can stay in the same tonality, Cmaj7, as in Track 259, figure A, or be directed to the ii chord, Dm7, figure B. In both cases, the G–G#–A cell strengthens the arrival to a chord tone.

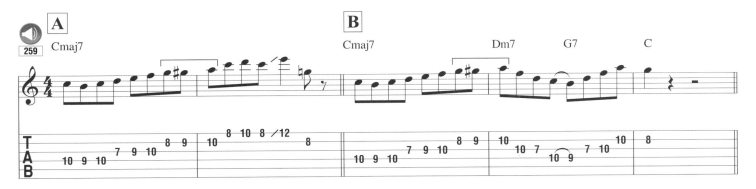

Like the hexatonic and dominant bebop scale, the major bebop scale offers plural applications over different chords. This scenario shows the most obvious. C major can be played over a Cmaj7–Am7 progression (I–vi) in a major-to-relative minor strategy. Here the descending A–Ab–G cell creates motion into a Dm7 via its eleventh tone, G.

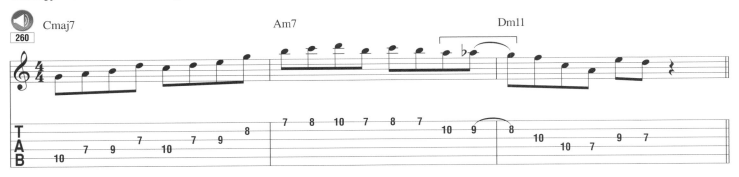

The strategy can also be applied to motion into an A7 chord. This time the G note is the target, the 7th of the altered dominant chord, A7♭9, and begins a stepwise line into its harmonic goal, Dm.

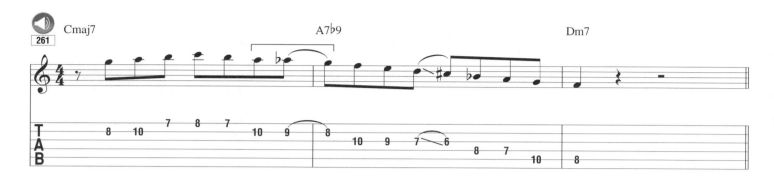

The same melody can be used to navigate to and connect with more remote tonalities. This phrase begins in C major and cadences on Fm7, a progression found in the first four bars of "Lady Bird." Note that the Fm9 arpeggio figure from the hexatonic chapter is used as an Fm9 extension.

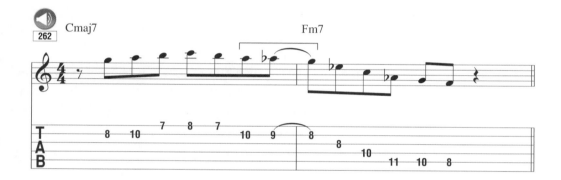

In this variation the same melody is played over a Cm7 chord, the parallel minor, as in the opening changes of "On Green Dolphin Street," "How High the Moon," "Ornithology," "Call Me," or "I'll Remember April." The targeted G note is 5th of C minor. The Cm7 bebop scale (see previous section) is used to demonstrate the connection of two complimentary bebop scales within a single jazz line. The same connection can be applied to I–IV7 or I–i–IV7 progressions, Cmaj7–F7 or Cmaj7–Cm7–F7. It is also effective in progressions with IV–iv7–♭VII7 changes (Fmaj7–Fm7–B♭7). This progression occurs in "Misty," "God Bless the Child," "Triste," and many other tunes.

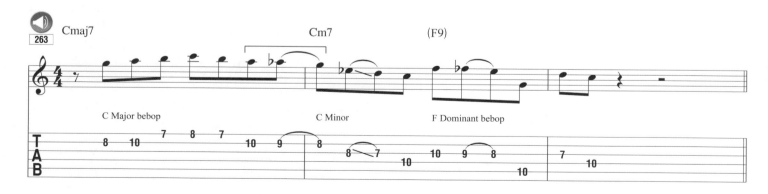

Alternate Bebop Scales

Practically any diatonic scale can benefit from the bebop transformation, the insertion of a chromatic tone into the pitch collection, and made into alternate forms. By minorizing the third degree of a major bebop scale the melody can be repurposed into a parallel-minor form. This sound dovetails nicely with enriched minor chords in a modal context and altered dominant chords related to the melodic minor scale. More on this in the next chapter. Play these minorized variations of Track 258 and listen to the transformed effect. Compare the sound of the melodies over Cm tonic chords and F9#11 altered chords.

John Coltrane used the parallel-minor transformation in his modal improvisations over "So What."

Pat Martino applied two transformations to this minor-mode line from his solo in "Along Came Betty." The first expands a G harmonic minor scale, played as an altered-dominant sound over D7alt, by adding a D–Db–C cell. This is similar to the primary dominant bebop scale except that is built on the minor mode. The second, at the end of the example, adds the D–Db–C cell to a G melodic minor scale and is played over the tonic minor.

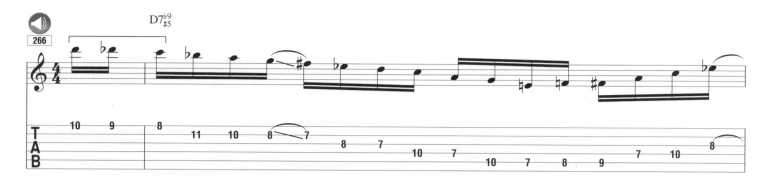

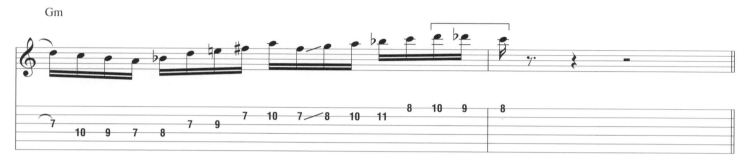

Joe Pass used the bebop transformation to add greater color to substitution melodies. In this ii–V–I phrase in C minor, from "There Is No Greater Love," he added the bebop cell to an Fm7 melody to enhance Dm7♭5 in the progression.

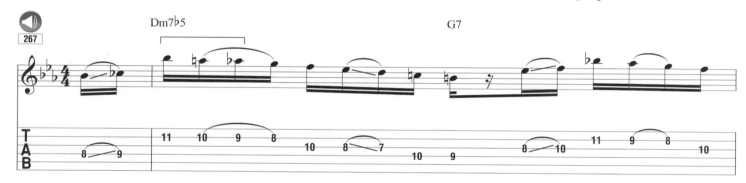

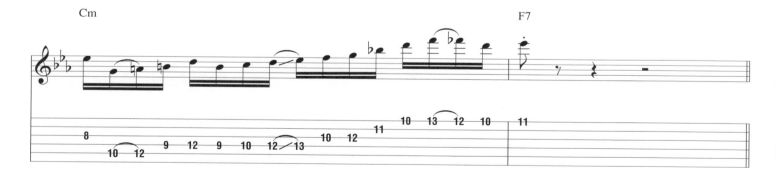

Bebop Scale Vocabulary

The next few pages contain idiomatic phrases from the jazz repertoire, illustrating bebop scale melodies in action. Make a note of the different rhythmic placements, emphasis of and connections to chord tones, and changes in melodic direction before or after a bebop cell is played. Sometimes, the cell creates its own phrase ending or period in the sentence, as in Tracks 258 (D and E), 266, and 267.

Charlie "Yard-Bird" Parker, the founding father of bebop, delivered, as expected, a wealth of bebop scale melodies.

His descendants added their own permutations in their use of the bebop language.

Clifford Brown, "Pent-Up House"

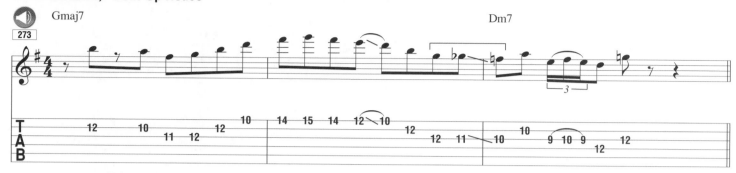

John Coltrane, "Blue Train"

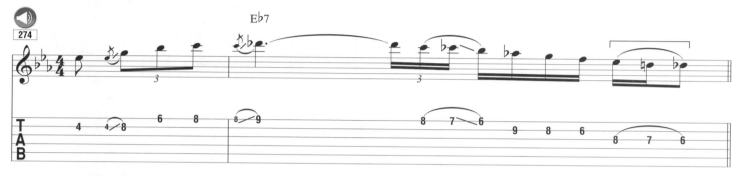

Sonny Stitt, "Con Alma"

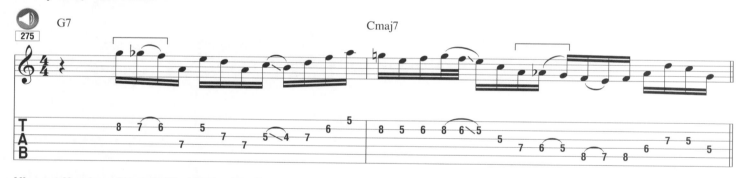

Vincent Herring, "Here's That Rainy Day"

John Coltrane, "Surrey With the Fringe on Top"

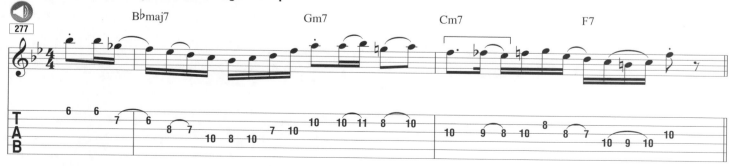

Vincent Herring, "Night and Day"

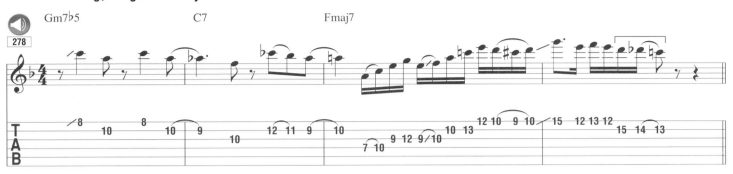

John Coltrane, "Tune Up"

Cannonball Adderley, "This Here"

Grant Green, "I'll Remember April"

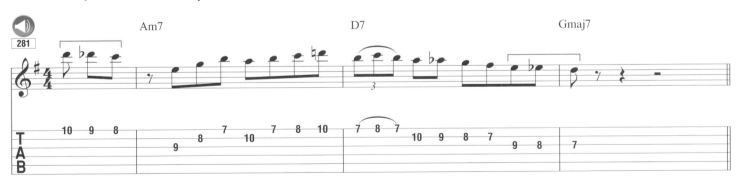

CHAPTER 11

FOUR ESSENTIAL SOUNDS, PART III: MELODIC MINOR

Melodic Minor Basics

The melodic minor scale has been used with such frequency in the jazz genre that it has earned the evocative nickname "jazz minor." Why the distinction in jazz? The answer lies in musicians' use of its unique melodic structure for improvisation and composition. The traditional melodic minor in classical music and common-practice theory has one form ascending and another descending. This example in A minor shows the differences in its pitch collection. Major 6 and major 7 intervals on the fifth and seventh degrees (F# and G#) are used when ascending in melodic minor. When descending it reverts to a natural minor scale or Aeolian mode with m7 and m6 (G♮ and F♮) intervals.

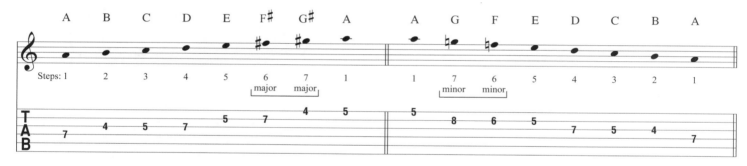

In jazz, melodic minor is generally played in the ascending form only. It is often used to define a tonic chord in minor keys because it contains raised sixth and seventh tones, which align with extended chords like minor 6/9 and minor (maj7) types and feel more stable. This simple ascending phrase merges the sound of melodic minor with a closely related parent chord, Am(maj9). Play the melody and listen for harmonic connection. After you've assimilated the sound, play the same phrase in ascending and descending form.

*T = Thumb on 6th string

Melodic minor contains the sound of a dominant 7th chord, its natural V chord, on its fifth degree, E. This phrase begins on operative notes of that portion. Listen for emphasis on the dominant 7th (E7) in the first measure and a resolution to Am via its 3rd, C, in measure 2. Link this phrase aurally to an indigenous sonority, Am(maj13), containing both F# and G# tones.

*T = Thumb on 6th string

Melodic Minor and Altered Sounds

Melodic minor bears a unique structure, making it ideal for playing over altered dominant 7th chords. Notice that half of the scale is a six-note portion of the whole-step/half-step series (F#–G#–A–B–C–D), yielding a *diminished* color. The other half is a five-note portion of the whole-tone scale (C–D–E–F#–G#), which produces an *augmented* sound. That's six out of eight tones of a diminished scale and five of six tones of a whole-tone scale. In the naturally occurring form of melodic minor, the two sounds overlap and converge. C, D, F#, and G# are common tones found in both portions.

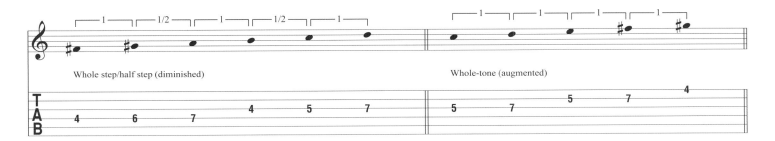

The colors of melodic minor and its symmetrical structure invite a variety of altered-chord applications. Modern jazz players routinely exploit its modes to improvise over the following extended and altered chords in A minor: A=Am(maj13), C=Cmaj7#5, D=D9#11, and G#=G#7♭5#5♭9#9 (fully altered). Sonny Rollins used the fourth mode thematically throughout his modern blues piece, "Blue Seven," as did Dizzy Gillespie in "A Night in Tunisia."

To develop an ear for these relationships, play melodic minor from different starting pitches and link them to their related chords. This ground-finding exercise illustrates the procedure. No language lines are yet offered. At this stage, simply listen for the relationship of the ending note with its related chord as well as chord tones on strong beats. The latter aspect defines chords in a horizontal melody.

A=Am(maj13)

C=Cmaj7#5

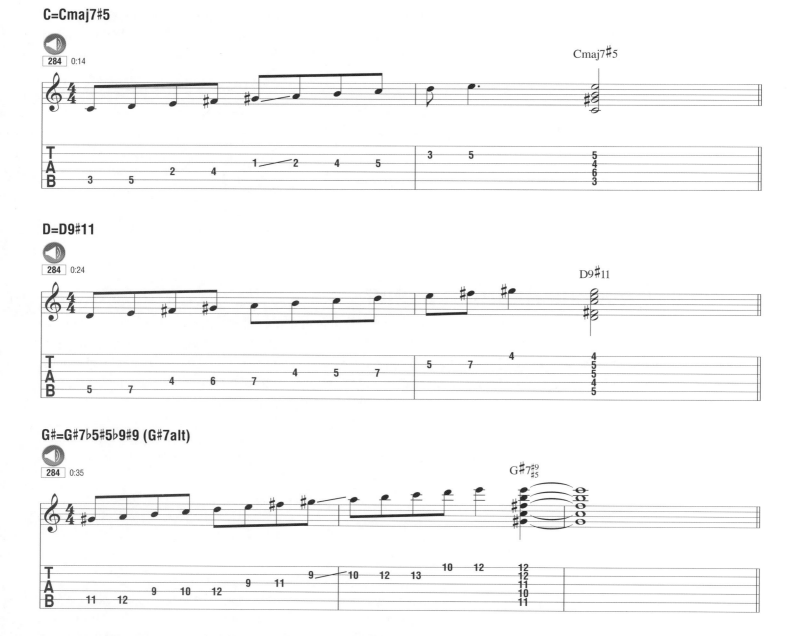

D=D9#11

G#=G#7♭5#5♭9#9 (G#7alt)

The B=Bm7♭9, E=E9#5, and F#=F#m9♭5 chords are largely theoretical and rarely used as derivatives.

Melodic Minor Superimpositions and Minor Conversion

When the pitch collections of three different melodic minors are applied to a single dominant 7th chord, things really get interesting. It's like combining the benefits of three tonalities into one key. When joined together melodically as superimpositions they attain uniformity, and impart varied color and motion to a particular chord progression.

Consider an altered D7: Apply the fourth mode of melodic minor cited above for D9#11 in Track 284 (third system). That produces an Am melodic minor sound for D7—the first step in minor conversion. The same melody functions as a motive or theme on three D7 altered dominant chords with differing relationships. The motive contains a G# augmented arpeggio (G#–E–C) and stepwise melody.

Play the first chord followed by the motive. Then, play the second chord. The D13#11/C is a quartal voicing for a D7 polychord with an E major triad in its upper structure (on the top three strings). The only altered tone in the chords and melody is the raised 11th, G# (or flatted 5th, A♭). This is the first level of dissonance.

The second sound, D7♭9sus4, is more exotic and represents the second level of dissonance. This is superimposition of a C melodic minor sound on a D root. It can also be seen as building the melodic minor on the D7's seventh step, another minor conversion. In any case, the procedure results in two altered tones, a flatted 9th and raised 9th (E♭ and F), as well as a suspended 4th (G) and 13th (B) in the D7 pitch collection—an interesting sound to say the least. Because it has no major 3rd (F#), but instead a suspended 4th (G), the chord and melody have a harmonically vague, mysterious quality suitable for modal and impressionistic applications. The same motive is played with different note-to-chord relationships. It's comparable to diminished harmony, in which the same information is moved in minor 3rd intervals, but still bears relationship with the underlying chord. Also note that the second chord, D13♭9sus4/E♭, is the same shape as the previous D13#11/C moved a minor 3rd higher, and has a G major triad in its upper structure. Play the chords and melody; listen and compare.

The third level of dissonance is achieved by moving the chords and motive up another minor third. In this configuration, it is called "fully altered" because it contains alterations of the 5th (♭5 and #5) and alterations of the 9th (♭9 and #9)—basically all the available alterations of a dominant 7th chord, in addition to the root, third, and seventh tones. At this level of dissonance, the motive and harmony have the most active and restless quality. They demand resolution to another chord, usually a 4th above: D7 to G (major, minor, or dominant). Bebop players use this form of melodic minor often to create enriched V–I cadence melodies. Regard this superimposition as E♭ melodic minor on a D root or an E♭ melodic minor built on the D7's flatted 9th step as a minor conversion. The final chord is D7#9#5/F#, again bearing the same shape as the previous two forms. Note that it has a B♭ major triad in its upper structure.

157

Conclusion: I describe this phenomenon as *three levels of dissonance.* In jazz, it is a biproduct of melodic minor usage with altered dominant chords. In jazz improvisation, the sounds can be mixed freely depending on the melodic goal of a line. In the previous three phrases, each motive and final chord have a specific sound relative to D7. They are a minor 3rd apart and generate different note-to-chord relationships yet they share the same interval shape. Howard Roberts likened this symmetrical activity to geometry, in guitar terms: using "sonic shapes." With it, a simple working strategy emerges when playing over D7. You have a choice of three distinct colors of melodic minor using the same intervallic shape:

1. A Melodic Minor over D9(13)#11
2. C Melodic Minor over D7(13)♭9sus4
3. E♭ Melodic Minor over D7♭5#5♭9#9

The first is a mild dissonance used often over a dominant II chord in standards and tonal jazz. The second is a more exotic late-bop and post-bop sound with modal tendencies. And the last is a stronger hard-bop color that suits all fully altered dominant chords. The last can be, and often is, played as a tritone substitute for A♭9#11. A♭ is a tritone away from D. Interestingly, the same notes that are altered in D7 are not altered in A♭7 and visa versa. Only the almighty tritone, C–G♭, at the center of both chords is interchangeable. And that's logical. It is the interval that defines the tritone in tritone substitution.

Melodic Minor Vocabulary

This idiomatic melodic minor line in Gm is typically played over tonic minor chords but can also be used to colorize vamps, blues tunes, and modal settings. Listen for the emphasis on E and F# tones in the melody, defining notes in G melodic minor. The cells in brackets (cell 1 and cell 2) are common melodic fragments found in many players' improvisations and compositions. Cell 1 is a favorite of John Coltrane and Pat Martino. Cell 2 was used as a central motive in Sonny Rollins' "Blue Seven"—there as an altered dominant sound.

These melodic minor phrases from the jazz language contain many characteristic patterns and uses of cells. Play and listen for pressure tones E and F# in the melodies as well as chromaticism in Tracks 291–294.

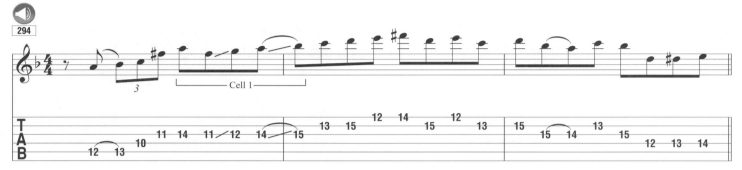

Altered Dominant Vocabulary

The fully altered chord and melodic minor have a close sonic relationship. These lines are based on E♭ melodic minor superimposed on D7. They can be played over D7#9, or A♭13, and can resolve to G major, G7, or Gm, making them extremely valuable as V–I cadence figures in a variety of harmonic situations. Play either D7#9 or A♭13 chords and resolve the line to B, the 3rd of Gmaj7. Listen to the connection and arrival point.

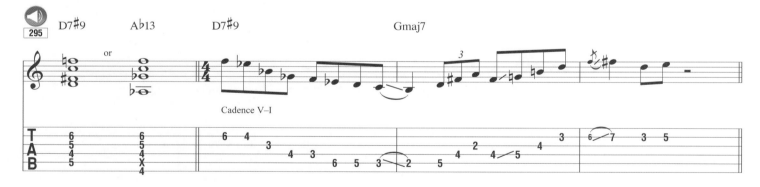

The same cadence can also be directed to a G7 chord. This maneuver is useful as V–I or I–IV in a blues progression.

160

This V–i cadence in G minor uses the melodic minor in E♭m as an altered V, D7♯9, as well as the G melodic minor for the tonic G minor. Here the altered line resolves to B♭, the 3rd of Gm.

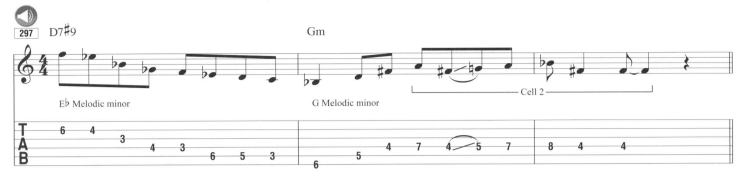

When the altered chord resolves to the fifth tone, D, it can continue from that note to Gmaj7, G7, or Gm. All three chords share the D. This variation uses a melodic cell known as an enclosure to target the D in a Gmaj7 line by enclosing it with chromatic notes.

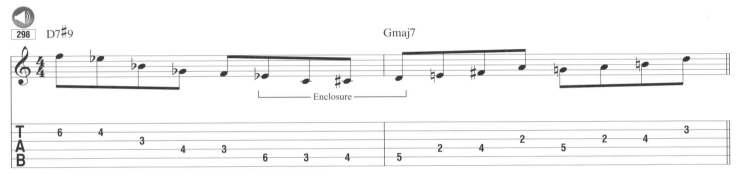

Stepwise motion provides another variation leading to D. This time the resolution is to a G7 blues melody.

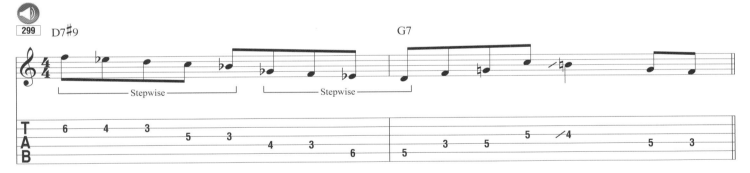

Changing the rhythm and the contour of the melody creates another variation. Note the bebop chromatic triplet figure that approaches the F tone (in D7♯9) from below with chromatic notes. The resolution contains a leap, D to A, the starting tone of cell 2.

The symmetrical nature of the melodic minor prompted John Coltrane to employ its innate whole-tone series for a pattern-oriented phrase over Cm in "Mr. P.C." The exploitation of these four-note groupings is a common strategy for improvising over augmented chords. Trane used the sound for the tonic minor. But you should also try it over an F9#11 chord. That's the strategy pursued by Sonny Rollins in "Blue Seven."

Pat Martino applied the sound of the melodic minor's sonic shapes in this symmetrical sequence from "Close Your Eyes." Note the use of a Bb melodic minor motive moving in minor 3rd increments to Db melodic minor and E melodic minor. This is like playing melodic minor ideas from a diminished perspective. It is played through changes in this phrase, but the horizontal nature and forward motion of the patterns and their imitations supersedes note-to-chord analysis.

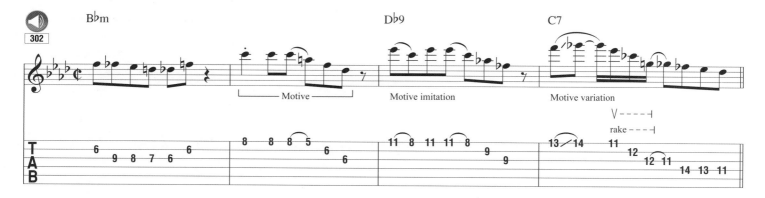

At the core of melodic minor is the augmented chord sound. The G melodic minor scale has three augmented triads based on the scale tones: G–A–Bb–C–D–E–F#–G. Augmented chords are based on equidistant intervals a major 3rd apart. This means there are Bb+, D+, and F#+ triads in the pitch collection, as well as the altered chord D7#5 (D–F#–Bb–C). Any of the augmented triads can be considered a triad in root position.

Wes Montgomery applied this reality in a telling horizontal phrase in "Four on Six." Here, the Bb+ and D+ triads are connected with a similar triad shape, C augmented (C–E–G#), not in the scale but indicative of the whole-tone scale. This creates a symmetrical pattern exploiting sonic shapes that goes in-out-in harmonically over Gm. Wes also used the melodic minor based on Eb (second level of dissonance) to address an F7 altered chord.

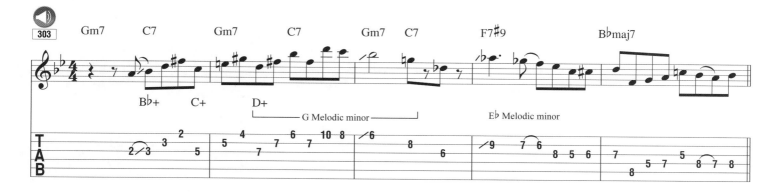

This hard-bop phrase from John Coltrane's solo in "On a Misty Night" (Tadd Dameron, *Mating Call*) illustrates his copious but thoughtful use of the melodic minor sound and stepwise motion over three ii–V progressions. C#m7–F#7 receive only the leading tone portion (C#–B#–C#) of C#m. Cm7–F7 receive a longer line with the full pitch collection. Note the G7 sound of the cell on beat 3. The melody over Fm7 is based on leaps and arpeggio outlines. Note that in all these lines the minor 7th of each m7 chord is replaced with a major 7th leading tone from melodic minor. The use of these ideas over dominant chords are examples of minor conversion and the first level of dissonance.

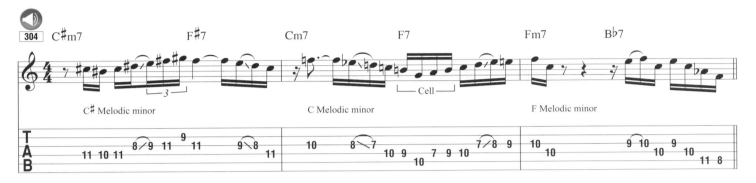

These two Pat Martino lines from "Lazy Bird" occur over an Ebmaj7–D7alt–Gmaj7 progression. They present definitive bop examples of the second and third levels of dissonance. The first phrase, Track 305A, depicts C melodic minor superimposed on D7. The second, Track 305B, poses an Eb melodic minor (fully altered sound) on D7. Note that they begin on a nearly identical Ebmaj7 hexatonic melody with slight rhythmic variation.

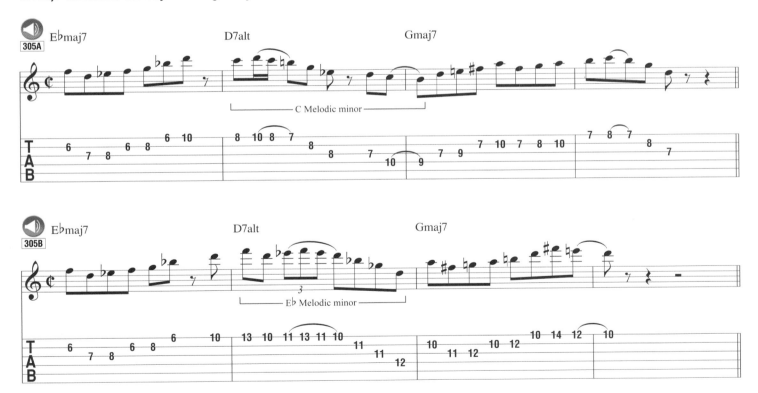

Charlie "Bird" Parker used melodic minor to emphasize the tonic chord in minor modes. This bebop phrase from "Segment" (on the next page) illustrates his approach in the key of Eb minor over a ii–V–i progression: Fm7b5–Bb7–Ebm. Here, he resolves to Eb melodic minor on arrival to the tonic.

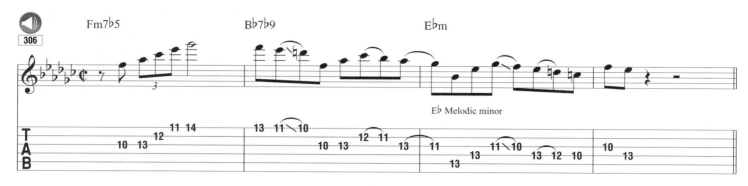

This phrase from "Ballade" is typical of Bird's intricate double-timed lines in slow ballads. He applies the B♭ melodic minor sound to the minor iv chord in a major-mode tune: B♭m in F major. This progression is common in standards and contrafacts based on standard changes. Though it is used as a subdominant sound over B♭m–E♭7 the minor melody has a powerful cadential effect, as if it was a V–I change. Note the mixture of pure stepwise melodic minor with extensive chromaticism and the suggestion of an alternate B♭m7 color on beat 4 of the first measure.

Cannonball Adderley employed melodic minor in modal situations and tunes with a minor tonality. This phrase from "Minority" illustrates his horizontal approach through i–ii–V changes in F minor. The ascending line in measure 1 is textbook melodic minor. The melody in measure 2 contains two cells frequently found in the bebop language, a four-note diatonic pattern of 5–3–2–1 steps and the bebop scale pattern B♭–A–A♭–E. Here, they are inflected with a melodic minor quality. Cannonball deviates momentarily to approach the Gm7 chord with an E♭ passing tone. This in effect connects and completes an F–E–E♭–D line. He returns to melodic minor to set up C7, demonstrating a jazz musician's ability to mix melody sounds in improvisation. The utility of the jazz language allows us to hear the final G tone as the 9th of Fm9 and the 5th of C7.

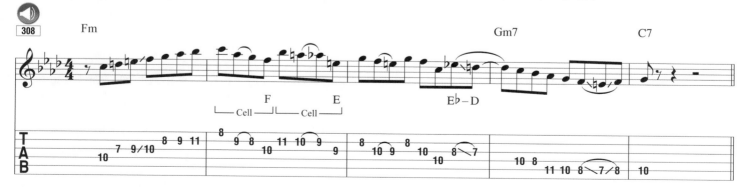

CHAPTER 12

FOUR ESSENTIAL SOUNDS, PART IV: HARMONIC MINOR

Harmonic Minor Basics

The harmonic minor sound is often described as exotic or ethnic. It suggests to many listeners a Middle Eastern or Spanish Flamenco quality, and it has been used specifically for that effect in improvisation and composition across genres. What gives it that sound? Harmonic minor has an unusual structure. Most diatonic scales are made of whole steps and steps. Harmonic minor is the only conventional diatonic scale that contains an *augmented 2nd* interval. That ingredient provides many possibilities. This example illustrates the structure of the harmonic minor scale in C minor.

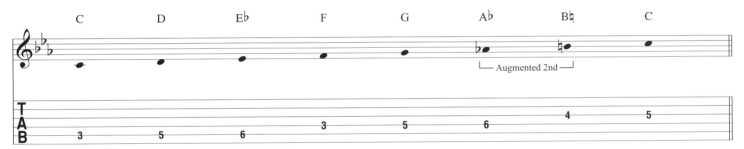

Harmonic minor has great harmonic potential. Besides the conventional harmonies of i, ii, and iv, Cm(maj7), Dm7♭5, and Fm6 (tonic, supertonic, and subdominant minor chords), it has an altered dominant 7th (V) chord, G7♯5♭9, an A♭maj7♯11 (VI), and a colorful, dissonant III chord, E♭maj7♯5, in its tonal center. Harmonic minor has an inherent richness as regards chord colors, however, it is made even more interesting with its naturally occurring diminished and augmented chords.

This example shows, in arpeggio form, augmented chords built on the scale's third, fifth, and seventh degrees (E♭–G–B) and diminished chords built on the second, fourth, sixth, and seventh steps (D–F–A♭–B). Conclusion: There are three augmented triads and four diminished chords in harmonic minor. Both are symmetrical. Both sounds are key dissonances in the jazz language. The sonorities of G7♯5 (based on the augmented triad with a G root—sometimes written as G7♭6 in deference to the scalar source)—and G7♭9 (based on a four-note B°7 chord with a G-root) are of particular interest to jazz musicians.

In jazz, the harmonic minor sound is especially valuable tonally as a ii–V sound. Consider a Dm7♭5–G7 progression in C minor. Both 7th chords are indigenous to the harmonic minor pitch collection: D–E♭–F–G–A♭–B–C and G–A♭–B–C–D–E♭–F. Play these forms and listen to the harmonically active sound of the stepwise melody over Dm7♭5 and D°7. D°7 is the substitution for G7♭9. Note the natural alignment of chord tones on strong beats in the phrase.

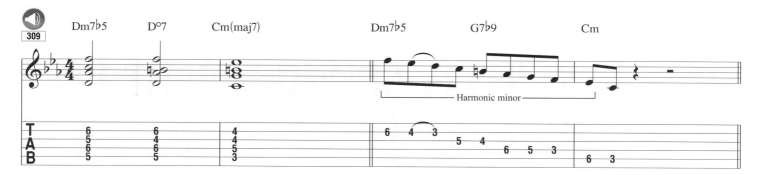

Harmonic-Minor Tonal Melody

The iim7♭5–V progression is found in countless jazz compositions and standards—particularly those in the minor mode. These two lines depict common harmonic minor melodies over the changes. Note the wide leap of B–A♭ that defines G7♭9. This is a natural attribute of the augmented 2nd interval in the scale. Also check out the use of *chromatic passing tones* (CPT) in the melodies. They are played in three-note cell groupings similar to the bebop scale transformations seen in Chapter 3. The phrase ending in Track 310, figure B contains a superimposition of G7 on C minor, typically used as a delayed resolution. It's borrowed from George Benson's solo in "So What." Interestingly, in this case, Benson used the tonal harmonic minor sound but in a modal context.

This next phrase is in the higher register. It exploits a characteristic melody favored by Charlie Parker. The wide leap from the 3rd to ♭9th (B–A♭) followed by stepwise descent played over an altered chord was a fixture of his style. The three-note lower neighbor-tone (LN) figure (B–B♭–B) emphasizing the major 7th, B, on the tonic C minor is an idiomatic melodic embellishment employed by Bird and later exploited by John Coltrane in the hard bop era.

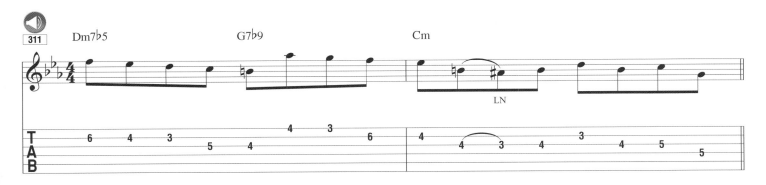

The same melody without the leap can be played stepwise to approach Cm, as in this longer line in the lower register. This phrase ending suggests a blues inflection with the chromatic F–F#–G tones over Cm.

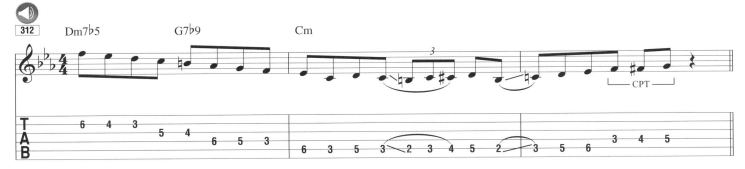

Harmonic minor works well with functional chromatic lines. Here, operative tones in Cm(maj9), D and B, are targeted from below by lower neighbor notes: C#–D and Bb–B. This was a strategy seen in Coltrane's minor melodies.

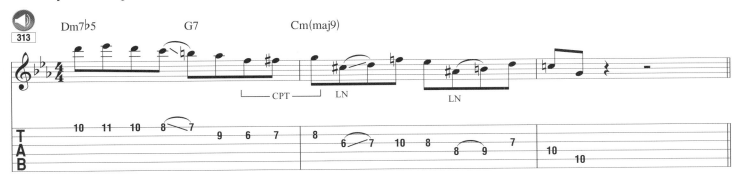

The harmonic attributes of harmonic minor are emphasized in this longer phrase. Note the chord-related outline patterns. The Fm9 arpeggio is used to define Dm7b5 and the Dm7b5 arpeggio is used over G7. Both are approached by chromatic passing-tone cells, as is the 5th of Cm in the resolution.

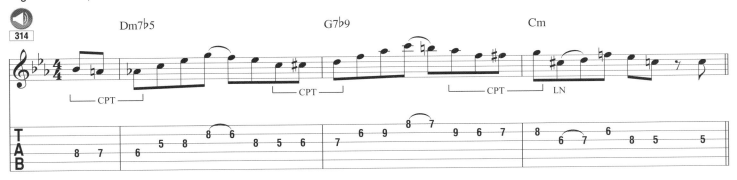

The augmented triad is often combined with the diminished chord to provide a more complex altered sound for G7 (G7b9#5). This phrase exemplifies the symmetry of 3rds-related forms and presents expanded possibilities of harmonic minor. The Dm7b5 is defined by a plural melody that can function as either the ii–V chord change or an Fm7–Bb7 progression. Note the Fm7 arpeggio and passing tones that approach B°7. Over G7 both B°7 and G+ are used in a typical pattern: ascending diminished–descending augmented. (See this in action on the next page.)

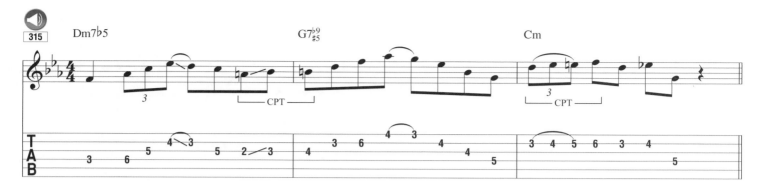

This variation also exploits the 3rds-related symmetry of diminished and augmented chords with one notable change. The B diminished/G augmented pattern has been moved a 3rd higher to produce a D diminished/B augmented pattern and approached with a similar chromatic cell. The phrase ending alludes to the motive of Sonny Rollins' "Blue Seven," which functions well as a tonic minor melody.

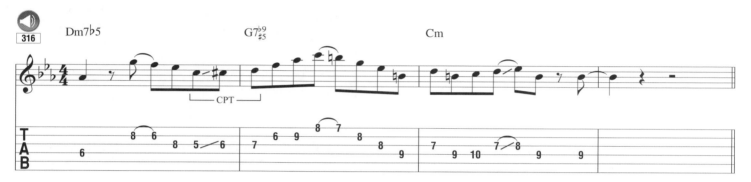

Minor-Mode Combinations

The ii–V–i progression based on harmonic minor is a vital part of the jazz harmony and its melodic language, found in tunes like "Autumn Leaves," "Summertime," "Manhã de Carnaval," "Alone Together," "What Is This Thing Called Love?," "Four on Six," "Hot House," "Airegin," "A Night in Tunisia," and many others. It is paramount that a jazz musician has a firm grasp on the sound and an approach to navigating the changes.

These ii–V–i phrases in E minor are offered as a starting point and could be readily applied to "Autumn Leaves." They contain key elements of harmonic minor in conjunction with altered dominant and tonic minor sounds based on melodic minor. Play and listen for the tonal effect of chord tones on strong beats, different colors of the m7b5 and altered dominant chords, mixtures of arpeggio, stepwise and chromatic motion, and the contrast of alternate but compatible tonic-minor sounds. The goal is to hear and feel them as an integrated whole in a horizontal melody.

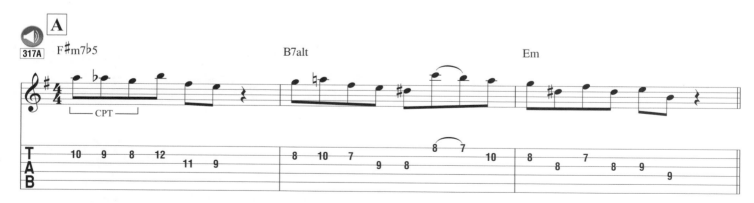

While assimilating the jazz language it is important to transpose music regularly and play your acquired melodies in several keys—and on the guitar, in different positions. Then, find a place in your repertoire where these new versions will reside and be performed as part of your statement. Practice the lines with the intent of attaching them to a particular set of changes in a variety of tunes. "Autumn Leaves" is often played in the alternate key of G minor. These ii–V–i phrases are in G minor and demonstrate several different combinations.

These ii–V–i phrases are in F minor. Listen for different colors and substitutions. The Fm pentatonic is used for the i chord in Track 319, figure A, which gives it a modal or bluesy quality and a nice contrast to a normally expected tonal melody. The Gm7♭5 in figure B is made more interesting with a B♭ melodic minor substitution line. In figure C, the melody is expanded with a stepwise, whole-step/half-step diminished run, another substitution over the Gm7♭5. A zigzagging Coltrane pattern, using lower and upper neighbor (UN) notes, decorates the phrase ending. Try using these lines in "Airegin" and "Hot House."

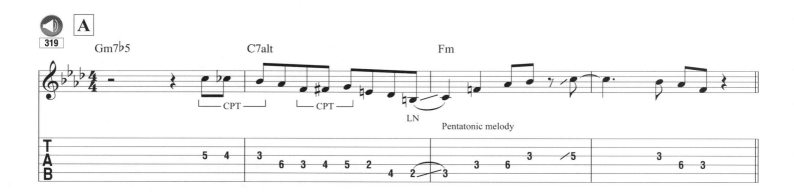

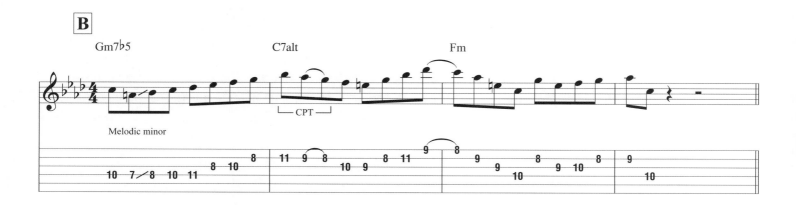

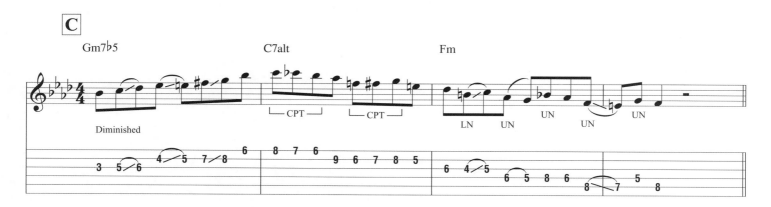

The sound of minor conversion is developed in these D minor phrases. Here, the ii chord, Em7♭5, is defined by converted Gm lines that resolve to the A7 chord sound. The connections make use of chromatic tones in Track 320, figures A and C, a Gm7 superimposition and delayed resolution in figure B, and a leading tone, C–C♯, in figure D. The lines all cadence on various Dm6 melodies to establish the tonic minor. They are based on a combination of the D harmonic and melodic minor sounds.

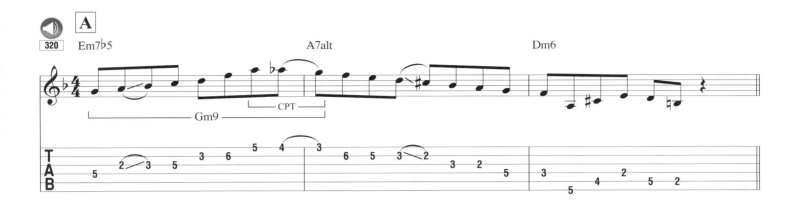

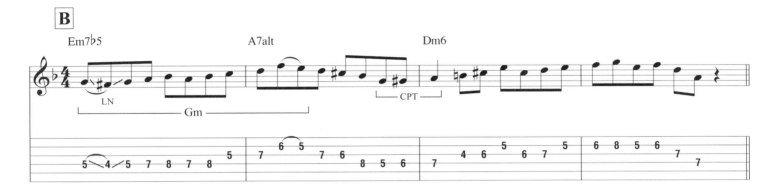

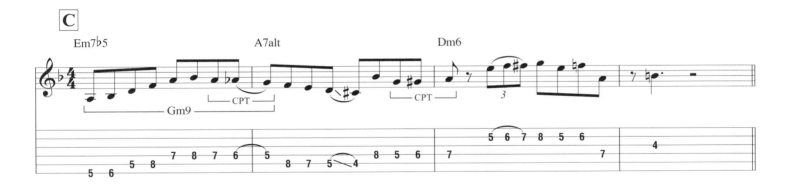

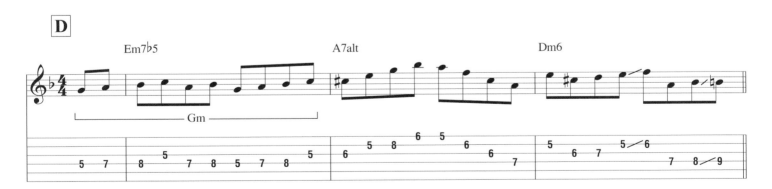

WOLF MARSHALL'S **JAZZ GUITAR COURSE**

Minor Modes and Deceptive Cadences

The harmonic minor ii–V–i is sometimes subjected to a deceptive cadence. In tunes like "Hot House," "What Is This Thing Called Love?," "Alone Together," "Stella by Starlight," "Night and Day," and "Once I Loved," an *evaded cadence* is used to imply one type of resolution, but it evades that expectation and actually goes somewhere else. There, a minor ii–V unexpectedly cadences on a parallel-major sound. These phrases demonstrate the process of *majorizing* the tonic-minor melody of several previous examples. Note that the melody in Track 322 retains the C+ arpeggio from C7alt on the F major chord. The resolution is delayed until beat 3 and the line is not majorized until that point. Play these modified versions and listen for the new major tonal center of F major for the I chord.

172

A minor-mode melody often requires more than just a simple parallel-major transposition. In some cases, "massaging" and even reworking the melody notes is necessary to produce a more satisfying idiomatic line. In this example, a G tone acts as the lower neighbor of G#, the major 3rd of E major, and the phrase ending is a chromatic, major-blues line with the same time span and rhythmic structure.

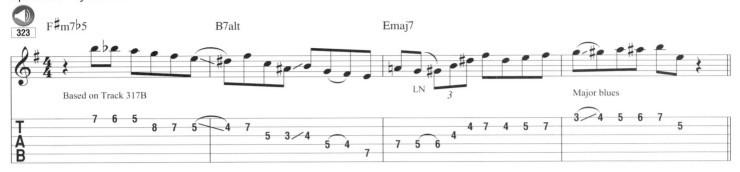

In this variation, the evaded cadence to G proceeds logically from a pedal-tone pattern begun in D7. However, the phrase ending substitutes a Gmaj7 hexatonic line with skips for the straight majorized stepwise melody. With practice and the acquisition of more vocabulary, decisions like this are made spontaneously "on the fly."

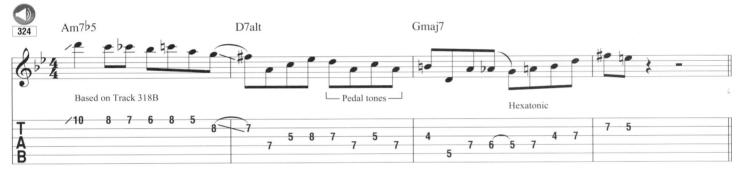

In the heat of improvisation, other adaptations take place. This majorized version maintains the bluesy spirit of the previous minor-pentatonic melody, but it replaces the line with a shortened variation along with slight rhythmic and contour changes.

This phrase doesn't revert to a majorized version until the second measure of Dmaj7. That's the beauty of the jazz language and the horizontal nature of its melodies, versus technical or theoretical scalar constructs. Common tones, melodic content, and logic supersede academic regulation. Again, the rhythm structure of the melody and its contours are retained for a line with the same feel and time span.

Minor-Mode Vocabulary

Countless jazz musicians have applied harmonic minor and the mixing of minor modes in novel and highly personal ways. This selected group of examples demonstrate typical expressions and situations in the repertoire.

Freddie Hubbard, "Moanin'" (live 1962 TV show with Jazz Messengers)

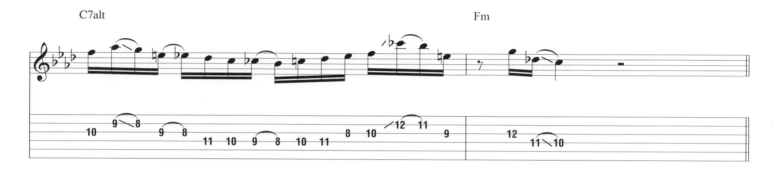

Wes Montgomery, "If I Should Lose You"

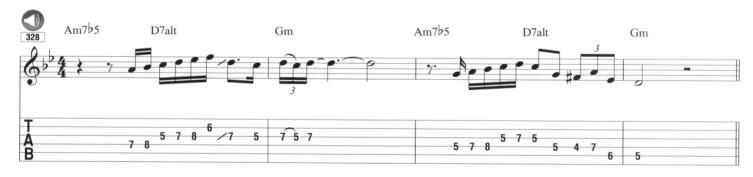

John Coltrane, "In Your Own Sweet Way"

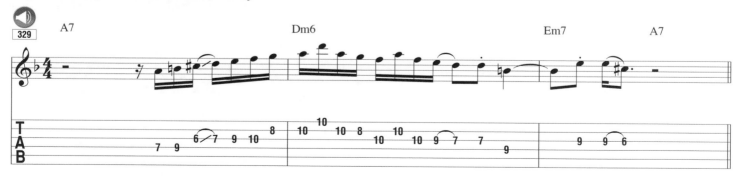

Wes Montgomery, "Come Rain or Come Shine"

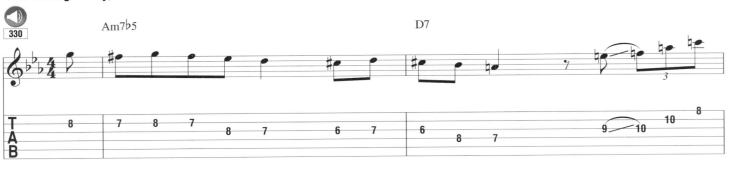

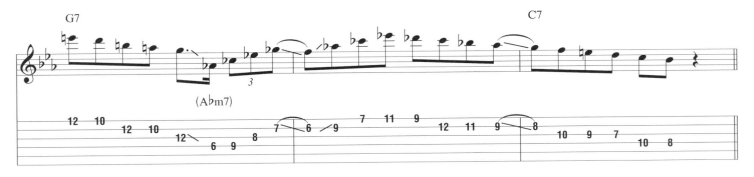

Vincent Herring, "Days of Wine and Roses"

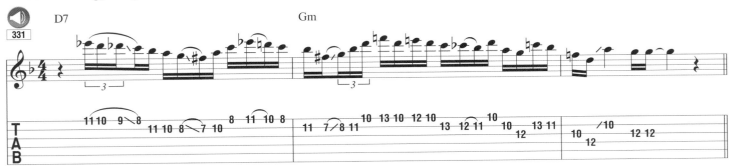

John Coltrane, "Mr. P.C."

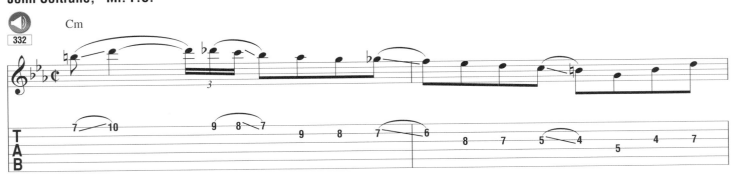

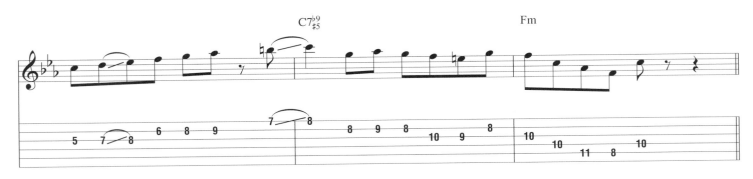

Pat Metheny, "Naked Moon"

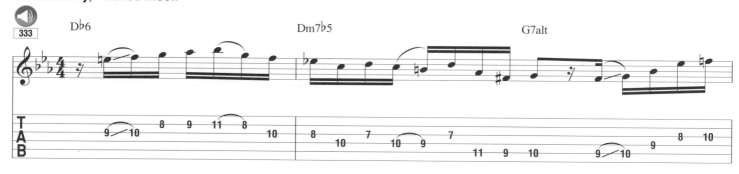

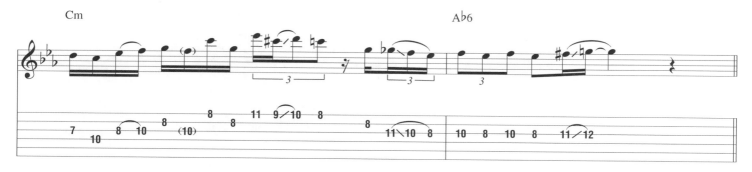

Pat Martino, "Alone Together"

Charlie Parker, "Diverse"

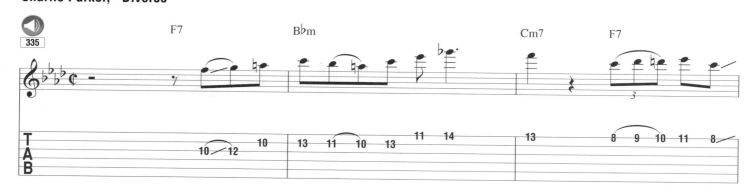

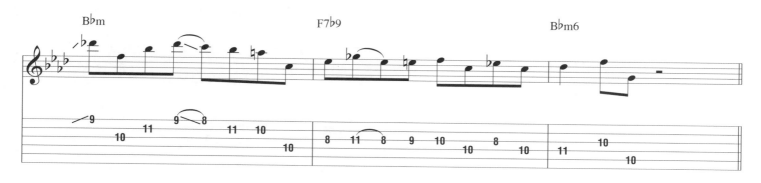

Charlie Parker, "What Is This Thing Called Love?"

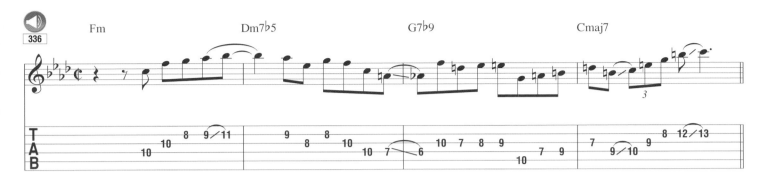

Charlie Parker, "A Night in Tunisia"

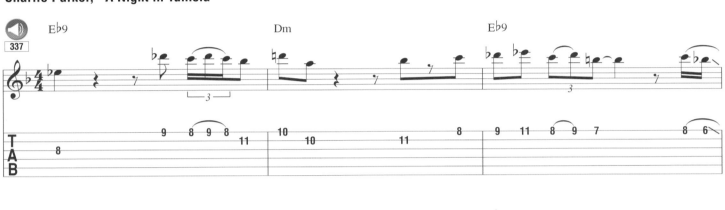

CHAPTER 13

BLUES MELODY

Blues Basics

Since its inception, jazz has enjoyed a close relationship with the blues. The blues ethic and its melodic/harmonic feeling are at the heart of much jazz. Consider some of the genre's greatest compositions of the last 90 years. "Mood Indigo," "Killer Joe," "Moanin'," and "Adam's Apple" evoke different eras and are not traditional blues tunes but are filled with blues feeling. The same principle holds true for standards like "Angel Eyes," "Stormy Weather," and "Cry Me a River." Much of that feeling comes from the composers' use of blues melody.

The Blues Scale

An explanation of blues melody begins with the blues scale. The classic blues scale is comprised of six notes. In G, the notes are: G–B♭–C–C♯/D♭–D–F. This example shows a G blues scale in descending motion. Note the minor 7th, F, and minor 3rd, B♭, as well as the flatted 5th (or raised 4th) in its structure. The latter two tones are often referred to as "blue notes."

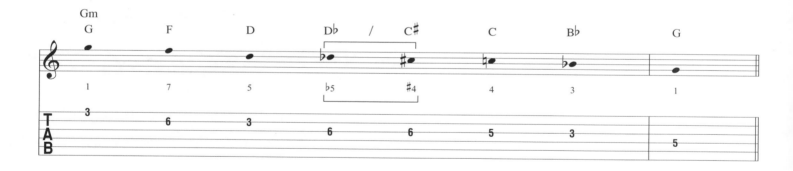

Playing a two-octave version of the scale in triplet rhythm produces an idiomatic stepwise blues melody.

With its minor 3rd and minor 7th tones, a blues scale conveys a minor sound. Consequently, many musicians have applied the blues scale to a minor tonality or a minor-blues tune. Pieces like "Birk's Works," "Midnight Blue," and "Mr. P.C." are emblematic. This phrase illustrates two common motives in a typical blues expression.

The blues scale is closely related to a minor pentatonic scale. It is essentially a minor pentatonic with an added flatted 5th or raised 4th tone. This simple melody is a requisite blues cliché. Note the quarter-step bend on the final note, a typical embellishment of a blues melody.

Adding the flatted 5th and applying triplet rhythms transforms the pentatonic melody into a deeper blues line.

Blues Melody

Harmonically, the blues sound is distinguished by its minor/major polarity. In traditional blues, a minor pentatonic or blues scale melody is played over a dominant 7th chord. Blues polarity is manifested in lines that combine minor and major sounds. This combination is often paired with blues scale melodies. A blues phrase may begin with a minor sound and end with a major sound. The polarity emphasizes the major 3rd of a dominant 7th chord yet still maintains the important underlying minor mood of the blues.

These blues phrases in G illustrate the minor-major polarity. Each is linked with an enriched dominant 7th chord commonly found in blues harmony. Play and listen to the blues scale melody, use of flatted 5th/raised 4th, and the blend of major and minor 3rds—and how they are reconciled with a G7-based sonority.

Swing Blues

In addition to the major 3rd, the 2nd and 6th degrees are often added as color notes producing an enrichment of blues melody. These are heard as 9th and 13th dissonances, found in the upper part of a dominant chord. The sound is sometimes referred to as "swing blues," because it predictably has its origins in the swing era—where those milder dissonances were prevalent. However, it has remained a common ingredient in jazz. Several notable jazz-blues standards, like Charlie Parker's "Billie's Bounce" and Sonny Rollins' "Tenor Madness," exploit the sound prominently in their themes.

This Charlie Parker phrase exemplifies a swing-blues melody realized from the bebop perspective. It contains a major-3rd addition to the blues scale and idiomatic use of a notable chromatic motive. This seven-note ascending chromatic line was heard in Track 342, figures B and D. In this melodic/rhythmic configuration it is associated with Bird's solos in "Billie's Bounce" and "Now's the Time." Because it lacks the seventh tone, it can be and is played as a major-chord sound in standard songs to impart a bluesy mood.

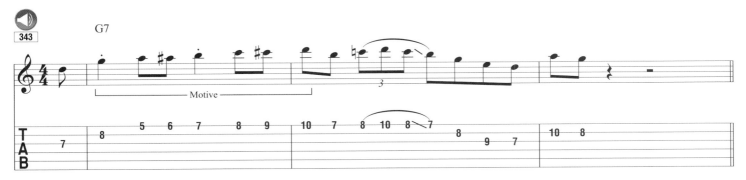

Charlie Christian embodied swing blues. This phrase from "Wholly Cats" begins with a central theme of blues music: Riff-based repetition of simple memorable cells. The string of eighth notes that follow in measures 3–4 contains the 6th and 9th tones as well as chromatic passing tones and a Dm extended arpeggio outline over G7.

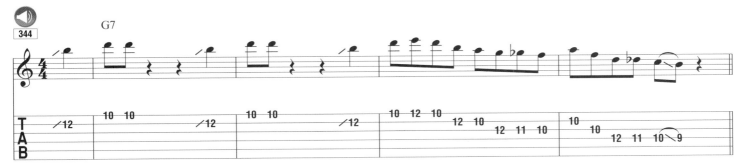

Kenny Burrell was influenced by swing, blues, bebop, and modern jazz. This line from "All Night Long" is played over a I–IV–I progression (measures 4–7) of a 12-bar blues in G. Check out the use of a G melodic minor sound over C7. It naturally produces a 9th and 13th (D and A) in the melody, but also the raised 11th, F#. The cadence melody contains a more traditional sixth tone over G7.

Hank Garland was fond of mixing overt blues scale sounds with swing melodies. This phrase from "Riot-Chous" demonstrates a characteristic line over I–IV–I changes (measures 2–7) of a B♭ blues. The practice of replacing the minor 7th tone A♭ with the 6th, G, to expand the blues scale is a swing gesture heard throughout. Also check out the toggling effect of the blue note E acting as a neighbor tone to F. The repetitions of similar melody lines over B♭7 and E♭7 typify the development of a common blues theme maintained through both chords.

John Coltrane applied some of the same elements during his harmonically ambitious phase in the early 1960s. This line from "Some Other Blues" is exemplary. Note the use of an interval-leaping cell, seen in Track 342, figure B, as well as the bebop scale over both F7 and B♭7. The final melody contains an added 6th and 7th tone in conjunction with B♭m pentatonic.

Blues Cadence Lines

The I–IV Cadence

In jazz, there are three important cadences in the 12-bar blues form, and they often affect the way a player interprets the changes melodically. Of primary importance is the I–IV progression that occurs in measures 4–5 of the form. This is the point at which many jazz performers apply more color and tension to the I chord, and create momentum into the change to IV. Devices like extended chords, superimpositions, alterations, substitutions, and a greater amount of dissonance are heard in this part of the progression.

The lines on the next page present several typical approaches to the I–IV change in A. Play, listen, assimilate the melodic language, and then transpose them to the common jazz keys of B♭, F, E♭, A♭, D♭, and G.

The A7 chord is colored with extended and substitution arpeggios: Em7 and C#°7. This effectively creates an A9–A7♭9 sound on the I chord as it cadences to IV, D7.

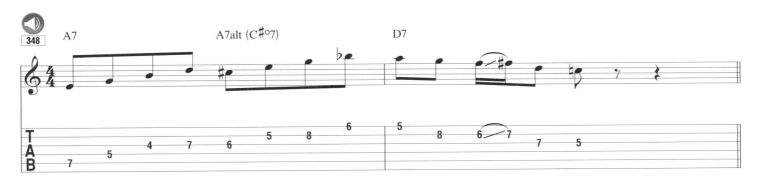

These lines are played in 16th notes—allowing for more melodic information and double-timed rhythm, both of which generate urgency in the chord change. The C#°7 melody contains stepwise motion plus an arpeggio, and emphasizes altered tones. Note the connections to different chord tones, the F# and A of D7.

The next group of phrases all begin with a simple swing-blues motive on the A7 chord. Note the use of the 6th in the melody. The idea is to apply different altered and substitution sounds as variants after the opening thought. Play the lines and listen to the possible colors. With practice, selecting a departure point by ear "on the fly" becomes an instinctive reflex, facilitating a greater command of the elements during improvisation.

These two phrases superimpose a Gm arpeggio on A7 creating different alterations, an A7♭9sus4 sound. The second example contains a delayed resolution on beat 3 of the D7 bar. It targets the A of a D7 chord.

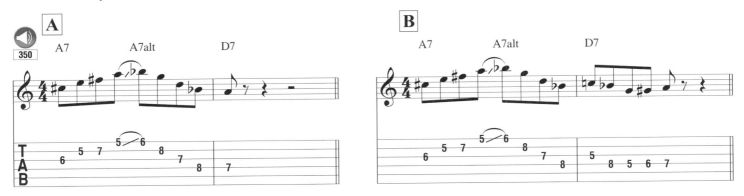

These two phrases exploit a B♭ minor substitution, producing more altered A7 sounds. Note the use of B♭ melodic minor in the second example. The line can also be heard as an E♭9#11 tritone substitution.

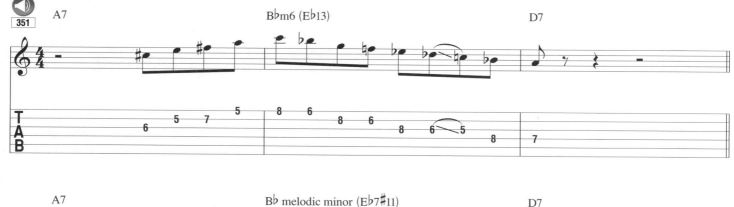

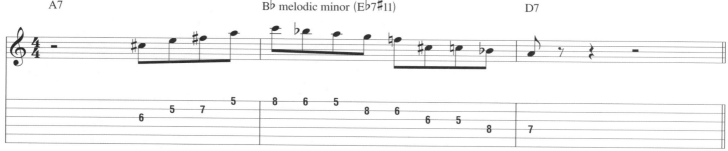

This phrase explicitly superimposes an E♭7 dominant sound on A7. Note the use of a transposed bebop scale line, which yields greater chromaticism and dissonance. Listen for a side-slipping, inside-outside-inside effect, similar to Wes Montgomery's transitional lines in "West Coast Blues."

These two examples contain common approaches to altered-dominant sounds using B♭m6 substitutions for A7. Note the Em9 arpeggios beginning the phrases and the different connections to the F# and A of a D7 chord.

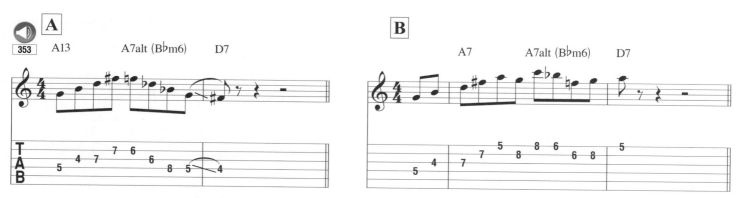

The I–VI7 Cadence

The VI–ii progression found in measures 8–9 of the 12-bar form is another important cadence. This is a common harmonic refinement in jazz-blues not typically heard in traditional blues. (See Chapter 3.) At this point in the form the melody reflects the changes. It moves away from the I chord in measure 7 to modulate to a ii chord in measure 9 via its secondary dominant, the VI7 or V of ii. In A, this progression is A–F#7alt–Bm7. The VI7 chord is usually altered to emphasize the tonality of the new key—here, that of the ii chord. The amount of alteration can vary from mild but dissonant to extremely dissonant and may involve a substitution. Typically, a harmonic minor sound and its altered dominant 7th chord containing ♭9 and #5 tones, G and D, would be applied to prepare motion to the minor mode, F#7(♭9#5) to Bm7. Note that these tones are shared enharmonic equivalents of A7 and F#7. In an A7 chord, they are the seventh and fourth tones. See Chapter 5 for details about the harmonic minor sound.

These phrases present various jazz-language melodies that define I–VI7–ii changes in the blues. Here, chords are added to the melodies. These emphasize the point of arrival to the ii chord and can also be effective as "chord punches" within improvisation. Play, listen, and note the different colors of F#7alt and how they resolve to Bm7. Then, transpose to other keys.

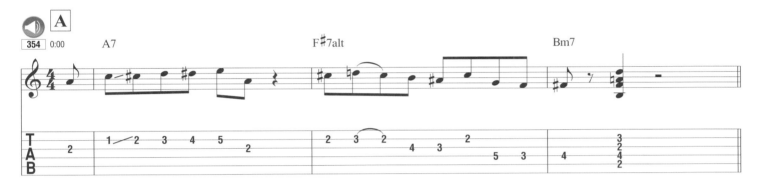

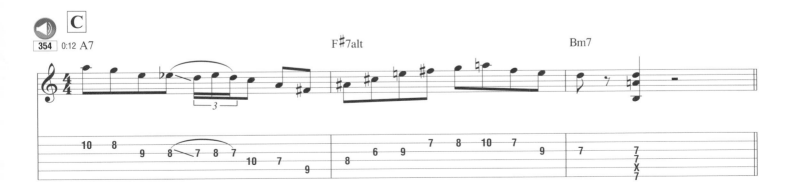

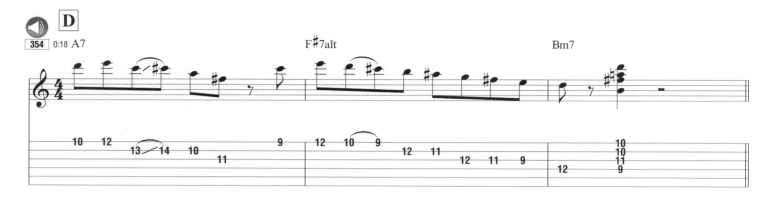

The V–I Cadence

The return to the I chord, A7, in measure 11 is commonly established with a strong harmonic sound over the preceding V chord, E7. Interestingly, the I–IV lines from Tracks 349–353 can be repurposed to fit the homeward-bound progression. These two phrases, originally Tracks 349 and 350 (figure A), played as I–IV (A7–D7), demonstrate the idea as a V–I sound: E7–A7. Play and listen to the sound of extended and altered melodies resolving to the tonic.

*T = Thumb on 6th string

This idiomatic phrase exploits the extended-chord sound of Bm11 on E7. It includes a progression of descending chords to complete the thought and form a turnaround pattern.

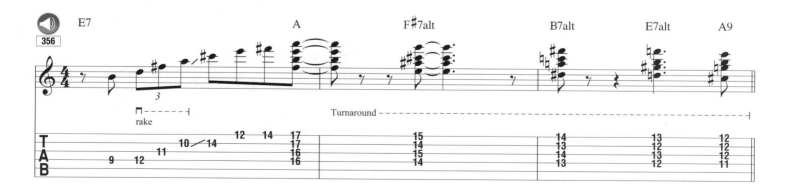

By contrast, this phrase emphasizes the diminished sound over an altered E7.

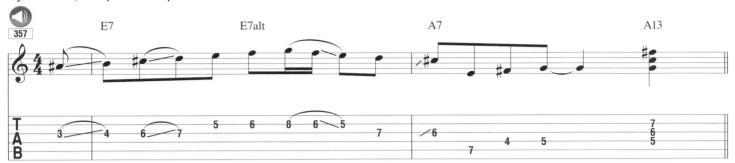

Call-and-Response Phrases

In traditional and modern blues, call-and-response phrases are important ingredients. Historically, blues phraseology is epitomized by melodies that answer each other in a dialoguing fashion. This group of phrases is based on Cannonball Adderley's call-and-response statements in "Barefoot Sunday Blues." Note the similar rhythmic structures and placement of melodies as well as the variation in the second call.

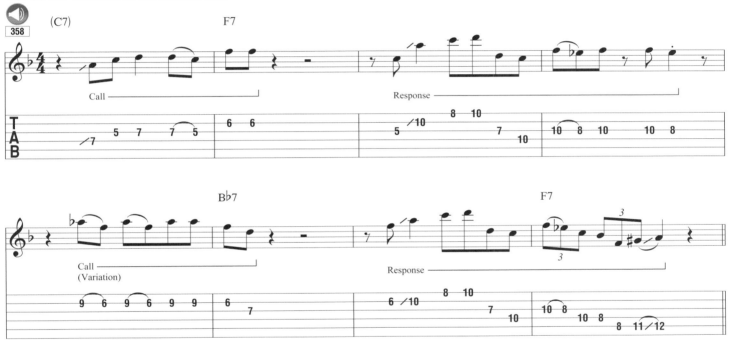

Call-and-response phraseology can be applied to the most modern blues settings. This telling example is based on McCoy Tyner's "Blues on the Corner." Note the riff-oriented phrase structure of simple imitative motives on the Bb7 and Eb7 chords. The final line is a very modern pattern made of 4th leaps arranged in whole tones. It depicts the idea of introducing a contrasting melody as the second response phrase.

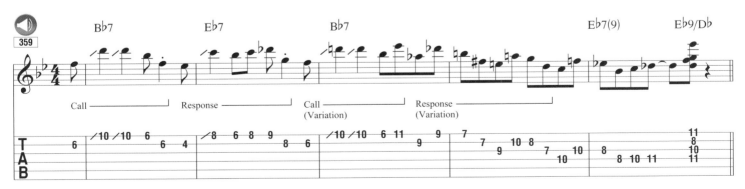

Many blues performances contain characteristic call-and-response phraseology. In your ongoing acquisition of sounds and ear training, listen for and strive to identify call-and-response melodies in conventional 12-bar blues tunes as well as standards and jazz compositions.

INTERMISSION

You've reached a milestone. Take a moment to pause, evaluate your progress, and consider your expectations. You have the essential tools—what Pat Martino called "the components from which music is made." You have ideas and insights gleaned and conveyed from my personal interaction with the masters—that includes sax players Jimmy Heath and Benny Golson in addition to the requisite guitar sources. You have many transcribed examples documenting and demonstrating notable jazz performers' usage of these components as functional vocabulary. Most importantly, you have the sounds. With regular repeated listening to key players cited here, your sense of musical perception improves, along with your ear, and the topics given as scholarly steps take on a living, transcendent quality and gain traction in your playing.

Your work ahead involves both the acquisition and assimilation stages of learning with the intention they will coalesce as mastery and innovation. Acquisition is the lifelong process of adding material to your vocabulary. Assimilation occurs through cultivating and implementing good habits following acquisition. Habits are made through the repetition of sounds in tandem with physical motor skills, be they chord or single-note expressions. Small chunks and parts of phrases must be isolated, studied, understood, memorized, played slowly and precisely, and practiced regularly so they'll become instinctual and prompt innovation. Ten minutes of focused practice is better than an hour of pointless rambling. Strive to balance and integrate the intuitive, instinctive side of your brain with the deliberate, calculating side. Your ear is the arbiter. If it sounds good, it is good. That tenet's been proven throughout jazz history—often to the consternation of incredulous bystanders.

The next step is to address the goal of fashioning your personal statement in real time. Improvisation, in group performance or solo, is the act of responding to the musical environment with confidence in the moment, in the process automatically shaping your materials into a coherent form that embodies your message. This doesn't just happen. It begins with perseverance in mastering the fundamentals of the craft and then actively pursuing creativity, not as an abstraction but a definite and clearcut agenda in the practice room. In the next section, you'll receive tools and suggestions to achieve this goal. You'll personalize and expand your expression beyond the basics through application of idiosyncratic embellishments, patterns and thematic development, and variation as reliable procedures. You'll increase your collection of sounds with new colloquialisms like turnaround cycles and over 100 ii–V–I phrases. You'll put it all together in model solos, the point at which an extemporaneous sketch becomes an improvised statement.

Someone brilliant once said of *individuality*: "Everything's been said (played) before; it just hasn't been said (played) by every-body." That could easily refer to speaking the jazz language. Remember, you always have something new and interesting to say/play if that's your priority. Kenny Burrell stressed this aspect of the jazz message with the final conclusion: "Be Yourself." But be the best and most interesting self you can be.

PART III:
IMPROVISATION

CHAPTER 14

PATTERNS AND ORNAMENTS

Music is a language; that's a guiding principle of this course. In the jazz dialect, the combination of melody, rhythm, and harmony supersedes scales, much like interesting stories supersede grammar books and spelling contests. Let's look deeper into the music-as-a-language analogy and begin with the smallest elements. Notes are like letters of the alphabet. Arpeggios, melodic cells, nuclear motives, and short patterns are words. Phrases and licks are sentences. Groups of phrases make points, develop themes, and convey the message of the storyteller. A memorable improvisation is like an inspiring extemporaneous speech. When meaningful content is conveyed with the decorative nuances, timing and delivery (rhythm), dramatic flourishes, and expressiveness of a gifted orator, the speech is transcendent, just like a Charlie Parker or Wes Montgomery solo.

When the raw materials of stepwise melody and arpeggios have been assembled, practiced, and internalized, you have completed the spelling phase. The next phase, covered in the previous chapters on essential sounds, necessitates acquiring and expanding vocabulary. Then, the fun begins: the task of repurposing acquired resources creatively to fashion and improve your musical storytelling. This phase involves using tools like patterns, embellishment, and thematic development.

Patterns

Patterns play a vital role in melody making. In the creation of a melody line or the combination of melodic segments and phrases forming an entire solo, patterns are at the core of what a player recalls, responds with and performs, and what is heard as spontaneous. Like traditional composition, improvisation is initially learned as a craft. The source material for the craft can come from the melody of the tune used or different tunes altogether, from the harmonic inferences of a chord progression, from the work of influential musicians gleaned through oral tradition or transcribing, or from the pursuit of pattern practice and development in personal study.

The command of patterns involves physical, intellectual, and, most importantly, *aural* habits. The emphasis on listening to what you play as you learn and practice is invaluable, as is the ability to apply favored habits in the heat of the moment during improvisation. An effective improviser must develop the ability to pre-hear where an upcoming musical event will occur. What the pre-heard patterns are and how and where they are recalled and applied to make melody is what differentiates one player's expression from another.

Patterns and Cells

Patterns are melodies with certain fixed elements that serve as the basis for repetition, variation, and development. You hear a good musical idea, you want to hear it again—maybe with a little different spin? This can mean elements that are repeated exactly, with slight changes, or as intricately developed themes. An understanding of patterns in jazz begins with building a pattern from a simple cell. Consider the first three notes of a major diatonic, pentatonic, or hexatonic scale—three notes a whole step apart. In C: C–D–E. This simple stepwise structure can produce a variety of patterns. Two initial choices are: 1) the cell intact as a three-note pattern; or 2) the cell reordered and expanded to create a four-note pattern.

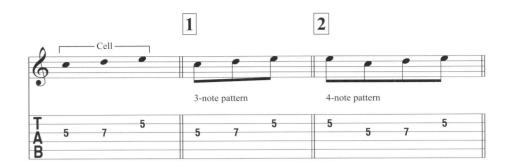

Pat Martino, a master of pattern manipulation in jazz, used a three-note cell based on these intervals to generate a long and exciting chromatic line through chord changes in his solo in "Lazy Bird." The three-note cell is repeated and moved chromatically to form a pattern. It is played in straight eighth-note rhythm in 4/4 meter, which has two eighth notes to a beat. This causes a three-against-four *rhythmic displacement* in every other pattern repetition, through an alternation of the cell on accented strong (down) and weak (up) beats. This technique underscores the importance of rhythm in jazz and generates an interesting *tension-and-release* effect during the time span of a phrase.

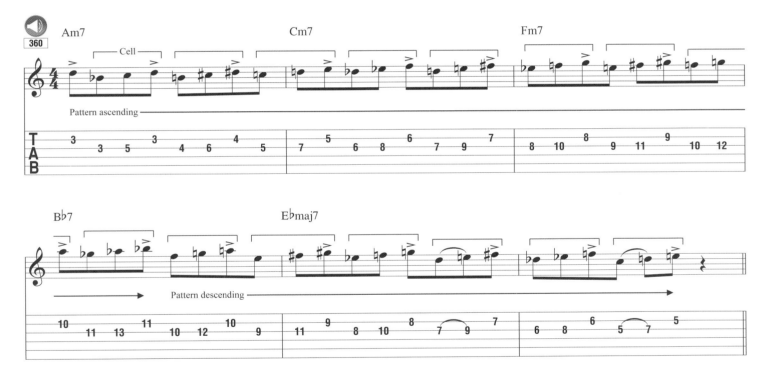

This is the epitome of a pattern's horizontal motion dominating a melody. Many of the notes don't necessarily align with chord tones vertically, and several are downright incongruous. Why does it work? Robben Ford put it succinctly: "Some patterns break a lot of rules, but work because repetition creates its own logic." (*Guitar Edge*, January 2003). Pat himself summed it up this way: "No bad notes, just bad connections."

The same pattern is also played more conventionally in straight, descending motion as on-the-beat triplets. This line from Pat Martino's "Little Shannon" solo (*Opus De Don*) demonstrates the idea as a chromatic approach figure to the iv chord, Gm, in a D minor blues. (Turn to the next page to see this in action.)

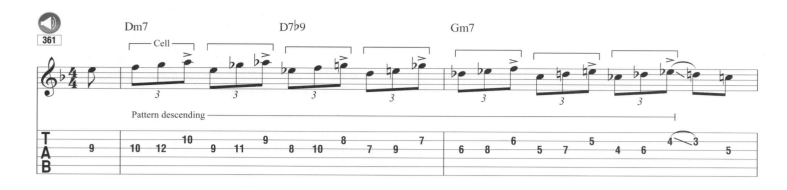

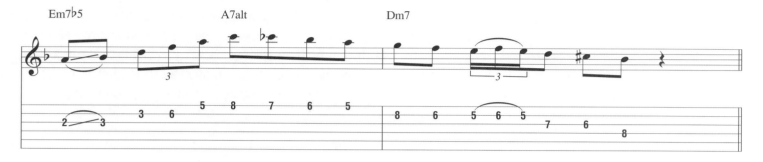

This line illustrates rhythmic manipulation of a repeated cell and the use of *side-slipping*, the technique of moving material a half step. In this type of application, the pattern takes on a greater meaning and becomes a motive or theme.

Patterns and Sequences

The *sequence* is often used to develop a pattern. A sequence is the repetition of a cell, pattern or motive at a higher or lower pitch. It usually moves in one direction on steps of a diatonic scale. For example, an ascending pattern begun on C will generally continue on D, E, F, and so on. This sequential phrase is an exercise based on the four-note pattern in the first figure of this chapter. It demonstrates a common mechanical practice phrase used by many musicians. The skip in the pattern allows the sequence to be used to outline different chords in the key of C major. Listen to the sequence and notice its activity, which creates the impression of moving through chord changes in ascending steps.

A sequence is usually *goal-directed* and represents the simplest type of melodic development. Typically, when developing a theme in improvisation or composition, a sequence contains three segments. The first states the pattern, the second restates the pattern on another step—commencing the sequence activity with imitation—and the 3rd (sometimes the 4th) completes the sequence on another step and progresses to another idea, the goal.

This Vincent Herring phrase from "Triste" illustrates the sequence principle in microcosm in an improvised solo. It exploits a very simple cell, the tones of a B♭ major arpeggio (B♭–D–F). Notice the activity: pattern statement on F and pattern restatement on the next step of the arpeggio, B♭. The third segment, begun on D, is the goal and becomes a variation moving to another melody.

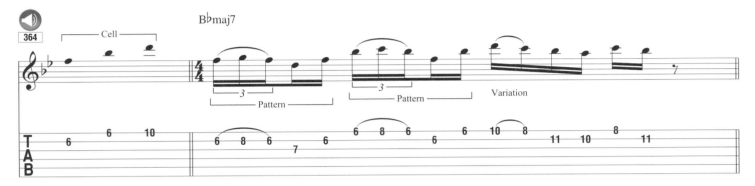

A sequence can stay in the same tonal center or mode, outline chromatic changes, or modulate to other keys. Consider this phrase, a mixture of tonal and modal patterns, used by John Coltrane to begin his solo in "Mr. P.C." It begins with a four-note pickup figure implying G7 that establishes the rhythm group for each cell. The next three cells are modal but contain chromatic neighbor tones. They ascend and are sequenced on diatonic steps in C minor.

Improvisation is akin to a living organism. Consider melody on a molecular level. A note is like an atom. Two or more atoms grouped together form molecules or the smallest identifiable particle. Molecules become cells that are the smallest *functional* unit of an organism. In different combinations specialized results are produced in the form of skin cells, bones, organs, connective tissue, and so on. In the music analogy, cells can be combined and developed to become longer patterns, motives, or themes. This set of chord-related intervals (3rds) or molecules defines the patterns and guides the harmonic thinking behind John Coltrane's sequence.

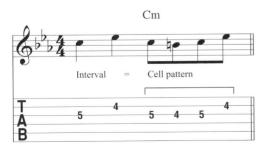

In jazz improvisation, a sequence is often used to outline chord changes. This Joe Pass phrase from "Django" exemplifies the idea. It is a *modulating sequence* based on moving through a cycle-of-4ths progression: C7–F7–Bb7–Eb7–Ab7. Notice that the longer sequence pattern consists of two cells: pattern 1, stepwise descent to the 3rd of a chord; and pattern 2, an ascending leap (highlighting the flatted 9th of a chord) and descending stepwise motion rejoining pattern 1. This type of sequence has a strong tonal sound suitable for cycle progressions and conveys a classical impression with its logic and contours.

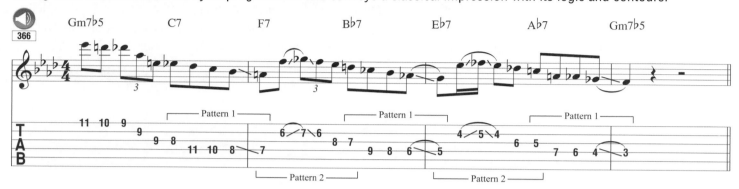

Many jazz musicians use four-note groupings to define chord changes. This sequential phrase from Joe Pass' "Django" solo illustrates the motion. Each cell is a four-note group of steps 1–2–3–5, sometimes called a "pentatonic pattern" because they are the first four notes of a major pentatonic scale. These cells typically define major or dominant 7th chords, and are found routinely in the improvisations of John Coltrane, Cannonball Adderley, and McCoy Tyner. This modulating sequence is based on a repeated cell played in three consecutive iterations. It gives way to contrasting lines over Ab7 (stepwise descent) and Db7 (a leap and stepwise ascent). The sequence outlines F7, Bb7, and Eb7 chords of a cycle progression. A very specific ascending pattern is produced.

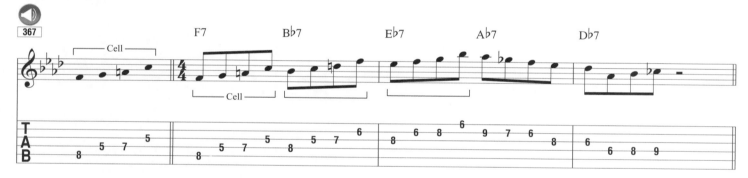

Patterns and Ostinato

Short melodic phrases are often repeated verbatim to produce rhythmic tension through persistence. This type of pattern is called *ostinato* (Italian: obstinate or stubborn), or the colloquial term, *riff* (repeated figure). It is a very effective and unifying tactic employed by musicians of many genres. Though it's static, the constant repetition of a simple pattern can generate a lot of music, especially when extended past the stage of a predictable phrase ending. George Benson used an ostinato built from a three-note cell (G–A#–B) to generate activity into the sixth chorus of "Clockwise."

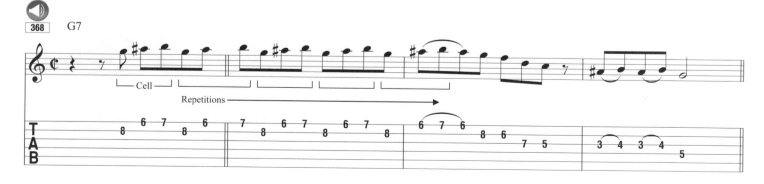

194

Pat Martino used ostinatos regularly in his improvisations. This phrase from "The Great Stream" is based on a repeated three-note cell (C–E♭–F) played over B♭7 and C7. As in Benson's application, the ostinato poses three-note groups over a pulse in 4 or 2 (4/4 or 2/2). This subjects the ostinato to rhythmic displacement, which heightens the tension.

Ostinatos are even more effective rhythmically and musically interesting when changes are made in the pattern. This Pat Martino phrase from "The Great Stream" is an example of an ostinato with several variations. The underlying pattern is constructed from a D♭m9 arpeggio melody. Only the last two statements are identical. Listen for the expanding and contracting effect of playing an ostinato with slightly different time spans and rhythmic placement.

Patterns and Pedal Tones

A pedal tone is a form of melodic repetition. In a typical application, a repeated note is re-articulated below or above other parts of a moving melody. Consider this demonstrative pedal-tone phrase based on a pattern from John Coltrane's solo in "My Favorite Things." It alternates diatonic notes in E major under a high B pedal tone and is played over an Emaj7–F#m7 vamp. Notice the *hemiola* effect of a two-note pattern within steady triplet rhythms.

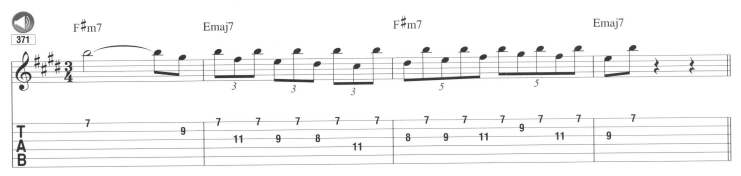

Howard Roberts applied the pedal-tone approach to chord changes in "What Kind of Fool Am I?" This phrase is played over a standard progression: Cmaj7–Em7♭5–A7. Note the melody notes C, A, E, D, and B♭ played over a repeated G–F#–G cell, the pedal-tone pattern. Here, the pattern enlarges what is typically a single-note melody.

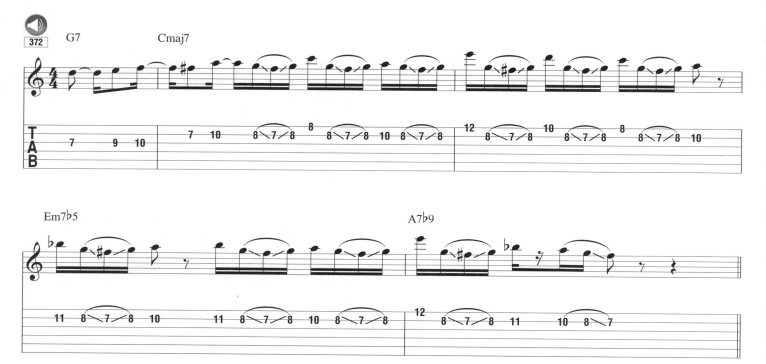

Jazz Ornamentation

Patterns are enhanced and developed into more elaborate melodic statements through ornamentation. In music, how a melody is decorated often affects its character, even on the simplest level—think of the first five notes of Beethoven's "Für Elise." In jazz, with its strong tonal implications, ornamentation attains great functional importance in emphasizing a chord or chord progression. Terms like approach tones, passing tones, enclosures, neighbor-note patterns, and voice-leading figures are used regularly to describe the melodic effect of this ornamentation.

Approach Tones

An approach tone targets a particular note of a chord, usually in horizontal motion over chord changes. Chromaticism is the most common form of the approach tone and occurs naturally in the bebop scales of jazz. (See Chapter 10.) Besides bebop scale applications, chromatic passing tones can be used to decorate any type of line. They are most commonly *functional* in the bebop sense and emphasize chord tones and the harmony. However, they can also be used freely to create what Joe Pass called "melodic flow."

This phrase demonstrates a typical practice scenario designed for improvisation and marks the first example of melodic modeling in this course. Two motives have been joined with the expectation of playing them in a future blues improvisation. This idea takes acquisition and assimilation into the most basic form of innovation. The first motive, played over F7, is a Coltrane cadence line for a V–I progression and has descending chromatic passing tones (CPT) from A♭ to F, targeting the F in a B♭7 chord. The next motive is borrowed from "Straight, No Chaser." It is repurposed rhythmically in its placement and relation to the beat. It has two cells with ascending passing tones targeting the 3rd and 4th of B♭. Play and listen for the chord-tone target effect in both motives.

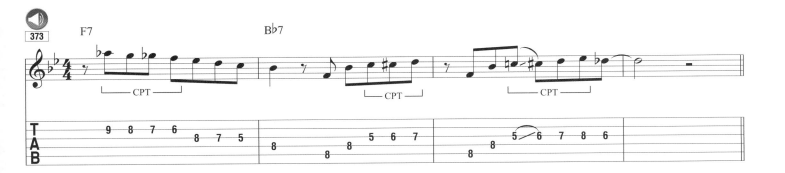

Charlie Parker used infinite variations of this ii–V–I phrase in his improvisations. Check out solos in "Anthropology," "Blues for Alice," "Celerity," "Au Privave," "Constellation," "Kim," "Ko Ko," "Barbados," "Now's the Time," "Billie's Bounce," "Ah-Leu-Cha," "Klaun Stance," "Card Board," "Bird Gets the Worm," "Merry-Go-Round," "Passport," and many others. Clearly, he felt this melody was ideal as a template pattern for application in a variety of tunes. It has two cells of chromatic passing tones targeting the sixth and fifth steps of Gm7 and a *lower neighbor* (LN) approach (F#–G) to the Gm7 arpeggio. Bird also used the phrase as a stand-alone dominant 7th line over C7 in "Passport." There, he played it in 16th-note rhythm and targeted the 3rd and 9th of C7.

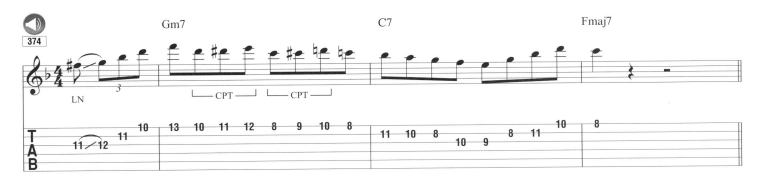

Bird played the same phrase with these variations. Note the elongated melody with more chromatic passing tones and straight-eighth rhythms and the use of E in the arpeggio pickup instead of the lower neighbor, F#. The last note is A instead of C, the phrase ending in "Passport."

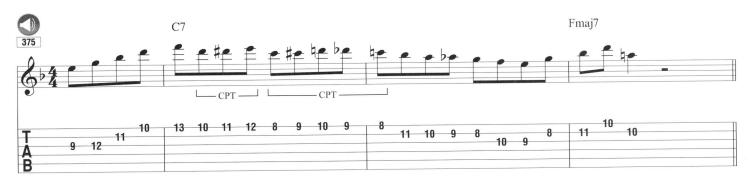

This variation on the next page exhibits other typical Bird changes. The original lower-neighbor pickup is played as eighth notes, the melody is shifted over one eighth note, and the second set of passing tones (D–Db–C) is inverted. A voice-leading figure (VLF) has been added to reinforce the C7 sound. It combines elements of chromatic passing tones and the enclosure, an extremely prevalent pattern in jazz melody. The final arpeggio, previously E–G–Bb–D, has been changed to its diminished form (E–G–Bb–Db) generating a stronger dissonant approach to the F chord via C7b9. The arpeggio is played over Fmaj7 producing a delayed resolution on beat 3.

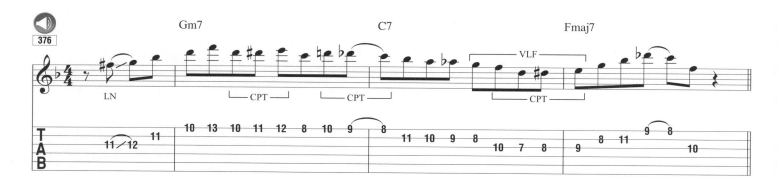

Bringing in other ideas and influences creates further variations. The pickup line connoting the melodic minor sound is borrowed from Trane and elongates the approach melody. A stepwise diminished line produces a different lower-register approach to the A note in the Fmaj7 chord.

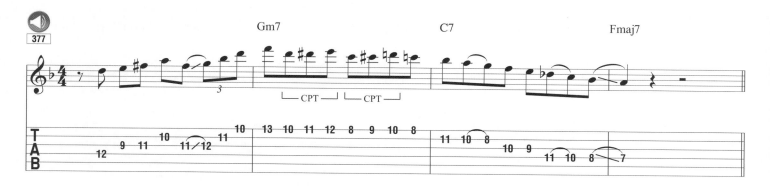

Melodic Targeting

Chord-tone emphasis is an important aspect of improvising over changes. The emphasis is most often achieved through targeting melody notes that have strong chordal identities. Any chord tone can be targeted, however the 3rd and 5th are most common, as well as the tonic in blues.

In this phrase, chromatic passing tone patterns are used deliberately to target chord tones. Play the first skeletal hexatonic melody in Track 378. Then, play and compare the ornamented version in the second figure. Listen to the emphasis of A, E, and G in this melody through approach from above and below with passing tones.

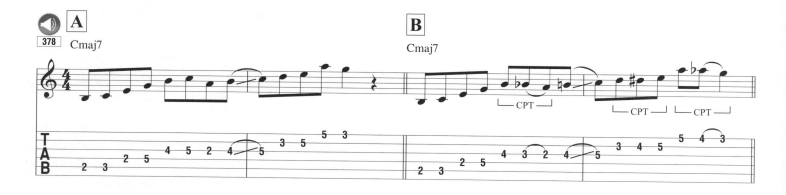

There are several idiomatic targeting procedures in this phrase. Note the longer chromatic passing-tone line connecting B to G. Enclosures are used to approach E and C chord tones. They exploit lower (LN) and upper (UN) neighbor-tone patterns. The final chromatic passing-tone pattern is derived from the major bebop scale.

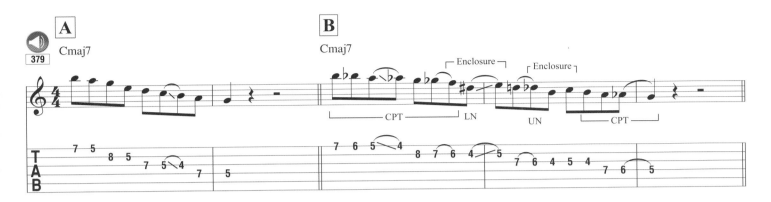

This ornamented phrase contains different types of horizontal motion: arpeggio, chromatic passing tones targeting G, a voice-leading figure targeting E, an enclosure targeting G, and melodic leaps targeting C and E.

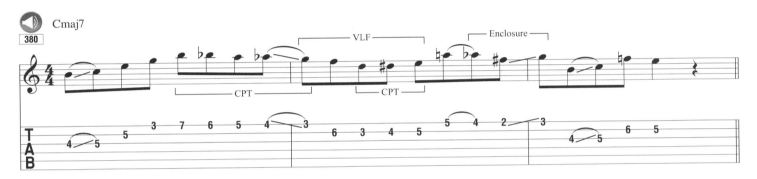

It is beneficial to practice different types of melodic targeting from a central motive. This process builds a sense of confidence in navigating and making variations spontaneously. The next group of phrases present a motive, first two beats, and several possible phrase endings. This is a practical way to prepare for improvisation; develop different approach cells and resolutions as habits through practice. These two phrases demonstrate two possible pathways to chord tones via chromatic passing tones to G or a G7+ arpeggio to E. The first figure of Track 381 targets a common tone, G, and can connect to Cmaj7, C7, or Cm.

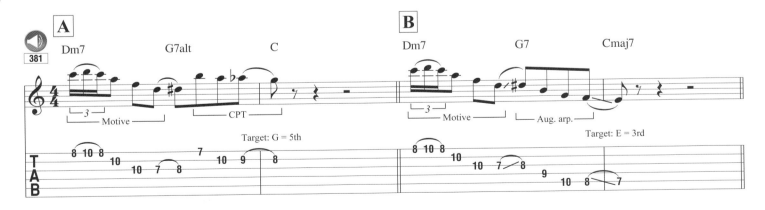

The example on the next page simulates a more ambitious practice scenario using the same idea. The central motive is navigated to several other phrase endings. Play the motive in the boxed area and pivot on the D# tone into these five different resolution lines.

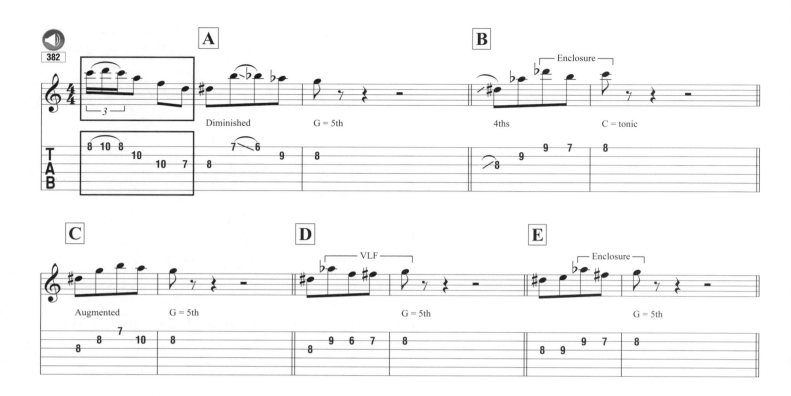

These practice phrases demonstrate six additional possibilities containing more diverse sounds. The goal is to hear how different melodies pivot on the D# tone and then enter surprising areas to approach resolution tones. The lines exploit motion into the lower register and contain altered and substitution options.

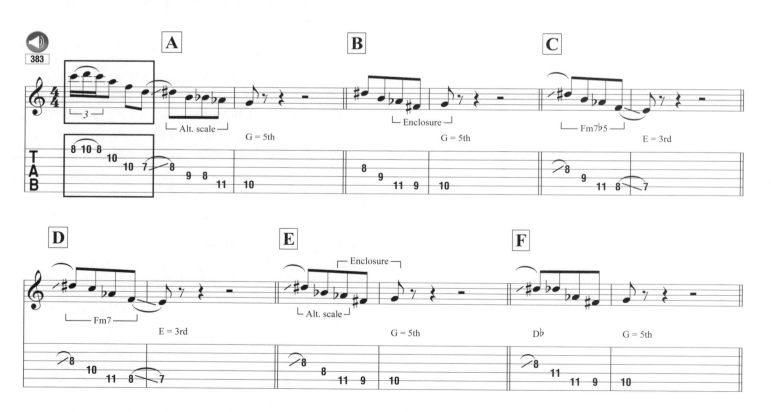

Pattern and Approach-Tone Vocabulary

The jazz language is replete with patterns, sequences, functional ornamentation, and approach figures in conjunction with idiomatic rhythms. This sampling depicts characteristic usage by the masters and presents object lessons in phrase construction.

Hampton Hawes, "A Night in Tunisia"

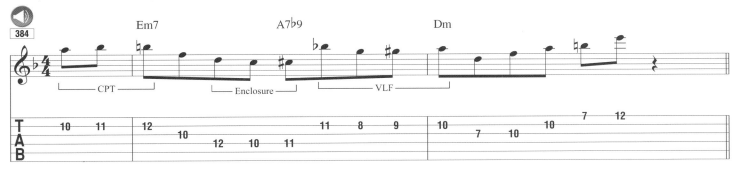

Cannonball Adderley, "Minority"

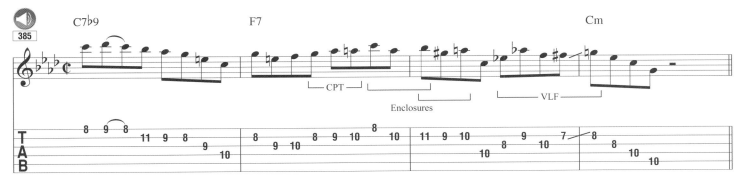

Tadd Dameron, "Hot House"

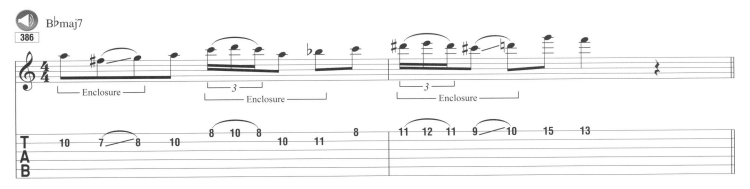

Joe Pass, "Satin Doll"

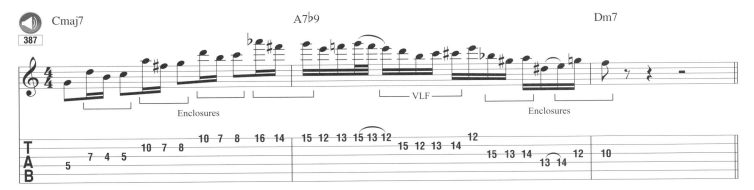

Pat Martino, "How Insensitive"

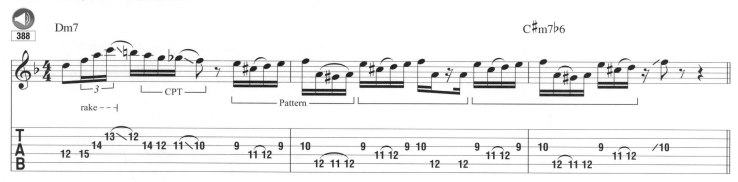

Wes Montgomery, "Misty"

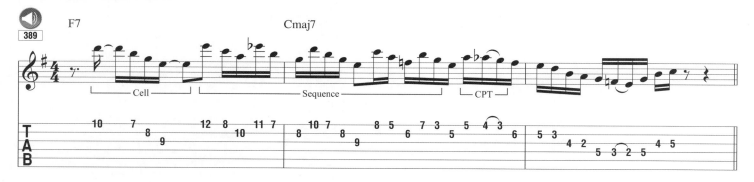

Cannonball Adderley, "Milestones"

John Coltrane, "Tune Up"

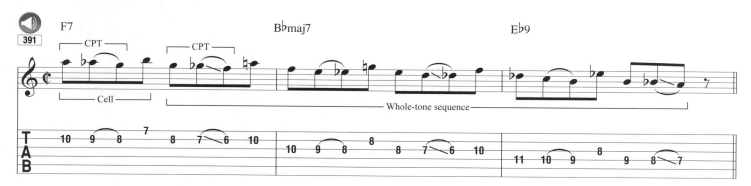

CHAPTER 15

TURNAROUNDS AND BACK-CYCLING

Turnarounds, sometimes called "turn-backs," are found in countless tunes—popular standards, traditional and modern blues, and original jazz compositions. The turnaround progression typically directs, or *turns around*, harmonic motion from the end of a tune's form to the beginning of a new chorus or repeat of a section. It commonly occurs in bars 31–32 of 32-bar standards and in bars 11–12 of a 12-bar blues. However, it can also be part of a tune's internal chord progressions, such as "There Will Never Be Another You," where the same changes are in bars 30–31, "Days of Wine and Roses" in bars 29–30, or "Rhythm Changes" in bars 3–4, 11–12, and 27–28. The turnaround progression can also be added to a song's basic changes when it doesn't occur there normally. This type of addition happens in tunes that cadence on a static I chord for two measures, like bars 7–8 of "Take the A Train."

The turnaround is arguably the most prevalent pattern, harmonically and melodically, in the form of a song and has survived many changes in style and genre. It is a crucial part of the jazz language. Addressing it melodically is a requisite in the skill set of any aspiring jazz improviser.

The Standard Turnaround

Most turnaround phrases are based on some form of a I–vi–ii–V–I progression. In the key of C major those changes are C–Am7–Dm7–G7–C. However, in jazz the first I chord is often played as a iii chord, Em7, a substitute for or inversion of Cmaj7, producing a *cycle-of-4ths* progression, Em7–A7–Dm7–G7–C, while retaining the function of a turnaround. The vi is typically a dominant 7th chord, VI7, and contains alterations that resolve to the ii chord, such as A7♭9 or A7♯5.

These straight eighth-note lines in C are examples of common turnaround melodies. Look for melodic elements introduced in the last section, such as combinations of stepwise motion, arpeggios outlining chord changes, interval leaps, enclosures and voice-leading figures, and chromaticism. Think of each chord as having its own melodic cell with varied characteristics, its own personality. Those small four-note cells link with the other cells to produce a longer line.

(A♭m7 substitute for G7 and
Target Note Figure: 5th of I chord)

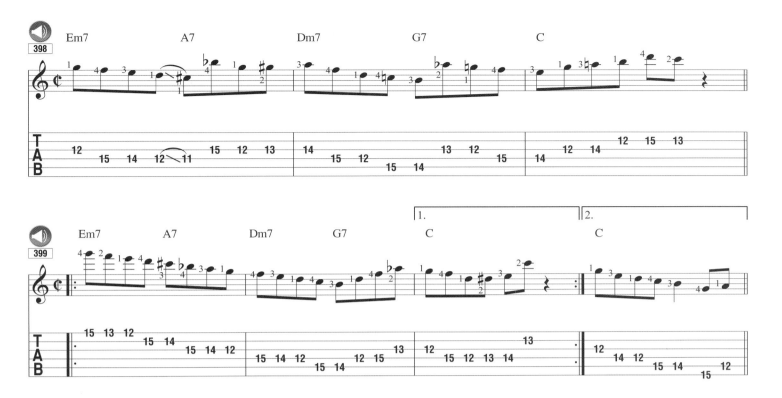

The phrases above can be harmonically aligned by combining them with chord progressions. Play the turnaround melodies and precede each with one of the following sets of changes. Listen and try to imagine singing the melodies with the chords. It is also useful to play each cell with its own chord and listen to the individual melody/harmony connection.

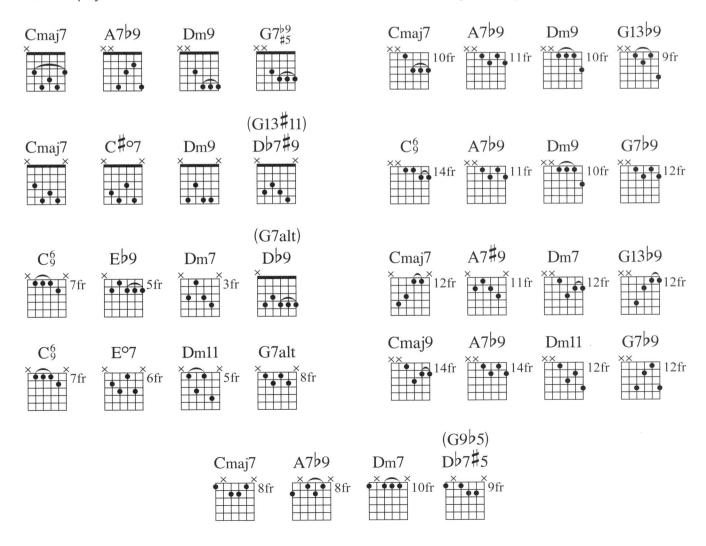

Several variations of the turnaround melody involve different starting notes. These three phrases illustrate characteristic alternatives.

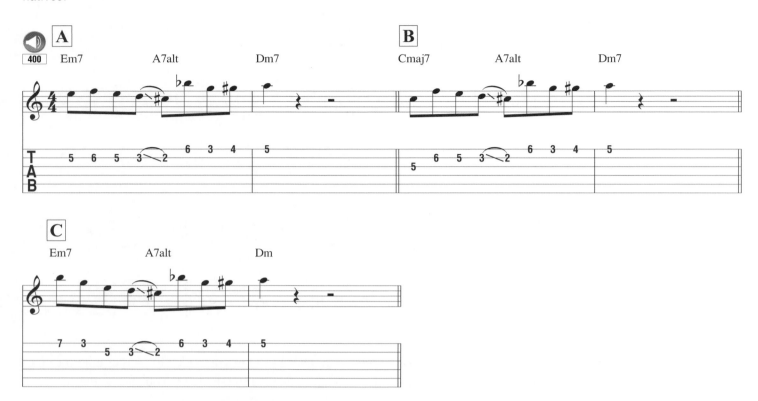

The standard turnaround pattern is usually based on a I–vi–ii–V–I progression or its alternate. Consider a tune like "Stompin' at the Savoy." The final two measures are typically written as D♭–E♭m7–A♭7, presenting an ideal opportunity to "drop in" a turnaround melody—here, as an intro to the first chorus of an improvised solo. This phrase depicts a turnaround added to the form in measures 31–32. A beneficial way to begin applying turnarounds is to pick a tune and insert the turnaround phrase into the final two bars.

Back-Cycling

From the preceding phrases we can draw several valuable conclusions about turnaround lines. The melody in Track 393, outlining Dm7–G7–C, is a short ii–V–I progression heading to a major chord while the melody for Em7–A7–Dm can be considered a short ii–V–I in a minor key.

Many harmonically astute jazz performers (Joe Pass and Sonny Stitt come to mind immediately) transfer, superimpose, and link these patterns to create more colorful motion, even when a turnaround is not indicated in the actual changes. Joe called it "back-cycling." In the most prevalent application, the previous phrases would be added to a section that remains on a single I chord or a I–V–I cadence, as in Track 396.

In coloring a minor chord, the melody for Em7♭5–A7alt–Dm7, a short ii–V–I progression from the turnaround phrase, can be superimposed into a static, Dm modal setting and played to produce a more active and harmonically interesting line. This phrase employs a portion of the turnaround melody as a short ii–V to resolve to a tonic D minor. The fragmented section is a cell and functions as a connector or linking melody.

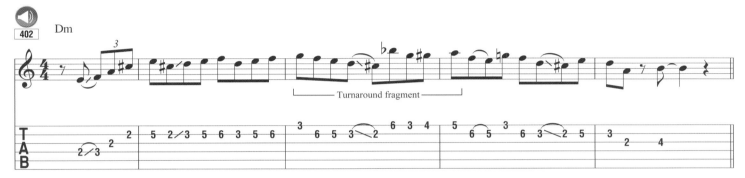

Turnarounds and Altered Chord Sounds

The examples in Tracks 393–400 contained some altered sounds on the VI7 and V7 chords. These phrases expand the idea and contain greater alteration, substitutions, and more chromaticism. The expansions are specified by text descriptions in the music.

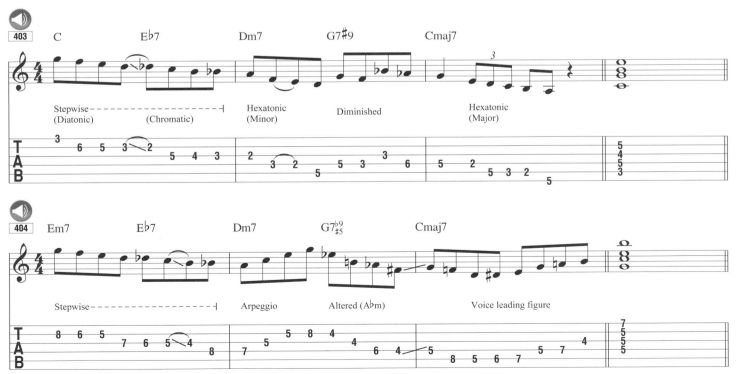

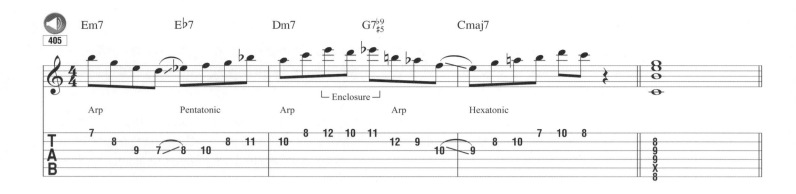

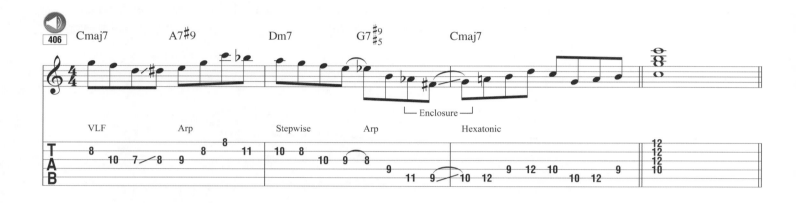

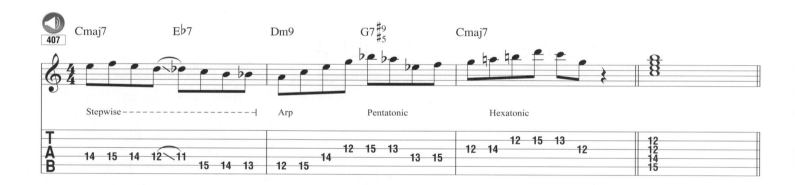

This example contains two enclosure figures, chromaticism, arpeggios, and a major-blues phrase ending.

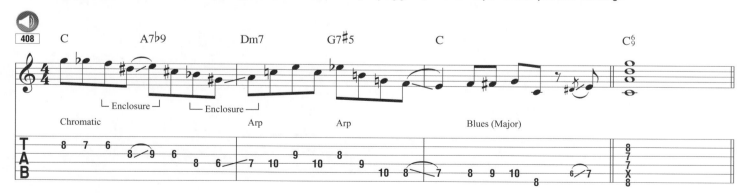

Turnarounds and 3rds-Related Substitutions

Thirds-related progressions are a key sound in modern jazz, used by many players and composers as an alternative to conventional changes. (See Chapter 5.) For an improviser, 3rds-related progressions are particularly effective and immediately applicable melodically as turnaround lines that generate greater harmonic activity and interest. Consider their use by important jazz artists like Wes Montgomery ("West Coast Blues"), Tadd Dameron ("Ladybird"), Toots Thielmans ("Bluesette"), and John Coltrane ("But Not for He," "Body and Soul"). The 3rds-related turnaround progression is commonly based on I–♭III7–♭VI–V chords, in C: Cmaj7–E♭7–A♭maj7–G7. Sometimes the final chord is played as D♭7, a tritone substitution for G7. These phrases are built on 3rds-related versions of the turnaround.

After learning and assimilating these sounds, apply them to standards and 12-bar blues progressions. By combining these alternatives with the standard turnaround phrases, an improviser's palette is expanded prompting innovation.

CHAPTER 16

THEMES AND VARIATIONS

Themes

A theme is defined as a musical entity that is a main idea in a composition or performance. It serves as the basis for development and variation. For jazz musicians, it is essential to compile and add to their thematic catalog and to also create new ideas that will become part of their future thematic catalog. One of the most enduring lines in the jazz lexicon is Charlie Parker's "famous alto break" in "A Night in Tunisia." There are many iterations of this phrase in Bird's catalog. Several come from the "Tunisia" session itself, where he played almost identical versions as a varied theme on different takes. The phrase is revealing and instructive in many ways, but it is also transcendent. It is clearly a preconceived and well-developed melody, reflecting countless hours spent practicing. It exemplifies the sound of numerous smaller, cellular motives woven together. Bird worked it up with the intention of making it part of a tune, yet retained its improvisatory "jazz" quality by leaving room for slight variations in each performance. He succeeded, and in the end, no two versions are exactly alike.

Playing this long and challenging phrase every day as part of a warm-up routine increases your technique and grasp of the language. It's a chops-builder and filled with requisite sounds—those are givens. However, in addition to assimilating the melody physically and aurally, great insights are gained by studying the pathways taken and decisions made in this horizontal tour de force. With emulation and assimilation comes innovation. It begins with small insights—understanding what is thematically important. Thinking as Bird might have thought fosters an intuitive sense of his maneuvers and produces a roadmap in this shifting mix of sounds. We're beyond the worlds of scales and rudiments here or even one type of sound. This is pure musical language from one of the greatest jazz artists of all time. Studying the details of his statement and deconstructing the melody into discrete sentences is rewarding. Try it and see; you won't be alone. The theme was studied and assimilated by legions of innovative players in their development.

Variations

The deconstructing process develops improvisation prowess and begins the creation of variations from themes. Consider Bird's break the theme, from which variations will be created. Playing the first two beats (and a quarter) yields a motive made from two small cells. Play and listen to the melody built from these two fragments.

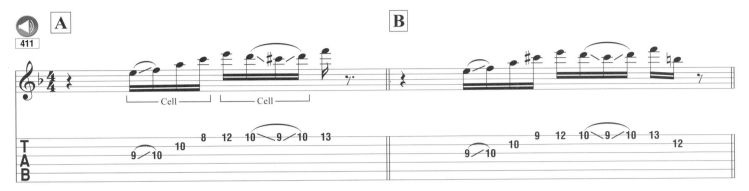

By making a couple of slight changes the sound of the melody can be modified to produce a stronger character for a Dm13 tonic minor. Note the C# and B notes in the new motive.

Play a variation in the lower register with a different phrase ending. This time, an augmented arpeggio gives the motive a Dm(maj7) sound. It could also imply or pivot into the V chord, A7#5.

Rhythm is an important fundamental aspect of making variations. A variation can *shift* along the time line to another beat creating a new rhythmic placement, can have different durations and values, be played across the bar, or stay in place and changed in its feel. A different variation is created by "editing out" some internal material and letting the melody move organically to another cell sooner. This phrase shifts the melody along the time span so that it begins on beat 1 instead of beat 2. The combined changes result in a F major or Dm7 sound.

This variation on the next page takes material from measures 2 and 3 of the original phrase, shifts the rhythmic structure, and repurposes it to function over a C7alt–Fmaj7 V–I cadence. Note the "filled-in" hexatonic line in measure 2 (a D note is added to the melody) as well as an Fmaj7 phrase ending with a skip instead of stepwise motion and the two 16th notes on beat 3, a common bebop rhythm. It is important to be aware of *beat orientation* as you build variations. Bird's melodies had a powerful melodic/harmonic logic based on *chord tones sounded on strong beats*. Strive to maintain that rhythmic-melodic relationship during your initial experiments.

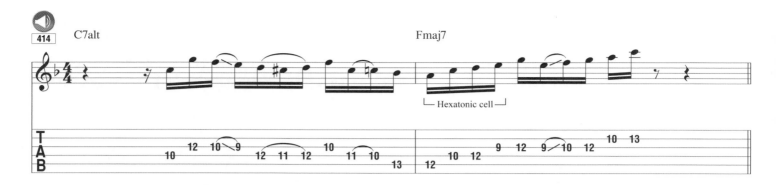

Any portion of Bird's long theme will yield cells and produce motives with similar possibilities. This variation takes the final section and reworks it to fit an A7alt–Dm (V–i in D minor) cadence. Note the skips implying a diminished arpeggio, chromatic passing tones, and an ending that, by targeting A, emphasizes the harmonic-minor sound and produces a resolution to Dm instead of Eb7.

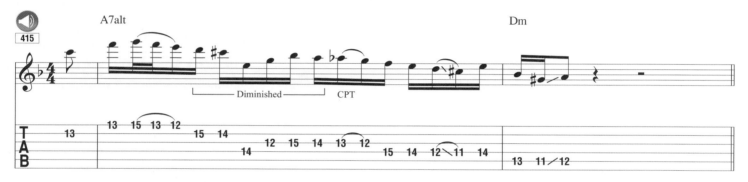

Combining the beginning (first two beats) with the ending (last four beats) and editing out the middle two-plus bars of 16th-note lines generates this less obvious variation. The first cell is re-fingered to expand its utility and produce a different expression on the fingerboard. Note the phrase ending with an emphasis on the tonic, Dm6, with a melodic minor sound.

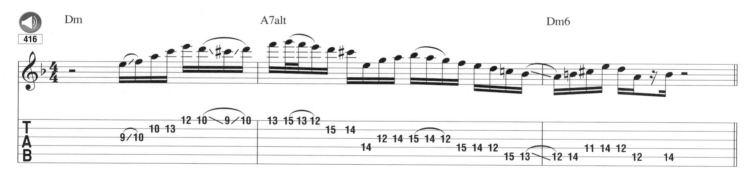

Extemporaneous Melodies and Improvisation

Preparing themes, variations, melodies, and patterns is part of an improvising musician's real-world practice regime. After the raw materials of basic sounds are internalized, assimilation requires a player to build a personal catalog from which they will create or innovate. The more comfortable one is with the process the more organic and natural will be the improvisation. As Joe Pass put it, in practical terms, "I never practice anything I wouldn't play on the gig."

Extemporaneous performing in public speaking or musical improvisation means, "carefully prepared but delivered without relying on notes." It's akin to creating a satisfying solo without reading or adhering to pre-written licks on a page. It goes without saying that these basic elements should be memorized and performance-ready. A performer knows the subject—the tune, knows what they will say about it, and says it in a conversational fashion. That takes practice.

Today's aspiring improvisers have tools with which to hone this craft in the hopes it will become an art form and a way of life. Excellent backing tracks of virtually any tune are available and should be used in the interim to explore ideas, create and develop themes, and prepare for a live performance.

Creating Variations with Turnaround Phrases

Consider the turnaround phrases from the previous chapter as potential material to be used for theme-and-variation subjects. Where to begin? Begin at the beginning, of course! This phase of development will be a focal point in practice sessions, the goal of which is to explore alternate paths for improvisation through the manipulation of cells.

Keep it simple initially. Pick a phrase. Let's apply the theme-and-variations process to the first turnaround line in Chapter 15. Here are some basic guidelines: Leave the first cell intact; it will link to a second cell that will be a variation. Use variations in motion and contour: stepwise or melodies with leaps that are changed to simple arpeggios, or melodies with different leaps in different directions. Add chromaticism and different motion. Aim for different target notes in measure 2. Consider simple substitutions, like E♭7 for A7.

This is the operative portion of the original melody, Track 392 in Chapter 15. Think of the first cell (cell 1) as a theme in either Cmaj7 or Em7. It will be played the same way in the next 12 phrases as a stepwise descending melody that sets up the second cell (cell 2). Cell 2 is a more active melody, reflecting dominant 7th harmony (A7, C♯°7, and E♭7) on beats 3–4. It will be changed throughout these examples to create variations, but it still conveys motion into the Dm chord. The first note in measure 2 is the target of cell 2 and will be a chord tone of Dm7. Play this phrase and listen for those elements.

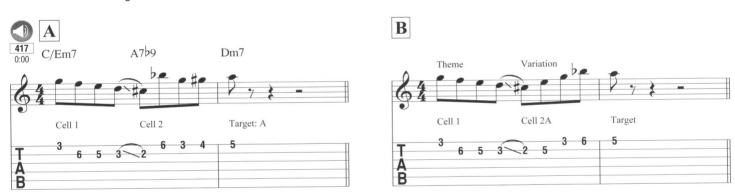

The first variation (cell 2A) applies a simple diminished 7th arpeggio, C♯°7, to the phrase and still targets A, the 5th of Dm7.

This variation (cell 2B) contains a wide descending leap (C♯–E) and then continues a diminished arpeggio to target a lower A note.

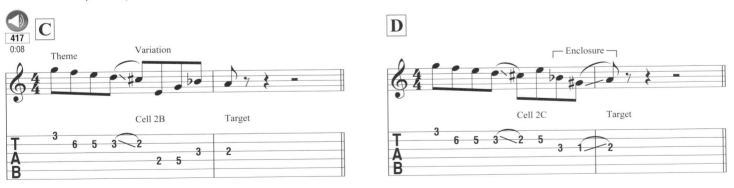

The C♯ diminished arpeggio and leaps (cell 2C) produce an enclosure of the A note. This is a favorite bebop approach figure.

This variation on the next page replaces the C♯ diminished arpeggio sound with a straight, stepwise line (cell 3). In doing so, it varies the contour and redirects motion through a harmonic-minor line to F, the 3rd of Dm7, a new target note. Play, listen, and anticipate the different melodic connections.

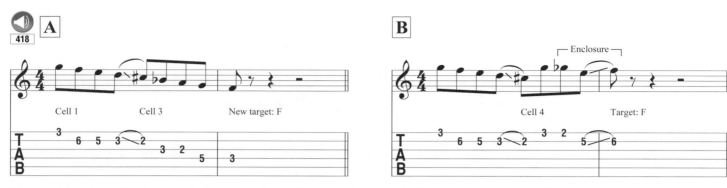

That variation benefits from melodic expansion with a new line, cell 4. The pattern begun on C♯ contains a tritone (C♯–G) leap that emphasizes the A7 sound and forms a connecting enclosure with chromaticism targeting F.

This closely related variation uses the same connection, C♯, and a very similar enclosing figure (cell 5) but leads to a different target, D, the tonic tone.

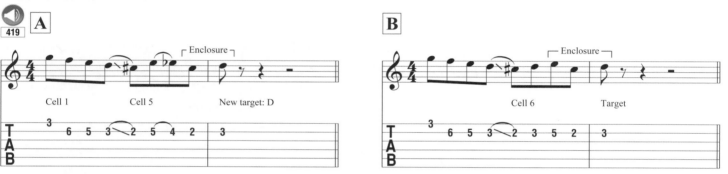

This variation applies a diatonic enclosure (cell 6) in D minor to accomplish the same melodic goal.

The C♯°7 arpeggio (cell 2D) is emphasized in this variation and presents the most common substitution for A7♭9. Note the zigzag contour. Play and listen to the effect this has on the connection. Rhythmic variety is very effective in improvisation. This variation adds a chromatic triplet figure (cell 7) as a connection to target D. Melodies like this are prevalent in the bebop vernacular.

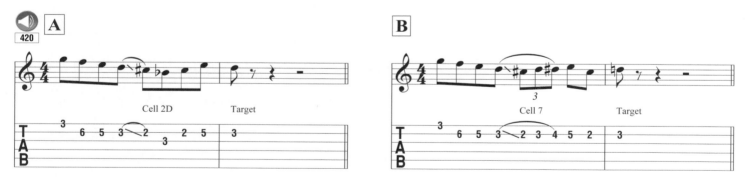

Modern jazz is filled with unpredictable intervallic lines. This variation contains a leap to a chromatic note (cell 8) and tweaks the harmonic-minor sound.

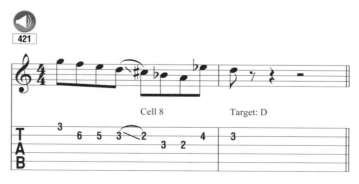

Substitution is emphasized with side-slipping melodies. These two phrases contain tritone subs, E♭, for the A7 sound. Both target the A note in Dm7. (Note the connections.) In the first figure of Track 422, the C♯ becomes the enharmonic D♭, the 7th of E♭7, a common tone in another key. It doesn't sound like it's left the key until after the connection is made. In the second figure, the first cell itself, C/Em7, is an enclosure targeting the E♭ tone of a pentatonic melody (cell 10).

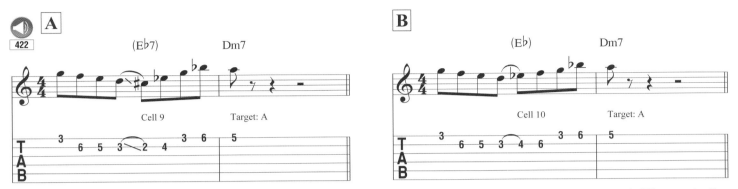

These three lines demonstrate other possible variations of cells in turnaround melodies. Listen for the use of different starting notes in each of the phrases and their effect on the line. The Em7 or Cmaj9 is expressed as a pentatonic cell in the first figure of Track 423, an arching stepwise contour in the second figure, and as an ascending leap and stepwise descent in the third figure.

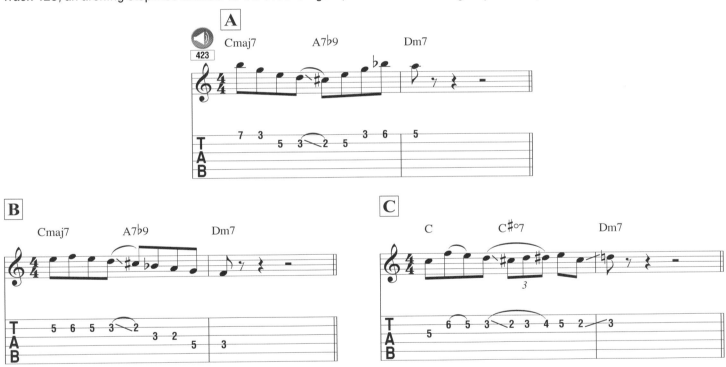

These two phrases demonstrate simple rhythmic variation. In Track 424, first figure, the melody is established as a sequence in straight eighth notes. In the second figure (next page), the same melody is converted into a syncopated line with a pickup effect because the notes on beat 4 have been subtracted and replaced with rests. Very effective variations can be created with such basic transformations.

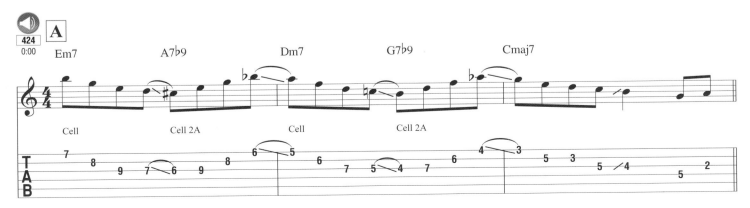

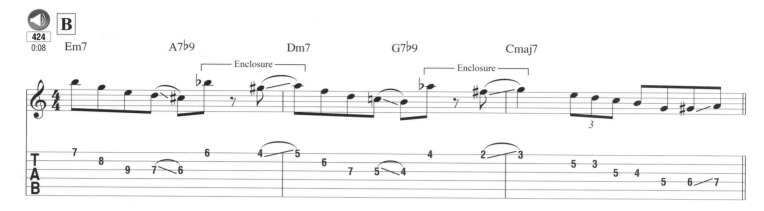

These four variations present further options. Note rhythmic changes in the use of rests as punctuation of the cells, varied chromatic approach figures and enclosures, interval jumps, stepwise versus arpeggio lines, and different colors of the chords: Tritone subs in Tracks 425 and 427, and Dm7b5 (half-diminished ii chord) in Track 428. Play these variations, listen, and then experiment with your own combinations.

CHAPTER 17

ii–V–I PHRASES

The ii–V–I progression is one of the most pervasive and essential in the jazz language. It is incumbent upon any improviser to develop a solid command of the harmonic pattern and acquire a large vocabulary of melodies that outline and horizontally define ii–V–I chord changes. In the most fundamental ii–V–I progression, the I chord is the destination while ii and V chords provide motion to that destination and produce their own activity along the way. In C, the ii chord is Dm7, the V chord is G7 (often an enriched or altered dominant), and the tonic I chord is C major (major 7th, major 6th, or 6/9). Envision a horizontal melody moving through and defining that harmonic pathway to reach and resolve to the I chord.

This four-bar phrase, from Vincent Herring ("Take the A Train"), demonstrates an idiomatic ii–V–I line. Notice the consonant melody made largely of arpeggios over Dm7, contrasted by a more dissonant, chromatic line over G7(#5♭9), and its resolution to a consonant Cmaj7 sound. Listen and strive to hear and feel a sense of motion and arrival.

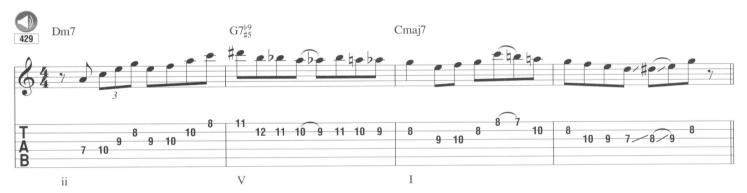

ii–V–I Phrases: Harmonic Rhythm

The ii–V–I progression is subject to harmonic rhythm. It is typically found in two forms of rhythmic duration: the long ii–V–I and the short ii–V–I. The Herring phrase above is a long ii–V–I. The long ii–V–I is a four-bar phrase with ii in the first measure, V7 in the second, and I, resolution to the tonic, in the third and fourth measures. The short ii–V–I is a two-bar phrase with ii and V in the first measure and I in the second measure.

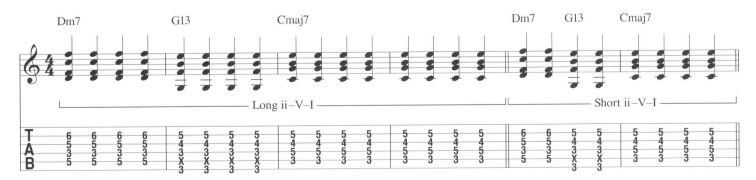

These two-bar phrases from John Coltrane's solo in "Giant Steps" exemplify short ii–V–I melodies.

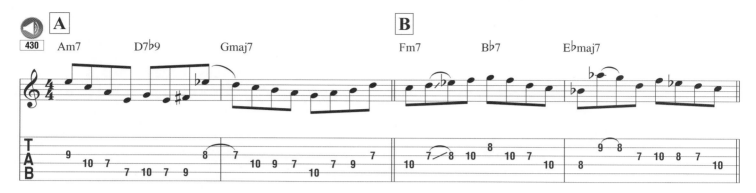

Short ii–V–I Phrases: Vocabulary

This collection of short ii–V–I phrases gathers 101 idiomatic lines transcribed from the jazz language presenting numerous possibilities for the improviser. Play and listen for differing degrees of dissonance, connections, imitative cells, enclosures, direction-defining chromaticism, leading tones, neighbor notes, rhythmic elements, and the varied characters of the phrase endings.

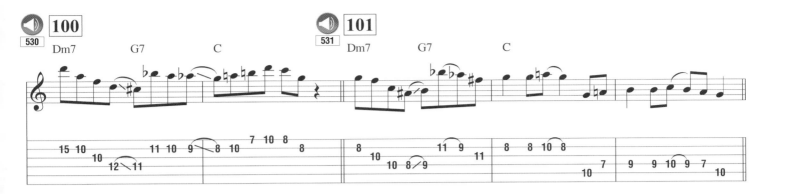

Working with ii–V–I Phrases

Many variations are possible using short ii–V–I phrases and their thematic cells. In these transformations, the basic material in No. 97 is varied by using cells borrowed from No. 64, 29, and 86.

Variations for improvisation: ii–V–I

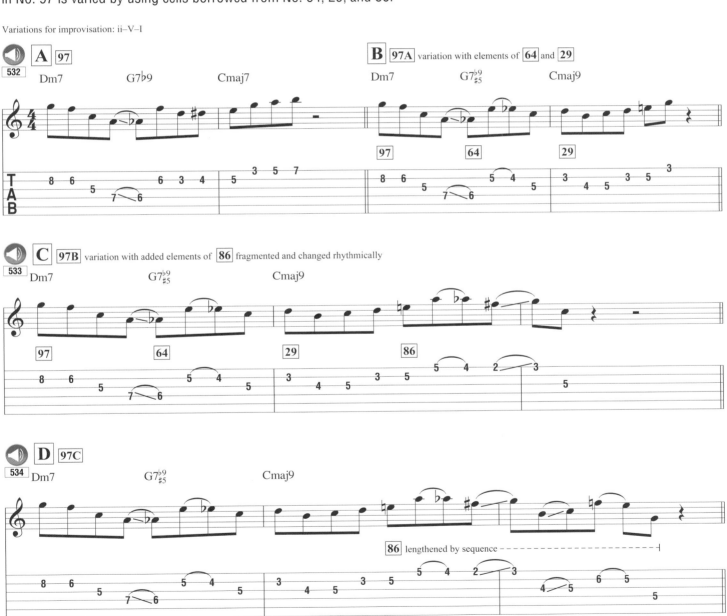

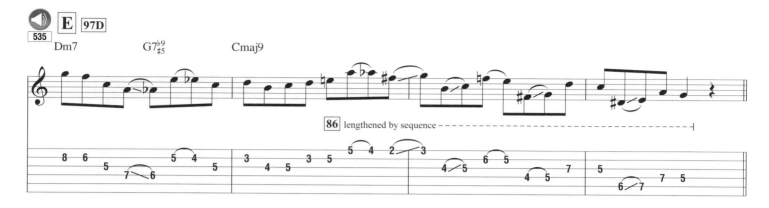

A short ii–V–I can be developed into a long ii–V–I. Consider No. 30 as a starting point. Notice the extended arpeggio played over Dm7.

By expanding the Dm7 arpeggio with neighbor notes, the same phrase is lengthened into a longer ii–V–I. The connection from G7#9 to C is maintained in the melody.

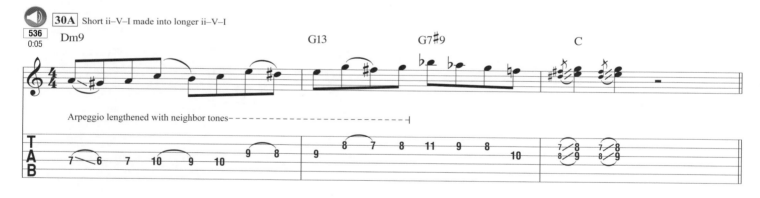

Now, consider the short ii–V–I in No. 101. In this variation, the phrase ending is shortened and altered. The "All This and Heaven Too" quote is abbreviated and becomes a one-bar line.

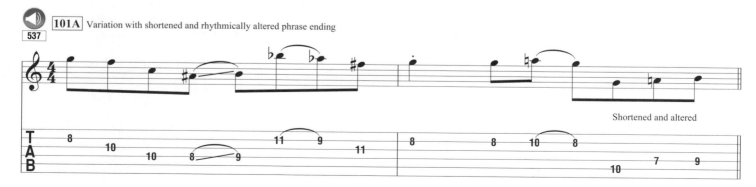

The same phrase can be lengthened into a long ii–V–I by inserting new material. Here, the new material consists of a common Dm7 cell played in measure 1. The melody of No. 101 is then rhythmically "nudged" over into measure 2 to function as a G7 line. That's a valuable biproduct of applying the jazz language—its malleability.

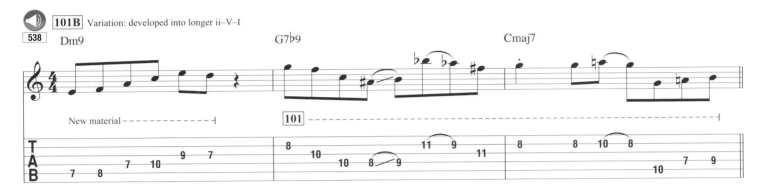

These phrases are improvised lines over the long ii–V–I progression. Once assimilated in the woodshed, their cells can be manipulated and altered through fragmentation and recombination, as in the previous lines.

ii–V–I Phrases in Context: Vocabulary

The jazz repertoire teems with examples of ii–V–I phrases played by the greatest improvisers in the genre. It is incumbent upon any aspiring player to become familiar and fluent with the melodic possibilities of the progression and begin to gather a personal collection aimed at increasing and strengthening your vocabulary. These lines of differing characters and configuration are offered as a starting point. Listen to your favorite jazz musicians and absorb some of their thinking by transcribing key phrases over ii–V–I changes.

Stanley Turrentine

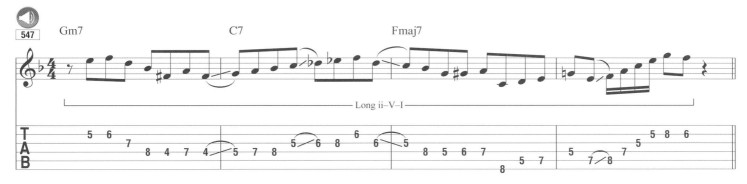

Freddie Hubbard

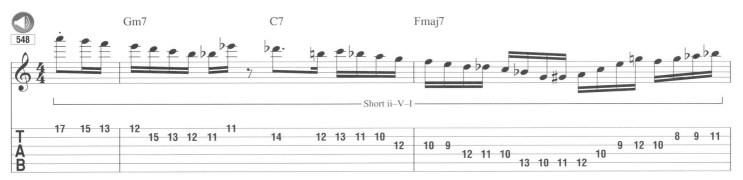

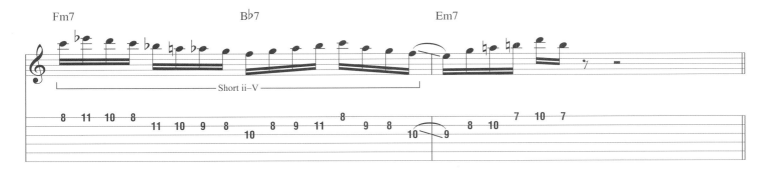

Cannonball Adderley

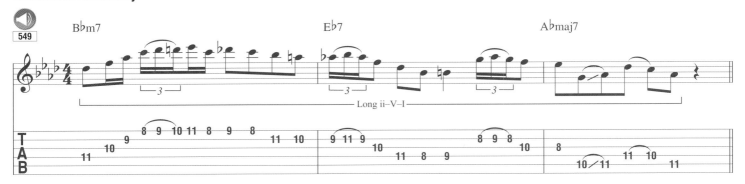

John Coltrane

Charlie Parker

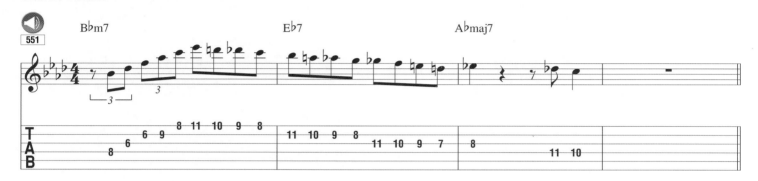

Vincent Herring

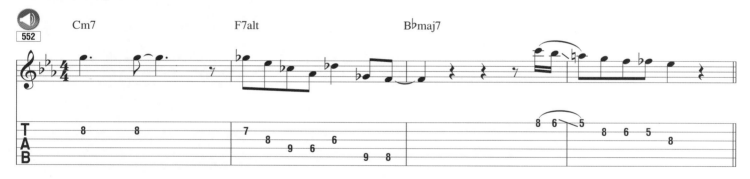

CHAPTER 18

THE MODEL SOLO

Creating a model solo puts an aspiring improviser on a solid path to applying accumulated and developing knowledge and mastery of the jazz language. We liken our efforts at this point to the *contrafact* of the jazz repertoire. Tunes like "Donna Lee," "Koko," "Hot House," "Oleo," and "Countdown" are well-known contrafacts, using new melodic material over the chord changes of "Indiana," "Cherokee," "What Is This Thing Called Love?," "I Got Rhythm," and "Tune Up," respectively. They represent the refining and formalizing of melody from the jazz language in the works of Charlie Parker, Tadd Dameron, Sonny Rollins, John Coltrane, and many others. You could say these tunes represent their "model solos," pieces in which they worked out and composed new melodies from their own vocabulary and exerted their preferences over standard chord changes.

Building a Model Solo: Blues

The construction of a model solo begins with selecting a set of chords from a tune or a chord progression that could apply to a number of tunes. An example of the former is the "Rhythm Changes" progression, which is derived from "I Got Rhythm" and has a 32-bar structure with an eight-bar bridge. The latter could refer to any 12-bar blues progression, from "Crossroads" to "Bessie's Blues." Let's begin building a model solo by addressing the most ubiquitous: a 12-bar blues progression.

This 12-bar blues progression in F is our starting point. It could apply to "Now's the Time," "Billie's Bounce," "Au Privave," or any number of blues tunes in F. It will serve as a container for the improvisational resources we are accumulating—typical licks, language lines, idiomatic rhythms, melodic/harmonic connections and linking materials, and the like. Visualize this blues progression as a template of the 12-bar form and a road map of the chord changes. Note the turnaround, F–D7–Gm7–C7, in measures 11–12.

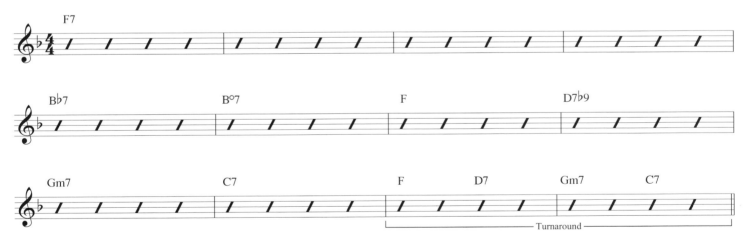

The same progression is often played with slight variations. In this case, a "quick IV" (Bb7) has been added in measure 2, and there is no diminished chord in measure 6. That variation will be used in the second chorus of this solo.

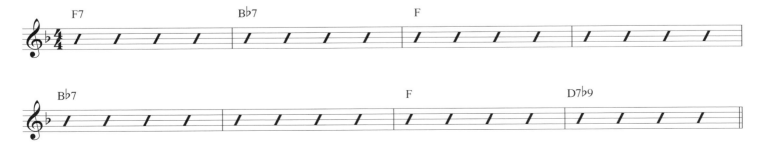

This three-chorus model solo harnesses many elements of the jazz language. Let's examine the options. Specificity as to the musical pedigree of these melodies is presented and stated with certainty, as the source material originated from my own personal listening, transcribing, and performing experience. It is played, as all the solos, after a theme statement and into a recap.

Third Chorus

C

A: First Chorus

Measures 1–3

A variation of the Charlie Parker blues phrase used in "Now's the Time" and "Billie's Bounce." This melody is a must-know line in the jazz language assimilated by countless players. Wardell Gray used it to begin his "Twisted" solo.

Measures 4–5

This altered line (F13–F7#5) resolves to the IV chord, Bb7. A variation of Bird's cadential melody from "Blues for Alice."

Measure 6

A simple major-blues motive leading back to I.

Measure 7

A voice-leading line, implying F–Bb–B°7–F, from John Coltrane, heard often in his hard-bop period. (Think the "Blue Train" solo.)

Measure 8

An altered, secondary-dominant connecting line. This bebop motive establishes the move from D7b9 to Gm7. It can be thought of as a V–i from G harmonic minor. Note the characteristic enclosure figure (Eb–C–C#–D) that targets the destination chord Gm7.

Measures 9–10

A triplet arpeggio sequence borrowed from Trane. This ii–V phrase outlines Gm9, Gm7, and C7#9#5 chords and sets up motion to I.

Measure 11

The resolution to I cadences on the 9th, G, and continues with a Bird motive played into the turnaround. It shares common tones with F and D7.

Measure 12

The final line contains F–F# voice-leading motion that signals a possible second chorus.

B: Second Chorus

Measures 1–4

A reinterpreted quote from Sonny Rollins' "Tenor Madness." This riff-based motive and its *major-minor polarity* suggests a simpler, traditional blues quality. The idea is to create contrast with the more explicit bebop of the first chorus.

Measures 5–6

A funkier blues lick borrowed from Cannonball Adderley embellished with microtonal string bending.

Measure 7

A chromatic major blues line I first heard played by Oscar Peterson.

Measure 8

This D7 altered line sets up Gm by using its dominant. Joe Pass made frequent use of this bop connection in the blues and standards.

Measures 9–10

A chord-outlining ii–V pattern that spells Gm11–C7alt and sets in motion a strong resolution to I. This line was used often by Wes Montgomery.

Measure 11

The return to I is emphasized by a traditional blues melody that implies F–C7–F. In a jazz blues turnaround, this simpler line can be an effective agent of contrast and melodic surprise.

Measure 12

The idea of leaving space for a pickup into the next chorus is also effective. This tactic is so pervasive it can't be attributed to a particular player. Suffice to say, B.B. King as well as John Coltrane and George Benson have routinely used this storytelling strategy.

C: Third Chorus

Measures 1–4

A paraphrase of Clifford Brown's "Blue Walk" riff.

Measures 5–6

A swing-blues figure involving bent double stops and a major-blues sound. This is like a big band "shout" figure reinterpreted on guitar. To me, it feels like a Count Basie-meets-Buddy Guy affair.

Measure 7

A recall of Trane's voice-leading melody in a higher register. (Think thematic development in its simplest form—nothing says "development" like the repetition of a key phrase.)

Measure 8

A transition line addressing D7alt. Notice stepwise and interval-jumping contours. The zigzagging contour melody was borrowed from Joe Pass.

Measures 9–10

Two essential Bird motives played back-to-back, one over ii (Gm7) and the other over V (C7). The latter applies jumps in the diminished scale as an altered C7 sound. It was heard in "Blues for Alice" and was a favorite pattern of Cannonball Adderley.

Measures 11–12

The turnaround is outlined with a specific sequential melody that spells out the chords with stepwise motion and arpeggios. Dexter Gordon used this type of tonal line to begin "Smile." Listen for the targeting of chord tones. That's the key to making these types of pattern-based lines work over changes. It resolves to a closing blues line in F7 defined by a descending C–A–F–Eb arpeggio that overlaps into the next bar. Delayed phrases like these are effective when "handing over the solo" to another player, as the next musician can easily imitate the melody as an interaction that acknowledges the previous solo. Those ingredients are elusive in an exercise format, yet must be cultivated to be brought forth and functional in live performance.

Model Solos and Variations

We can only imagine how many different ideas and motives Bird and others tried and discarded before they decided on the final phrases of their contrafacts. The process is an instructive and joyous one—provided you're interested in melodic exploration. These variations are offered to start your ball rolling. They are reinterpretations of the opening Bird blues phrase of the first five measures. Similar experiments should take place regularly in your "woodshedding." Try substituting these for the opening line of the solo.

Building a Model Solo: "Rhythm Changes"

After the 12-bar blues, the most prevalent form used for jazz contrafacts is the chord progression of "I Got Rhythm," called "Rhythm Changes" colloquially. Let's examine its musical terrain. The progression occupies a 32-bar structure and is divided into four sections of eight bars each: 8+8+8+8=32, labelled AABA, arguably the most common form for standard songs with a bridge (B). The first two and last eight-bar A sections, here designated as A(1), A(2), and A(3), are similar or nearly identical.

B

A3

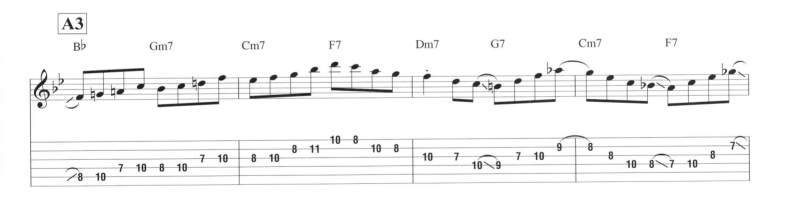

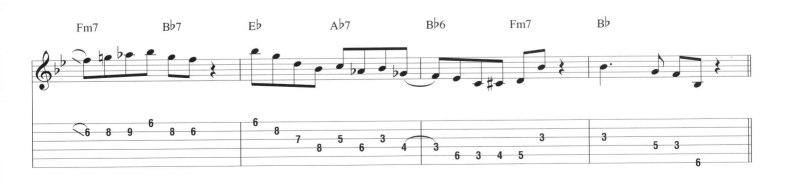

A(1)

Measures 1–2

A Cannonball Adderley line from his "Oleo" solo with Miles Davis. Think of this melody as the "call" in the call-and-response phraseology, vital to a cohesive jazz message in your improvisation.

Measures 3–4

A iii–VI–ii–V turnaround phrase functions as the "response" to the opening line. Typical altered-chord harmony is reflected in the melody of measure 4, for F7#5♭9. This produces tension generating forward motion into the fifth bar.

Measures 5–6

A sequential phrase exploiting arpeggios outlines the harmonically active Fm7–B♭7–E♭(6)–E°7 progression.

Measures 7–8

The first A section is concluded with a quote of "All This and Heaven Too"—an indispensable melodic cell that has been used for a phrase ending by John Coltrane, George Benson, Vincent Herring, and many others.

A(2)

Measures 1–2

A chromatic line (C#–D–E♭–E–F) played as a sequence pattern. This is the "call" melody setting up an expectation for a response.

Measures 3–4

The response outlines a iii–♭III–♭VI–V *alternate turnaround* progression associated with Trane and Dameron. This phrase exploits arpeggios and a pentatonic line (D♭7). An A°7 arpeggio, substitution for F7♭9, provides tension and motion into the next phrase.

Measures 5–6

Two cells used as "twin" patterns define Fm7–B♭7 and form a ii–V–I progression to E♭. The contour changes to an ascending stepwise line made of two connected arpeggios: E♭ and E♭m. The D (leading tone) is used to begin each arpeggio.

Measures 7–8

A phrase ending containing two staples of hard bop. The first is ubiquitous and originated in Bird's improvisations. The second is a rhythmic phrase ending favored by John Coltrane.

B

The "Rhythm Changes" bridge cries out for contrast and thematic development, as the chords are all dominant 7ths and arranged in a standard *cycle-of-5ths* (4ths) progression: D7–G7–C7–F7. It's up to the improviser to give each their own character. Those decisions distinguish players of "Rhythm Changes" in a crowded field.

Measures 1–4

Two imitative phrases played over D7 and G7. The first is in Am, and it is largely diatonic and decorated with neighbor tones. The second is a similar melody moved down a half step. This poses both A♭m and A♭°7 on G7 and produces an altered/substitution sound. It connects with a Dm7 hexatonic motive (extension of G7) in bar 4.

Measures 5–6

A variation of the previous two motives. It is an example of Gm used over C7 and exploits the F♯ tone (raised 11th of C7) prominently.

Measures 7–8

The final bridge phrase begins movement back to the A section. It is made of two motives, the first is "inside," a diatonic F7 with neighbor-note embellishment, while the second is an answer with an "outside" side-slipping quality, G♭m/F7. The idea of layering the two faces of the same chord in an in-out imitation within the same phrase came to me via Dexter Gordon.

A(3)

Measures 1–2

The return to A is emphasized by three sequenced pentatonic cells ascending in 4ths through B♭–Gm7–Cm7 changes. The resolution to B♭ in bar 5 is made via a descending pentatonic cell that is a quote from "Fools Rush In."

Measures 3–5

A sequential turnaround line made of two ii–V cells. Note the imitated diminished arpeggio contours and flatted 9ths for both dominant chords. The resolution in bar 5 cadences on a minor cell for Fm7–B♭7.

Measures 6–8

The E♭–A♭7 harmony is underscored with a whole-tone line: D–B♭–C–A♭–B♭–G♭. It resolves to the tonic via a bebop enclosure and quote of the "Blues Walk" riff.

Many variations of the "Rhythm Changes" chord progression are possible, and some options are presented in this solo. This chart adds more other options to the mix. The top line depicts the most common changes. The lines below the staff contain increasingly more involved substitution and altered possibilities.

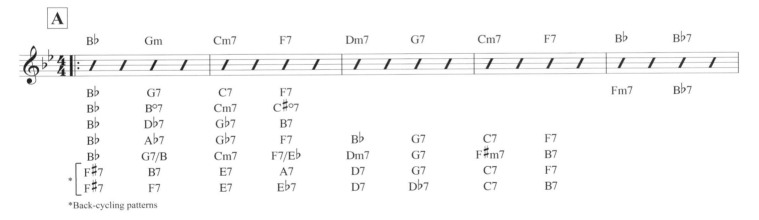

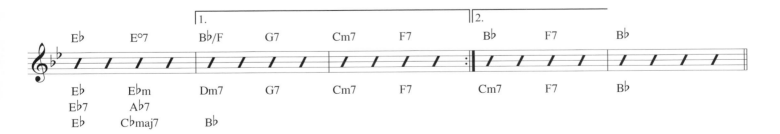

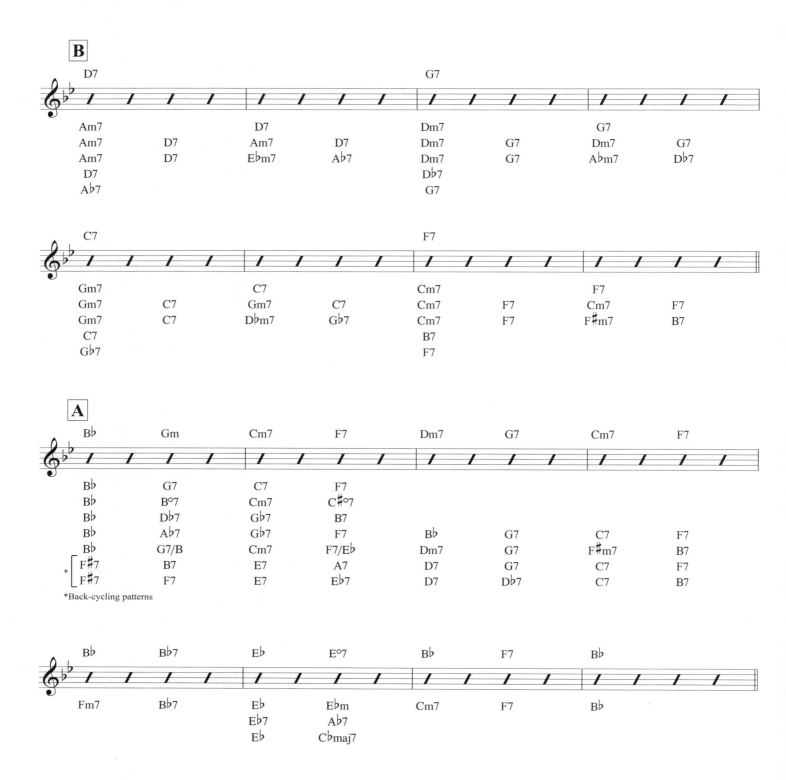

*Back-cycling patterns

Building a Model Solo: "Cherokee"

Charlie Parker once stated that learning the blues, "Rhythm Changes," and "Cherokee" prepares a jazz musician for almost everything. Indeed, the musical DNA for countless tunes resides in those changes. Bird himself built his contrafact "Koko" around the "Cherokee" progression during his first official recording as a leader.

"Cherokee" has a larger AABA, *64-bar form* (16+16+16+16) and is usually played in Bb major. The progression contains many characteristic harmonic moves, like motion from I to IV and then its dominant IV (Bb–Bb7–Eb–Ab7), heard in tunes like "Misty," "There Will Never Be Another You," and others, *tonicization* of the ii chord (making ii a temporary key center: Cm–G7 [or Dm7b5–G7]–Cm, and several ii–V–I progressions [especially in the modulatory bridge section]). This chart presents the basic harmonic landscape of "Cherokee" changes.

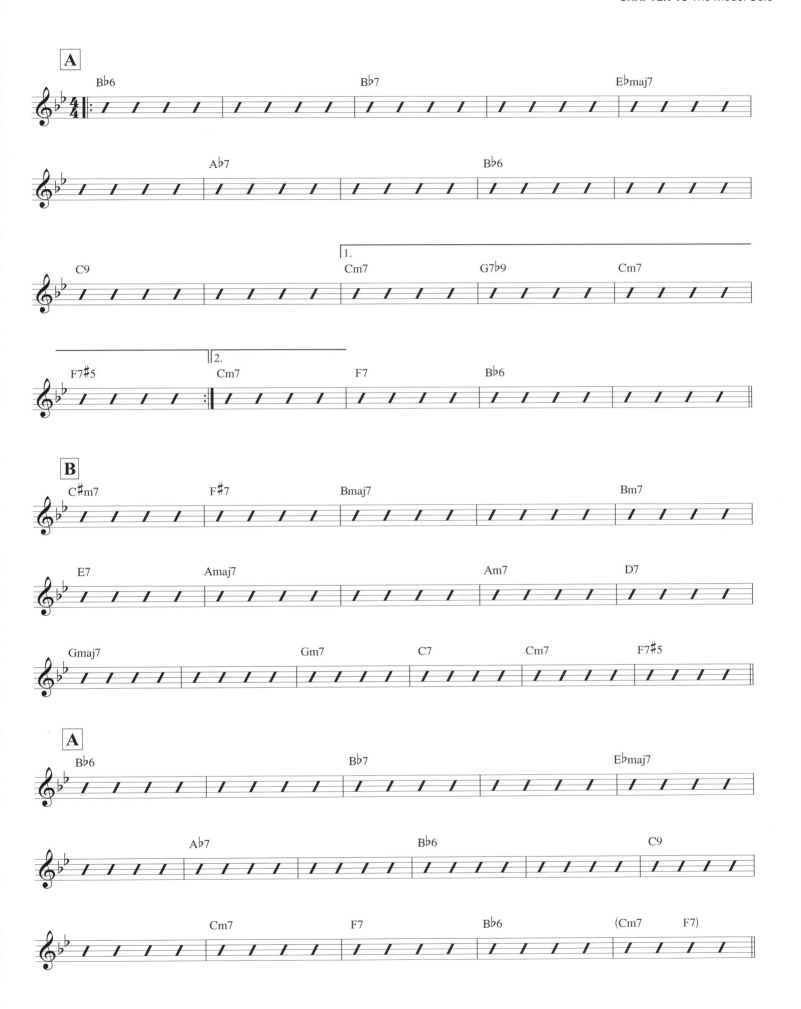

This 64-bar solo is built on the "Cherokee" changes. Many of the key elements of jazz improvisation are represented and cited in the descriptions and commentary.

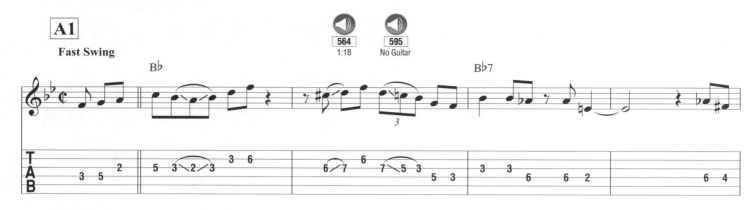

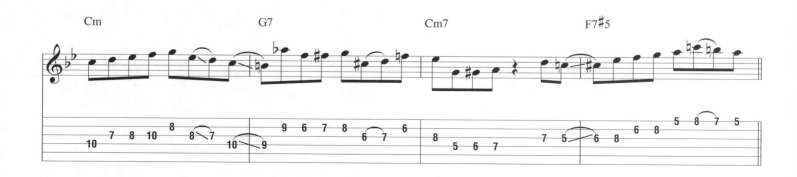

A2

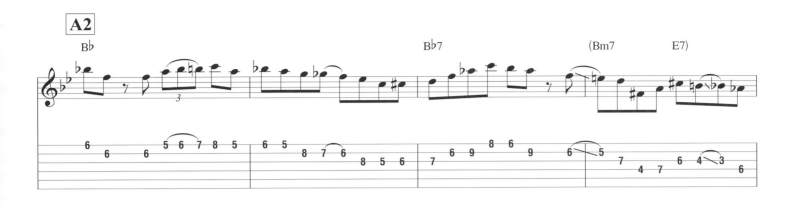

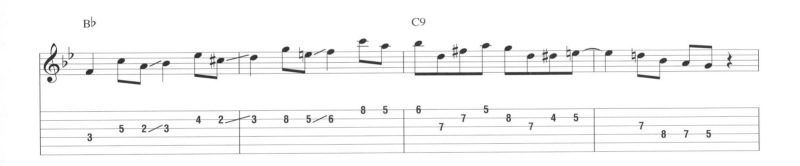

B

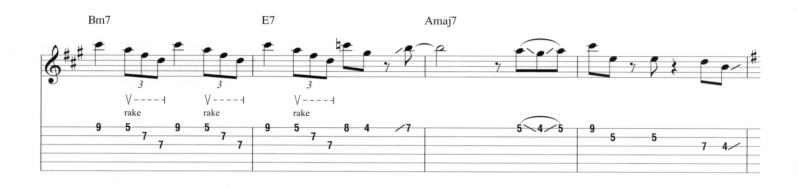

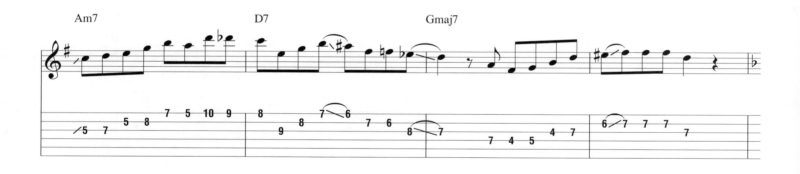

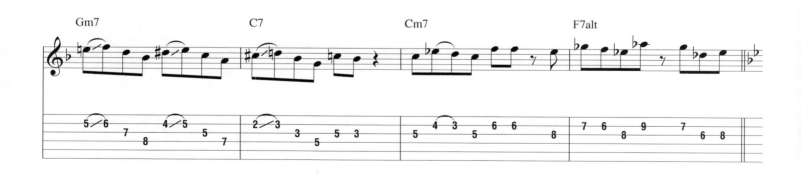

A3

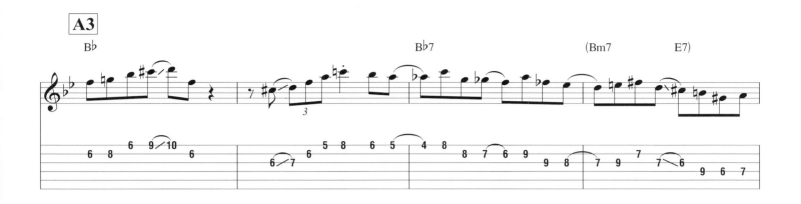

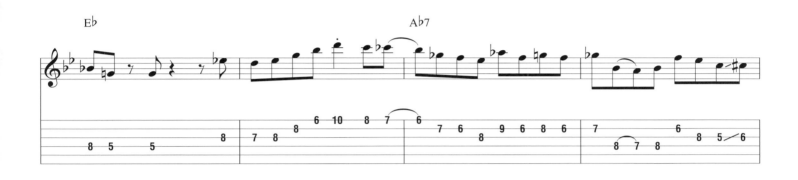

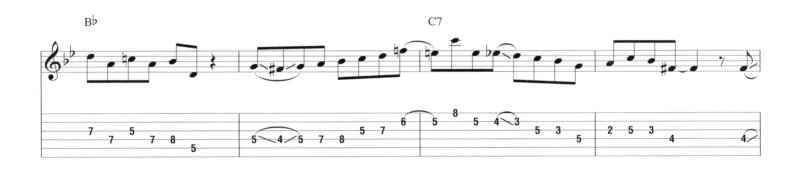

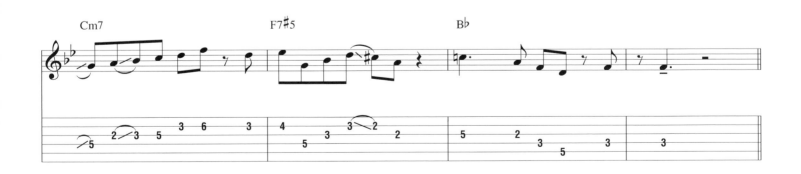

A(1)

Measure 1

An opening pickup line heard in many jazz solos. Consider this an entrance phrase and the "call."

Measures 2–4

The "response" is a paraphrase of the coda line in Clifford Brown's "Cherokee" arrangement. Note the cadence on E, the ♭5th of B♭7♭5.

Measures 5–8

A parallel major/minor development of a Bird motive. Listen for imitation and the thematic toggling effect of G and G♭ in the two melodies over E♭ major and A♭7.

Measures 9–12

A string of eighth notes weaving through a I–II7 progression. Note the bebop enclosure opening, leaps, and extended arpeggios over B♭ and the 13#11 altered sound, made by substituting a Gm(maj9) extension for C7.

Measures 13–15

A line tonicizing the ii chord, Cm, generated by back-cycling through its dominant, G7. Note chromatic embellishment in approaching important chord tones.

Measure 16

A whole-tone stepwise ascent emphasizing F7#5. The enclosure opening and closing allude to the phraseology in measures 8–9.

A(2)

Measures 1–2

An essential Bird phrase using chromatic approach chord tones and the stepwise major bebop scale.

Measures 3–4

An in-out melody that begins with diatonic outlining of B♭9 (in). It's followed by a substitution, Bm7–E7, a ii–V in A (out), to side-slip above the destination chord, E♭ major—a move gleaned from Wes Montgomery in tunes like "West Coast Blues" and "Road Song."

Measure 5

A Gm pentatonic cell used over E♭maj7. This sound was employed by Trane over major 7th chords. It mixes pentatonic and diatonic melodies.

Measures 6–8

The major-minor polarity of the melody alludes to "Just Friends" and contains a Pat Martino quote from his version.

Measures 9–10

A zigzagging pattern targeting a B♭ major triad. This ubiquitous figure has been used by Joe Pass, Oscar Peterson, and Sonny Rollins as well as Bird.

Measures 11–12

A C7 phrase begun with a chord-outlining figure. Note F# in the melody, chromatic approach notes to E, and a G minor phrase ending.

Measure 13

A Dizzy Gillespie sequential pattern outlining C minor, the ii chord.

Measure 14

A substitution line from Bird's "Kim" solo. This melody superimposes B7 on F7, a tritone sub, and includes a specific cadence lick with chromaticism, approach tones, and an interval leap.

Measures 15–16

A major-blues phrase ending that has roots in the swing era.

B

Measures 1–4

A four-bar Charlie Parker ii–V–I line from his "Cherokee" solo. Note arpeggios and chromatic passing tones on C#m7, the deliberate targeting of the D, augmented 5th, on F#7, and a characteristic hexatonic phrase ending in B major.

Measures 5–8

Bird commented that playing on the higher intervals of the chords in "Cherokee" informed his style. This ii–V–I phrase illustrates with one of his common motives. It exploits arpeggios outlining Bm9–E7#5–Amaj9 changes.

Measures 9–12

A ii–V–I phrase blending stepwise and arpeggio melody. The motive in measures 11–12 was a line Bird used in "Cherokee" and other solos.

Measures 13–14

A Trane pattern of triad arpeggios and lower-neighbor tones played as a sequence over Gm7–C7.

Measures 15–16

A quote of "Fascinating Rhythm" in two keys a minor 3rd apart, used over Cm7–F7. The first cell is in C minor and the second in Eb minor, a substitution for F7alt. This fragmentation principle can work with any appropriate minor melody with ii7 potential.

A(3)

Measures 1–2

A swing-blues line marks the return to the tonic. That ground-finding line leads to a Dm7 arpeggio acts an extension of Bbmaj7.

Measures 3–4

A spiraling chromatic scale pattern punctuated with leaps for Bb7. This figure is associated with modern jazz players like Cannonball Adderley and John Coltrane. It begins in the Bb7 bebop scale and moves incrementally into the side-slipping substitution Bm7–E7.

Measures 5–8

The parallel Eb major/minor polarity is emphasized again in this phrase over Eb and Ab7. Note the straight arpeggio on Eb major answered by a more complex line in Eb minor with chromaticism and interval leaps.

Measures 9–10

An interval-jumping hexatonic cell in Bb followed by a Gm line anticipating the C7 chord. Note the F# leading tone in the melody. It's the gateway note into the relative minor connection.

Measures 11–12

An interval leap mixed with chromatic passing tones and an altered phrase ending over C7.

Measures 13–16

The final ii–V–I exploits extended and altered chord sounds. Note the rhythmic imitation of syncopation on beat 3 of bars 13, 14, and 15. The phrase ending applies a rhythm used often by Trane to finish a line.

Building a Model Solo: "Take the A Train"

Our closing example pursues a more detailed but freewheeling approach to selecting motives and creating phrases for improvisation. The process has proven helpful to aspiring improvisers whose skills are increasing but require more guidance and steps for application of specific sounds. This model solo will be played over the changes of "Take the A Train," a perennial jazz favorite. Two sets of ten motives are offered for Cmaj7 and D9#11 in Tracks 565–584. Each set contains a potential group of themes for a tonic sound, using the major bebop scale in C and altered-chord sounds based on the A melodic minor scale for the II7 chord, D9#11. These represent your accumulated vocabulary and are applied to illustrate the assembly and connection of lines for the first four bars in each A section.

With repetition and substitution, the practice of deciding which theme goes where becomes instinctive to the hand and ear. Moreover, the motives can be treated as "markers" for inserting, or "dropping in," newly acquired vocabulary into future improvisations. The tried-and-true methodology mimics productive time spent in the woodshed experimenting with and deciding upon themes and melodic connections, and it is part of the oral tradition of jazz learning. Be creative and try all possibilities, and most of all, *have fun* with this exercise!

Major Bebop: Cmaj7

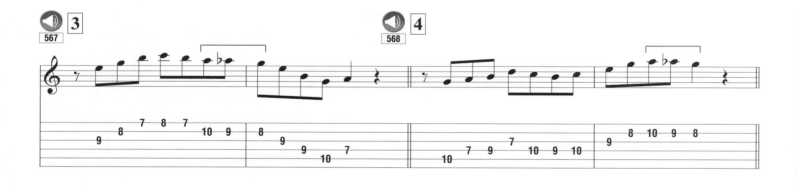

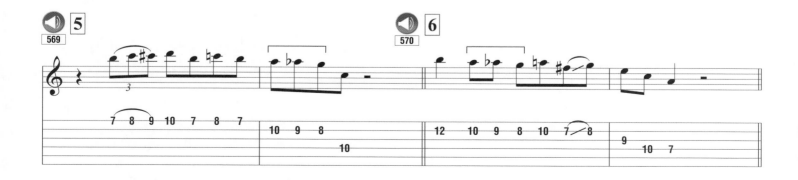

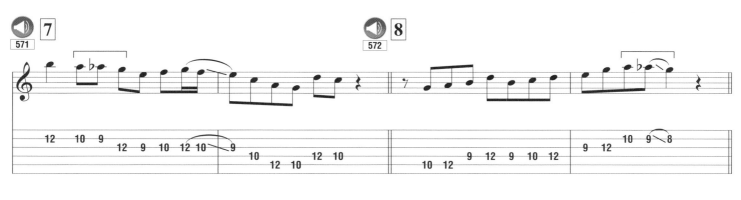

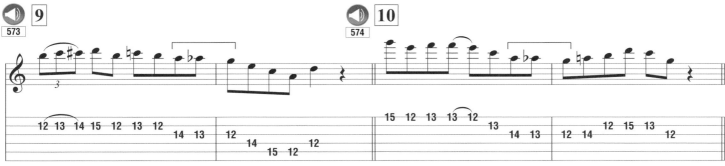

"Altered Scale" D9#11

Am (Melodic Minor)

This model solo is played over two choruses of "A Train," a 32-bar AABA structure in C. It draws heavily on specific motives for the first four bars of A sections. The second four bars are a place for long ii–V–I melodies from the jazz language. The B section (bridge) explores possibilities for longer lines over the IV chord, Fmaj7, different dominant 7th chord sounds for D7, and the return back to the tonic via ii–V material. The application and placement of specific motives is numbered in the music. This track begins with the piano intro as a count-in.

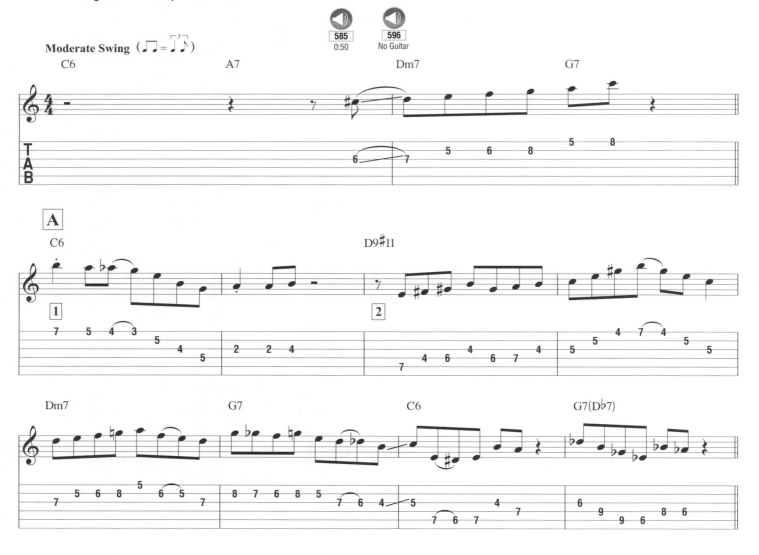

With regular practice, the process of recalling and connecting your motives, themes and melodic ideas becomes subliminal and flows out of your vocabulary automatically, affecting what you are saying in your improvisation. That's the beginning of *your* jazz message.

CHAPTER 19

IMPROVISATIONS

The following improvised solos are played on the changes of six indispensable standards. The emphasis is on deliberate application of the jazz language in improvisation over a variety of progressions and rhythm grooves. A brief description of the music and performance notes is presented along with recommended listening. It is vital to hear different versions. This shapes your aesthetics, and enriches and informs what you have to say as an improviser. *Listening is imperative.* It is of paramount importance that an aspiring improviser become familiar with multiple interpretations—classic and modern—of standards played by masters, as well as the theoretical elements and technical fundamentals of each song. Balancing these aspects is at the heart of the art form. It is expressed by an artist as the merging and managing of repertoire and performance requirements with the goal of delivering your own message, guided by aesthetics, in improvisation.

"Autumn Leaves"

The tune: It's hard to imagine anything rarer than an American jazz classic influenced by ballet music written by a Hungarian transplanted to Paris. Yet that's the case with "Autumn Leaves," one of the world's most enduring standards. A case of musical globalism, Joseph Kosma's 1948 composition was a one-hit wonder but has remained popular with instrumentalists and vocalists since the 1950s. It has been recorded more than 1400 times, was a crossover instrumental hit for Roger Williams, and has also been covered by pop artists Eric Clapton, Bob Dylan, and Eva Cassidy.

Musical basics: "Autumn Leaves" is a 32-bar tune in a minor mode, here E minor. Its form can be viewed as a two-part AB (16+16) or a smaller four-part AABC (8+8+8+8) structure. The music contains recurring cycle-of-4ths progressions and ii–V–I changes in related major and minor tonal centers: G major and E minor, both of which make it ideal for beginning jazz improvisers. "Autumn Leaves" is commonly performed in a medium-swing groove and sometimes in G minor as a favorite secondary key. One of the most malleable standards, it has been interpreted in Latin, bossa nova, slow swing, jazz waltz, uptempo, and ballad treatments.

Improvisation

This single-chorus solo gets the ball rolling. As you play through the music, pay attention to the use of essential melody sounds and connections of ideas. These include chord outlining, mixed minor modes in tonic and ii–V applications, hexatonic, bebop scale, and altered lines, as well as numerous ornamental and approach-tone figures and patterns.

First Chorus

A

Moderate Swing

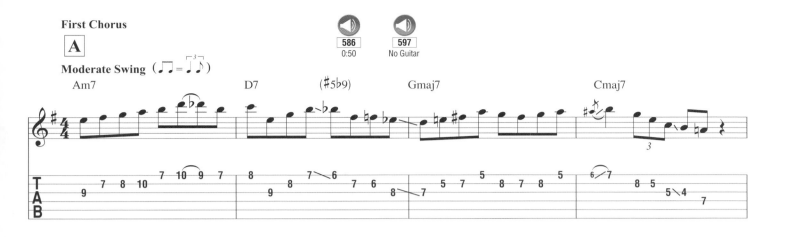

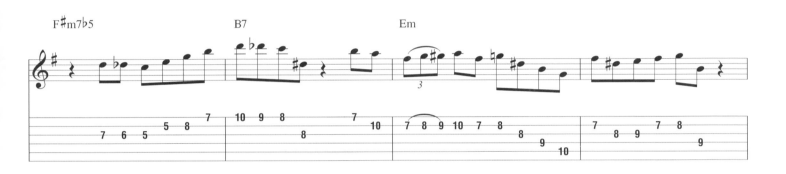

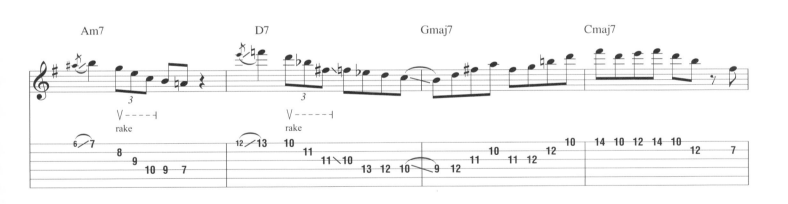

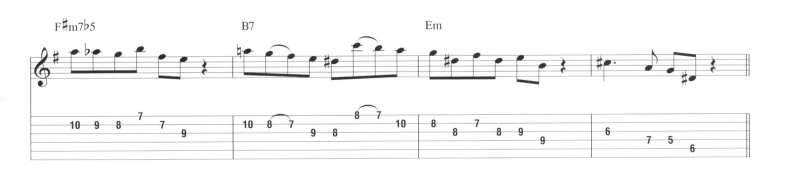

B

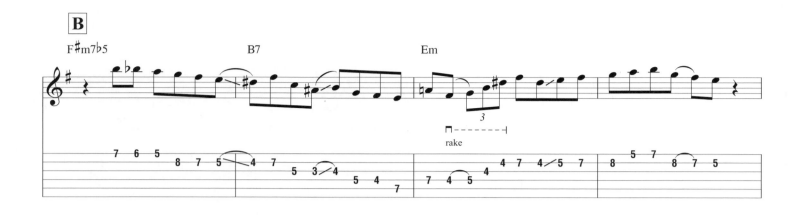

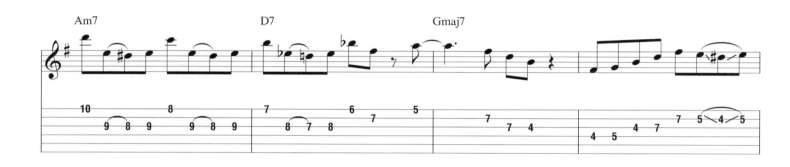

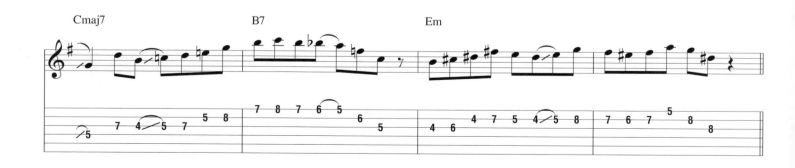

This additional chorus of "Autumn Leaves" is offered as a supplement. It can be practiced separately as an alternate solo for the previous example, concurrently as a series of variations, as a vehicle for *recombining*—exchanging motives and patterns between choruses—or as a possible continuation to produce a two-chorus solo by joining Tracks 586 and 587. These processes are used to develop a solo strategy and occur throughout jazz improvisation on a subliminal level by the great players. They are skills worth cultivating.

Second Chorus

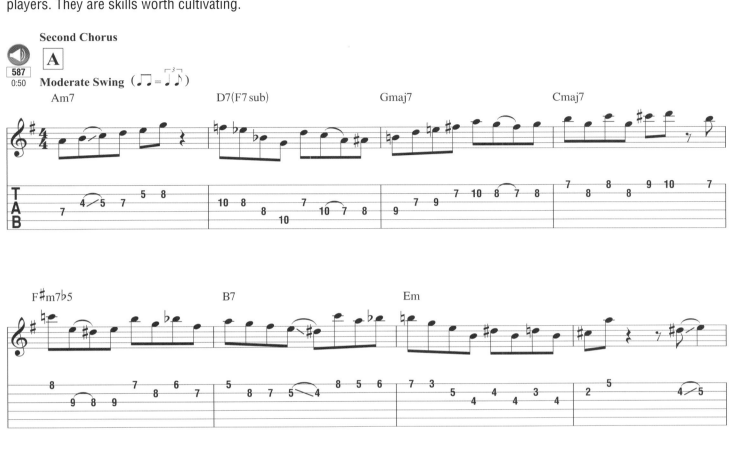

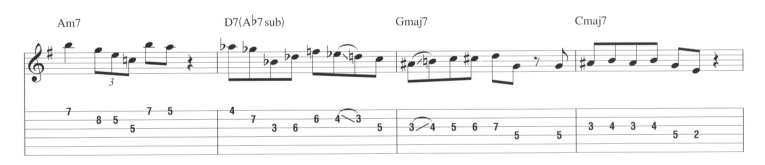

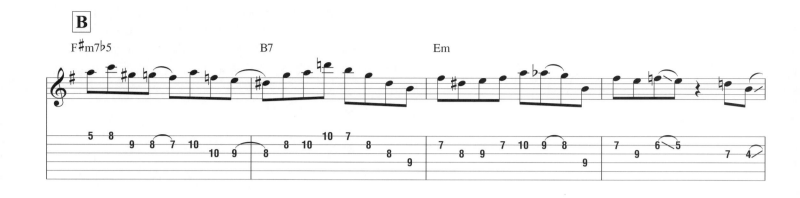

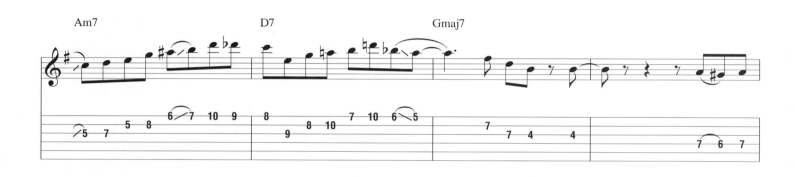

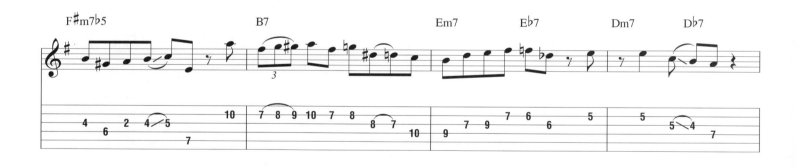

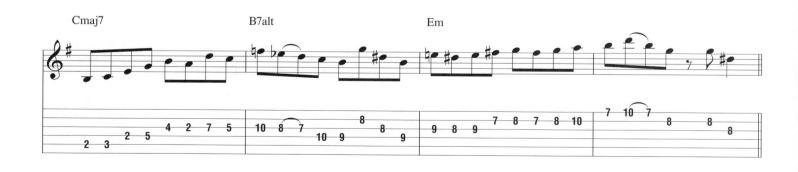

"All the Things You Are"

The tune: "All the Things You Are" is a true evergreen jazz standard. Written by Jerome Kern in 1939, it has remained essential since the swing era. Bebop and post-bop artists embraced it as a vehicle for improvisation and a template for contrafacts by Charlie Parker ("Bird of Paradise"), Dexter Gordon ("Boston Bernie"), Lee Konitz ("Thingin'"), Kenny Dorham ("Prince Albert"), Mal Waldron ("Anatomy"), and others. No wonder—it boasts ingredients that entice and tantalize modern and traditional players. The mix of tonalities presents countless harmonic possibilities for improvisation.

Musical basics: "All the Things You Are" is a 36-bar tune that modulates through a variety of keys. It is almost always played in Ab and commonly in a medium-swing groove. It has an ABCD (8+8+8+12) structure, though the A and D sections begin identically. There are numerous 3rds relations in the changes—that is, in fact, one of its most prominent aspects. The tune starts in Ab (on the relative minor Fm) with cycle-of-4ths changes and modulates to C in measures 7–8. That progression is then transposed and repeated in Eb (beginning on Cm) and modulates to G in measures 15–16. The bridge (C) continues in G and modulates to E in measures 21–23, before cadencing on Fm in measures 24–25. The final section (D) contains a parallel major-minor progression: Dbmaj7–Dbm(maj7) in measures 29–30, and a biii°7 chord, B°7 (Cb°7), that connects Cm7 and Bbm7 in measures 31–33. An additional four bars, measures 33–36, acts as a tag in the form.

Improvisation

This two-chorus solo focuses on the all-important harmonic pathways in the changes. Each new key center is approached with a ii–V–I progression, in either long or short form. Therefore, there are ample opportunities to use both types from your vocabulary. Measure 16 (second time) presents the option of using an altered-chord line as a dominant 7th substitution for a ii–V. The partial quote of "Fly Me to the Moon" in measures 25–28 demonstrates the idea of playing a common melody from a similar set of changes, in this case another well-known cycle tune.

"On Green Dolphin Street"

The tune: This Bronislaw Kaper film song from 1947 became a Top 40 pop hit when Jimmy Dorsey's orchestra covered it that year. It was transformed into a jazz standard in 1958 when Miles Davis, inspired by Ahmad Jamal, recorded it with John Coltrane, Cannonball Adderley, and Bill Evans onboard. The tune's engaging chord changes, inherent variety, and malleability have coaxed many interpretations from traditional to modern and everything in between.

Musical basics: "On Green Dolphin Street" is a 32-bar tune in ABAC form. It is frequently performed in alternating grooves: Half-time or Latin for the A sections and swing for the B and C sections. This is emphasized by jazz musicians with an emphatic *pedal point* under the parallel major-minor tonic chords and chromatic harmony in the A sections, which opens the door to tonal, modal, pentatonic, and outside (atonal) approaches. The variety in the A, B, and C sections (simplicity in the A sections, greater complexity in B and C) prompts diverse performance options for improvisers. The B and C sections have greater harmonic activity via a 3rds-related modulation from C major to E♭ major in measures 9–16, and cycle motion though related diatonic keys (A minor, E minor, and D minor) in measures 25–32. Long and short ii–V–I progressions are important aspects of these sections.

Improvisation

This three-chorus solo begins with a four-bar entrance phrase and pickup, built loosely from the last part of the melody, combined with a blues lick, and an altered-chord cadence line. This is a reliable, chorus-starting tactic that has ushered in many a solo. Note a number of quotes throughout the improvisation. The idea of a motive being minorized to portray parallel C major and C minor modes is also heard in the beginning of the third chorus. The chromatic D7–D♭maj7–C progression in the A sections allows for parallelism or melodic motion up or down—both options are exploited in the solo.

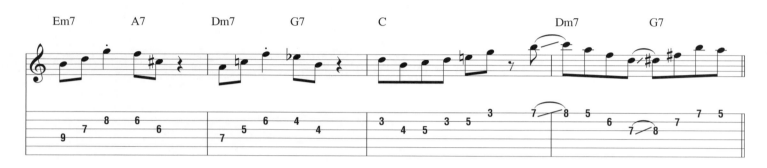

"Manhã de Carnaval"

The tune: Brazilian music of the 1960s exerted a powerful influence on jazz. The bossa nova form, via Antônio Carlos Jobim, João Gilberto, Luis Bonfá, Marcos Valle, and others, remains a prevalent Latin style in jazz, along with Afro-Cuban music. A true Pan-American offspring, bossa nova is particularly conducive to guitar since most of the repertoire was written on the instrument. Bonfá's "Manhã de Carnaval" (Morning of the Carnival) was one of the earliest bossa nova tunes, a featured song from 1959's *Black Orpheus*, and also goes by the name "A Day in the Life of a Fool" when sung. It is a standard in the jazz repertoire and has received diverse covers by Perry Como, Chet Atkins, José Feliciano, Joan Baez, Cher, and Luciano Pavarotti.

Musical basics: "Manhã de Carnaval" is a 32-bar ABAC tune situated in a minor mode. It is almost always played in the key of A minor with a medium-tempo bossa nova groove but was also recorded as a slow swing by Jim Hall and Jimmy Raney. It contains a blend of modal and tonal elements, a diatonic cycle-of-4ths progression in the second eight bars, modulation to Dm in the second part of the form, and numerous ii–V–I progressions.

Improvisation

This two-chorus solo on "Manhã de Carnaval" changes invites the improviser to explore and color the minor mode. In this setting, all pentatonic and diatonic modal sounds are fair game as well as chord-outlining tonal lines and bebop language elements. The second verse begins with a quote of "Água de Beber," a popular Jobim bossa nova classic. This phrase has a pentatonic blues scale sound, which provides contrast to the largely diatonic, modal, and tonal melody and bop lines of the improvisation. The final eight-bar section utilizes chord melody phrases to pass the solo to the next soloist.

275

"Someday My Prince Will Come"

The tune: Jazz from a cartoon—what? Strange as it seems, the Disney animated feature of *Snow White and the Seven Dwarfs* yielded a perennial jazz standard, covered by heavyweights like Miles Davis, Dave Brubeck, Bill Evans, and Herbie Hancock. And its allure was not lost on other artists, like Chet Atkins, Eugene Chadborne, and Julie Andrews, who created their own renditions over the years. "Someday My Prince Will Come" remains one of the greatest tunes in jazz to have emerged from an unlikely source.

Musical basics: "Someday My Prince Will Come" is a 32-bar ABAC tune in 3/4 meter. It is played in a variety of keys, the most common being Bb and F. The jazz waltz is a staple in the genre and brings out a different side of an improviser. (Many say it's their lyrical side.) Triple meter suggests a bouncy but relaxed rhythm approach to swinging, implicit in the lyrical improvising of guitarists like Wes Montgomery, Joe Pass, and Jim Hall—think "Full House," "Sometime Ago," or "Baubles, Bangles and Beads." 3/4 also prompts a player to adjust their jazz language lines rhythmically to suit the meter's different phrase structure. Many idiomatic bop lines are phrased over or through the bars. There are several intriguing harmonic twists in the tune, like the D7alt chord cadencing on Ebmaj7 in measures 1–2 of A sections, as well as a 3/4 version of the iii–biii°7–ii–V changes in measures 9–12.

Improvisation

This two-chorus solo pursues the elusive "lyrical style" of playing and phrasing, a subjective notion at best. It contains a number of transformed idiomatic lines modified for the feel of triple-meter generally and the jazz-waltz groove, specifically. Therein lies a challenge and opportunity for the improviser. How does one convert their existing vocabulary to address the meter? Several possibilities are explored in this improvisation. See if you can recognize characteristic 4/4 lines that are repurposed for 3/4 time. In addition to the reevaluated jazz lines is the emphasis on specific, "bouncy" rhythmic motives, the most prominent being the two eighth-note syncopated figure on strong beats, such as "1–and" in the first bar of the solo, and elsewhere.

"Body and Soul"

The tune: "Body and Soul" has been called the "granddaddy of the jazz ballad." You're in good company when living inside this venerable tune. It's one of the most played pieces in jazz, there are volumes written on just how to perform it, and it's a favorite of tenor sax players ever since Coleman Hawkins made it a part of the canon in 1939.

Musical basics: "Body and Soul" is a 32-bar AABA tune played regularly in Db major as a jazz ballad with *rubato* (free time) feel. Here, the 16th note prevails as the primary rhythmic unit. The harmonic rhythm is slower, allowing for more melodic development. This tune begins on Ebm, the ii chord, like many jazz standards. However, it is more minor in tonality than a typical minor 7th chord. This calls for tonicizing of the ii chord to have it function like a temporary i chord in Eb minor. The familiar chord progression involving the biii°7 chord occurs in the key of Db major in the A section (Fm–E°7–Ebm7) and in C major in the B section: Em7–Eb°7–Dm7–G7. "Body and Soul" is further distinguished by a chromatic modulation in the bridge, from the tonic Db to D major and then C major. The bridge returns to the A section via three chromatic chords: C7–B7–Bb7, the latter being the V chord of Eb minor. Many players mine an implied bluesy flavor in the tune and often the chromaticism is defined explicitly with arpeggio spelling of the chords or movable themes in parallel motion.

Improvisation

This one-chorus solo begins with an alternate turnaround phrase that creates melodic motion from Db major to Eb minor. Thematic imitation and development of an Ebm9 motive are pursued in the first two bars of A. Many players seize the opportunity to play Gb blues lines or Dbm sounds over the dominant IV chord, Gb7. Dbm is heard in the first and third A sections and Gb7 blues in the second. A chromatic blues line is also played in measure 32 to begin the turnaround phrase, a useful strategy in soulfulness. In the A sections, Ebm and Cm7b5 are treated as closely related and addressed with shared Ebm melodies. A common and effective approach in standards, particularly ballads, is the practice of alluding to the tune's melody in the course of improvisation—but only a snippet, more than that can sound too obvious. This idea is heard in the second A section in measures 1–2 and 7, and in B, measures 1–2. The transition from B to the third A section is made with a simple cell, manipulated and moved in parallel motion.

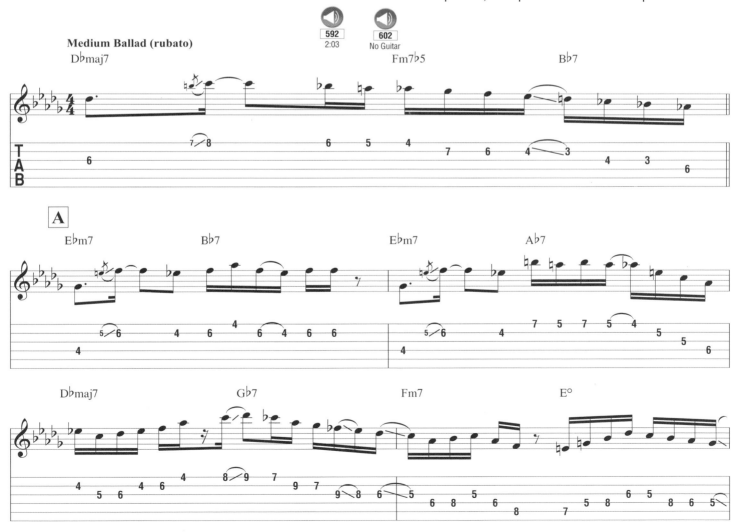

Octaves and Jazz Melody

Playing melodies in parallel octaves is an indispensable strategy. Closely associated with Wes Montgomery, it was one of his most identifiable traits and is a common dialect of jazz guitar. The themes of Tracks 564 and 588 and the intro/outro vamps of Track 590 are rendered in octaves. You can consider these to be "model solos in octaves."

Technique

The octave technique developed by Wes involves two locked-fingering shapes. Shape 1 is for low octaves played on the 6th and 4th strings and the 5th and 3rd strings. Shape 2 is for higher octaves on the 4th and 2nd strings and the 3rd and 1st strings. The other strings are muted, designated by Xs in the diagrams, with the remaining fret-hand fingers. Octaves can be articulated with the thumb, pick, or plucked with fingers.

The following four phrases are typical jazz lines played in octaves. Tracks 603 and 604 are ii–V–I phrases in C that may be used in "Take the A Train." Track 605 is a blues phrase in F over Bb7–B°–F7 chords. Track 606 (next page) is an A minor melody applicable to tunes like "Manhã de Carnaval."

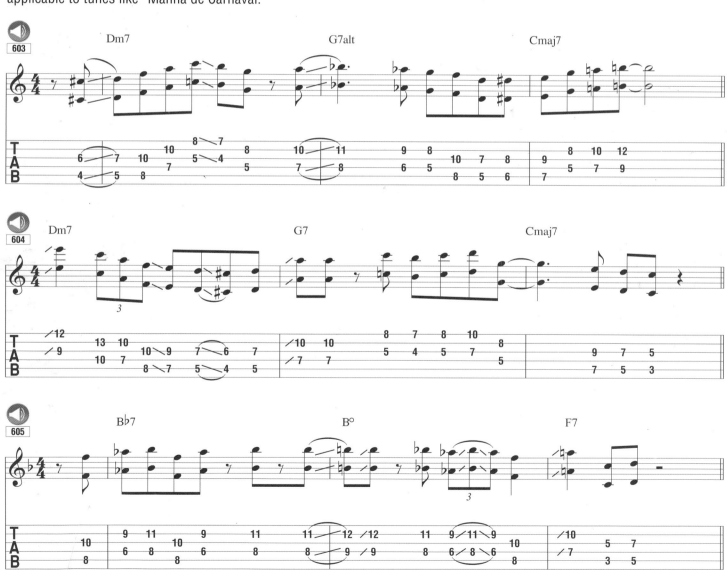

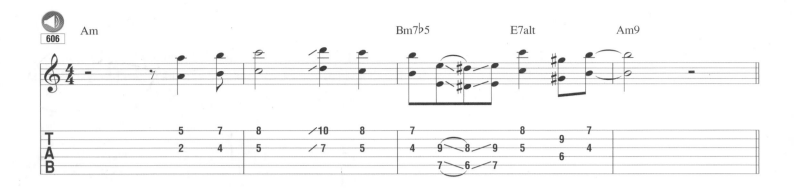

EPILOGUE

At the conclusion of any course, the inevitable question arises: *what next?* This course in the jazz language is no different. Consider the obvious. Language is comprised of words leading to sentences, statements, and finally, the *message*—that unique personal expression of what you're saying in totality. You have acquired the parts of speech (basic sounds), assimilated the lexicon in characteristic phrases, become fluent with the material through practice, repetition, and critical *listening*, and are ready to express yourself in a conversation through musical time and space. This is the next step in your journey of application and innovation.

In parting, here are some thoughts for your future endeavors. Mastering the jazz language means more in the context of application, specifically *performing*. All great jazz performers sprang from the language as a basis. You are now similarly equipped to produce your first set in a jazz performance. Focus not only on solos but, just as important, interpreting the *melody* of songs. These can be obtained from conventional sheet music, fake books, or preferably by listening to recordings and creating your own composites from favorite versions. You may also reinterpret my contrafacts from Chapters 18 and 19—or write new ones, which is recommended. Consider adding fills during melody statements, closing cadenzas (as in Tracks 553, 586, and 587), and breaks and pickup lines to begin solos (heard in 585, 588, and 589). Note the expansions of song form in arrangements: Simple outro tags in Tracks 563, 586, 587, 588, and 589, and ensemble intros and outros in 585, 590, 591, and 592. Imagine those possibilities in your own interpretations. If you intend to lead musicians, take charge by learning to count-in tunes. Use the opening clicks of 553 to practice out loud in time: "1–2–1-2-3-4." Track 585 conversely allows a band's keyboardist to set the pace with a traditional intro figure known to most players, a common scenario. Each arrangement is also presented as a full backing track (minus guitar) with counts; apply the same principles to each. Develop rhythm guitar and comping strategies based on material in the first seven chapters on harmony. Use the backing tracks to prepare, technically and aesthetically, for playing the melody, accompaniment, and improvisation in actual group performance.

Build your powers of improvisation by first learning the solos in Chapters 18 and 19. Treat them as etudes to get acquainted with call and response phrases, navigation, imitative melodies, quotes, various melodic/harmonic possibilities (diatonic, chromatic, altered, substitutions), and idiomatic rhythms. Then explore alternate sounds, pursue thematic development, choose different ii–V–I and turnaround phrases, and experiment with rhythmic placement. Create and refine your own model solos (written or aural), and regularly acquire additional vocabulary by transcribing the work of musicians that speak to you. While practicing, consider aspects like accenting and dynamics, legato versus staccato articulation, space (rests and duration), and incorporating substitute blues melody. Apply all these methods over the backing tracks, record them, and listen self-critically to your innovations. Transfer these assets to tunes outside this course to continue your individual improvement, expanding repertoire, and growing command of the jazz language. Make this a habit. Happily, it's a lifelong process.

Stay inspired. See you on the other side.
—Wolf Marshall